Distributional Analysis
of Tax Policy

Distributional Analysis of Tax Policy

Edited by David F. Bradford

The AEI Press

Publisher for the American Enterprise Institute
WASHINGTON, D.C.
1995

Available in the United States from the AEI Press, c/o Publisher Resources Inc., 1224 Heil Quaker Blvd., P.O. Box 7001, La Vergne, TN 37086-7001. Distributed outside the United States by arrangement with Eurospan, 3 Henrietta Street, London WC2E 8LU England.

Library of Congress Cataloging-in-Publication Data
Distributional analysis of tax policy / edited by David F. Bradford.
    p. cm.
    Includes bibliographical references.
    ISBN 0-8447-3891-3 (paper : alk. paper). — ISBN 0-8447-3890-5
(cloth : alk. paper)
    1. Tax incidence—United States. 2. Taxation—United States.
3. Income distribution—United States. I. Bradford, David F.,
1939–   .
HJ2322.A3D57   1995
336.2'94'0973—dc20   95-18681
                                                        CIP

1 3 5 7 9 10 8 6 4 2

Printed in the United States of America

Contents

FIGURES

Contributors

DAVID F. BRADFORD is professor of economics and public affairs at the Woodrow Wilson School of Public and International Affairs, Princeton University, and adjunct professor of law at New York University. He is an adjunct scholar of the American Enterprise Institute and a research associate of the National Bureau of Economic Research. Mr. Bradford was a member of the Council of Economic Advisers from 1991 to 1993 and was the deputy assistant secretary for tax policy at the Treasury Department from 1975 to 1977. He has served on numerous advisory boards and is affiliated with the American Economic Association, the Econometric Society, and the National Tax Association. Mr. Bradford is the author of several publications on tax policy, including (together with the U.S. Treasury Tax Policy Staff) *Blueprints for Basic Tax Reform* (second edition, Tax Analysts, 1984) and *Untangling the Income Tax* (Harvard Press, 1986).

ALAN J. AUERBACH, Robert D. Burch Professor of Tax Policy and Public Finance at the University of California, Berkeley, is also a research associate of the National Bureau of Economic Research. In 1992 he was the deputy chief of staff on the Joint Committee on Taxation. Mr. Auerbach has been a consultant to the U.S. Treasury, the Office of Management and Budget, the Swedish Ministry of Finance, the International Monetary Fund, and the World Bank on issues of taxation and has testified frequently before House and Senate committees. He is author of several books, including *The Taxation of Capital Income* and *Mergers and Acquisitions*. He has also written more than ninety chapters in books and articles for scholarly journals.

THOMAS A. BARTHOLD joined the staff of the Joint Committee on Taxation in 1987. He studies environmental and energy taxes, estate and gift taxation, the low-income housing tax credit, and tax-exempt bonds. Mr. Barthold was a member of the economics faculty at Dartmouth College. He has published studies on capital gains, charitable bequests, and the relationship between interest rates and inflationary expectations.

EDGAR K. BROWNING is the Alfred F. Chalk Professor in Economics at Texas A&M University, where he has taught since 1984. From 1969 to 1984 he was a professor of economics at the University of Virginia. In 1988 Mr. Browning was the president of the Southern Economics Association. He is the coauthor of two popular textbooks, *Public Finance and the Price System* and *Microeconomic Theory and Applications,* as well as numerous articles in professional literature.

GARY BURTLESS is a senior fellow in the economic studies program at the Brookings Institution. He was an economist in the office of the Secretary of Labor and the Department of Health, Education, and Welfare. Mr. Burtless is the coauthor of *Growth with Equity: Economic Policymaking for the Next Century* and *Can American Afford to Grow Old? Paying for Social Security.* He taught at the University of Maryland in 1993 as a visiting professor of public affairs.

DON FULLERTON is professor of economics at the University of Texas. He received his Ph.D. in economics from the University of California at Berkeley in 1978 and won the outstanding dissertation award of the National Tax Association in 1979. Mr. Fullerton taught economics at Princeton University, the University of Virginia, and Carnegie Mellon University. From 1985 to 1987 he was the deputy assistant secretary for tax analysis at the Treasury Department.

JAGADEESH GOKHALE is a staff economist at the Research Department of the Federal Reserve Bank of Cleveland. He holds a Ph.D. in economics from Boston University and does research in public finance, macroeconomics, and applied microeconomics.

MICHAEL J. GRAETZ is Justus S. Hotchkiss Professor of Law at Yale University. He was a professor of law at the University of Virginia and the University of Southern California law schools and professor of law and social sciences at the California Institute of Technology. During January-June 1992 Mr. Graetz was the assistant to the secretary and special counsel at the Treasury Department. In 1990 and 1991 he was the Treasury deputy assistant secretary for tax policy. In 1989 Mr. Graetz served on the Commissioner's Advisory Group of the Internal Revenue Service. He served in the Treasury Department in the Office of Tax Legislative Counsel during 1969–1972. His publications on federal taxation include a leading law school text and more than forty articles on tax and health policy and tax compliance issues in books and scholarly journals.

JANE G. GRAVELLE is a senior specialist in economic policy at the Congressional Research Service of the Library of Congress. On leave from CRS, she has served at the Labor Department, the Treasury Department, and Boston University. At CRS Ms. Gravelle specializes in taxation, particularly the effects of tax policies on economic growth and resource allocation. She has published papers in academic journals and serves on the editorial board of the *National Tax Journal*.

R. GLENN HUBBARD is Russell L. Carson Professor of Economics and Finance at the Graduate School of Business at Columbia University. He was the deputy assistant secretary of tax analysis at the Treasury Department during the Bush administration. Mr. Hubbard was a visiting professor at Harvard University's John F. Kennedy School of Government and at the University of Chicago and the John M. Olin Fellow at the National Bureau of Economic Research, where he continues to be a research associate. Mr. Hubbard has published numerous articles on public finance, financial economics, macroeconomics, industrial organization, and public policy.

WILLIAM JACK is an economist in the European 1 Department of the International Monetary Fund. He was on the staff of the Joint Committee on Taxation from 1992 until 1994 and was a member of the economics department at Sydney University. His current research includes optimal taxation, investment incentives, and health insurance. Mr. Jack has been a consultant to the World Bank on matters of public finance, project appraisal, and decentralization in China.

RICHARD A. KASTEN is the deputy assistant director for revenue forecasting at the Congressional Budget Office, where he has been on staff since 1985. Before the appointment as deputy assistant director, he was in the CBO's Tax Analysis Division, where he forecast individual income tax revenue. Mr. Kasten has been constructing microsimulation models for more than twenty years. He built his first complete microsimulation model for his MIT Ph.D. dissertation in 1975. At the U.S. Department of Health and Human Services from 1975 to 1985, he worked on models of welfare reform and social security earnings sharing.

LAURENCE J. KOTLIKOFF is professor of economics at Boston University, research associate of the National Bureau of Economic Research, and fellow of the Econometric Society. He was a senior economist with the President's Council of Economic Advisers in 1982 and 1983. Mr. Kotlikoff served on the faculty of economics at the University of California at Los Angeles and at Yale University. He is the author of *Generational Accounting, What Determines Savings?* and has been published extensively in professional journals, newspapers, and magazines.

ANDREW B. LYON is an associate professor of economics at the University of Maryland. He was an economist at the Joint Committee on Taxation until 1987 and on the staff of the President's Council of Economic Advisers from 1992 to 1993. Mr. Lyon has written articles on public finance focusing on corporate and personal taxation, including the alternative minimum tax, capital gains taxation, and problems of asymmetric information.

GILBERT E. METCALF is an assistant professor of economics at Tufts University and a faculty research fellow at the National Bureau of Economic Research. His research includes distributional analysis, investment policy, state and local public finance, and energy economics.

JAMES R. NUNNS is the director for individual taxation in the Office of Tax Analysis of the U.S. Treasury. He is the coauthor of "Measuring Tax Burden: A Historical Perspective" in *Fifty Years of Economic Measurement: The Jubilee of the Conference on Research in Income and Wealth.*

DIANE LIM ROGERS is principal analyst in the Tax Analysis Division of the Congressional Budget Office and assistant professor of economics at Pennsylvania State University. She received her Ph.D. in economics from the University of Virginia in 1991. With Don Fullerton Ms. Rogers wrote *Who Bears the Lifetime Tax Burden?* published by the Brookings Institution in 1993. Her teaching and research covers public finance, with an emphasis on the distributional effects of taxes.

C. EUGENE STEUERLE is a senior fellow at the Urban Institute and author of a weekly column in *Tax Notes.* He has served in various positions in the Treasury Department, including deputy assistant secretary of the Treasury for tax analysis. Mr. Steuerle was a federal executive fellow at the Brookings Institution and resident fellow at the American Enterprise Institute. He is the author of four books, including *Retooling Social Security for the Twenty-First Century, The Tax Decade,* and numerous reports and articles.

ERIC J. TODER is the deputy secretary assistant for tax analysis at the U.S. Treasury. He has been the deputy assistant director in the tax analysis division at the Congressional Budget Office, consultant to the Treasury of New Zealand, and deputy director of the Office of Tax Analysis, U.S. Treasury. Mr. Toder was an assistant professor of economics at Tufts University and senior research associate at Charles River Associates.

CAROLYN L. WEAVER is a resident scholar and director of social security and pension studies at the American Enterprise Institute. From 1981 to 1984 she was the chief professional staff member on social security for the Senate Committee on Finance and during this period also served as a senior adviser to the National Commission on Social Security Reform. Ms. Weaver has been a research scholar at the Hoover Institution, has taught economics at Tulane University and Virginia Tech, and has been a guest lecturer at Harvard and George Mason Universities. She is the editor of two AEI books, *Social Security's Looming Surpluses: Prospects and Implications* (1990) and *Disability and Work: Incentives, Rights, and Opportunities* (1991), and the author of numerous articles on social security, disability policy, and political economy. Ms. Weaver is a member of the U.S. Social Security Advisory Board and of the 1995 Social Security Advisory Council.

Acknowledgments

When I attend an opera or play, I am always impressed by the long list of people included in the printed program, those who play critical roles but do not appear on the stage. A book project of this kind also has its extensive supporting cast, whose hard work and attention to detail are essential to its success. The authors of the papers and the participants at the conference at which the first versions were presented—the players on the stage—are duly noted in the pages to follow. I thank the many others whose effort was behind the scenes at the American Enterprise Institute.

In particular, I would like to thank Molly Calahan, who was my assistant during most of the organizational phase of the project; Amy Smith, who picked up the reins when Molly left for business school; and Stephanie Rich, who ably stepped in when Amy took off for California. It was a pleasure to work with Isabel Ferguson and her collaborators, Hilary Laytham and Leanne Yingling, who know how to make a conference run like clockwork. Diana Furchtgott-Roth, with her assistants, Audrey Williams and Chelsea Haga, was critical in getting the book pulled together and offering editorial advice, and editor Ann Petty was upbeat and supportive.

These individuals are themselves part of a larger team of managers, secretaries, research assistants, chefs and food servers, computer gurus, and more who collaborate to make AEI an exceptional environment for policy research. I cannot name everyone in this group, here, but I do want to thank Christopher DeMuth, AEI president, for his enthusiastic backing of this project from start to finish. Getting to know him better was one of the many benefits of my stint as a visiting scholar at AEI during the spring of 1993.

Another kind of support is also critical to work of this kind. The Chase Manhattan Bank generously underwrote AEI's commitment to this project, and the John M. Olin Foundation's support of my work on tax reform helped to free some of my time to bring it to conclusion. I am very grateful to them.

DAVID F. BRADFORD

1
Introduction

David F. Bradford

The distribution of tax burdens is a central aspect of tax policy. Changes in the tax rules redistribute after-tax income and wealth among people in a variety of ways. Some are obvious, as when an increase in the top income-tax–bracket rates raises the burdens on high-income individuals. Some are much more difficult to identify, as when a change in depreciation rules affects the relative profitability of different industries and thereby the fortunes of the owners, workers, customers, and suppliers of different businesses.

The principal tool of distributional analysis currently employed in the federal tax policy process is the burden table. Particularly influential are burden tables prepared by the professional staffs of the Treasury Department, the Congressional Joint Committee on Taxation, and the Congressional Budget Office.

A burden table is apparently simple. In the left-hand column are income classifications, 0–$10,000, $10,000–$20,000, etc. Subsequent columns display information about the families or individuals with income within the indicated intervals. Normally, the main focus is on the taxes paid by those families or individuals under current law and under a proposed change. The pattern of increases or decreases in taxes by income category is the main information about the distribution of tax burdens available for policy makers.

This volume had its origins in my frustration with the uses of burden tables. Based on several years of experience with tax policy issues, as a government official and as an advocate of my view of good tax policy, I had two objections to the existing practices.

The first was a frankly partisan one. Since my experience in President Gerald Ford's administration as the chief tax economist in the U.S. Treasury, I had favored the consumption strategy as the preferred model for taxation. The methods used to analyze the distributional effects of consumption-based taxes were, I felt, inherently biased against this approach to taxation. Serious arguments can be made for and against my position. But because of flawed distributional analysis

1

by the official agencies, consumption-based proposals received short shrift in practical political life.

The second source of my frustration had little to do with my policy preferences. It was that income distribution issues were treated in too simplistic a fashion in the policy debates. Here the complaint was not that the standard analyses were wrong, but that they reflected too little of the complexity of distributional issues, reducing a multidimensional issue to one of rich versus poor.

Policy makers and the general public should be better informed about what burden tables can and cannot show. They should also have more dimensions of information available about the distribution of costs and benefits associated with tax and other policy decisions.

These frustrations were fresh in my mind at the end of my service on President George Bush's Council of Economic Advisers. I therefore leapt at the suggestion of Christopher DeMuth, president of the American Enterprise Institute, that I organize a conference to review the state of play in distributional analysis and to promote its improvement.

What follows are some of the problems that we set out to address.

How Should People Be Classified?

Burden tables typically aggregate across family size. That is, single individuals and married couples with any number of dependents having the same annual income are lumped together in the analysis of distribution. Two-earner families are lumped with single-earner families. Age may also be an important variable. Arguably, the true "deficit problem" is one of distribution between present and future generations. Traditional distributional analysis ignores these dimensions of the problem. They should somehow be brought systematically into the picture in the policy debate.

Another important variable is, What is counted as "income" in classifying people? Should the "imputed income" of those who occupy their own homes be included? Is income the most appropriate classifier, or would a measure of consumption give a better reflection of the economic status of families? Should it be recognized that in the normal course of events, for most people, earnings rise from early in the working years through middle age, then decline in later years, most obviously when they retire from the work force? Should the burden tables control for the age structure of the population? Should a measure of lifetime income or earnings be used instead of an annual measure that includes life-cycle and transient effects?

What Should Be Distributed?

As a general proposition, the appropriate framework for thinking about distribution is the entire fiscal structure, taking into account all taxes and transfer programs and at least some real expenditure programs, such as schooling. Data, conceptual and institutional factors (the committee structure of Congress, for example), and sometimes political factors may result in limiting the scope of burden-table analysis. But efforts should certainly be made to include all the major federal taxes—including excise, estate, and gift—and corporation income taxes in distributional analysis. Analyses that focus on the individual income tax alone are seriously flawed.

In a similar vein, it can be argued that failing to incorporate transfer programs systematically to the analysis leaves out what has probably been the most substantial source of redistribution over the past several decades. Economists have long recognized the essential equivalence between taxes and transfer payments. The "refundable" earned income tax credit (EITC) in the existing income tax provides an example of a transfer payment that typically *is* included in burden-table analyses. (The refunded portion of the EITC is counted as a positive transfer payment in the budget.) Why, however, should this transfer program be singled out for inclusion? It makes little sense to think about the distributional impact of tax policy in isolation from that of transfer policy.

An effort to incorporate payroll taxes to the distributional analysis must, moreover, take into account the transfers they finance, particularly in cases such as social security retirement, where the taxes and benefits are linked, person by person.

What Is Meant by the "Burden"?

By and large, burden tables have taken a pragmatic, cash-flow approach to identifying burdens—the taxes shown for an income category are the cash tax payments made during a year by the families in question. There are some serious problems with this approach. One of them corresponds to the "lifetime" versus "snapshot" classification of families. The person who makes a tax-deductible contribution to an individual retirement account (IRA)—or who makes an investment subject to accelerated depreciation—for example, receives a reduction in current tax liability. A price is paid, however, in the form of an increase in future tax liability at the time of withdrawal from the IRA or from realization of gross income from the investment. Burden tables are likely to ignore the latter effects, resulting in biases in the analysis.

3

Other issues are raised by the inadequacy of revenue as a measure of the burden of taxes. In response to an increase in tax rates, a taxpayer may engage in avoidance behavior, such as by working less. The change in taxes actually paid will understate the change in burden in that case, because it will not include any allowance for the fact that the avoidance itself is costly. Suppose, for example, an increase in marginal tax rates leads a taxpayer to reduce work effort to the point that less is paid in taxes. The *reduction* in tax liability would obviously be a nonsensical description of the change in burden. The avoidance behavior is itself costly.

Economists have a fairly well-developed set of tools for characterizing the burden of taxes. They think of the incidence of a particular change in tax rules in terms of a measure of the amount a person would have to be paid in order to accept the change willingly. In general, this is *not* the same as the amount of extra tax revenue that person would pay as a consequence of the policy change but includes as well the change in the cost of avoidance. Typically, a tax imposes a burden larger than the revenue generated, and the identity of the payer may be different from that of the person who bears the burden of a tax.

The price of inconsistency, or at least lack of clarity, in existing burden table analysis can be high. An interesting instance at the heart of an intense political controversy is the burden-table treatment of reintroducing an exclusion from taxable income of a significant fraction of realized long-term capital gains. This policy change was much debated between 1989 and 1992. Although the Treasury and congressional analytical staffs disagreed about the details, there was no disagreement that cutting the fraction of gain subject to tax would significantly increase the total gain realized, because of the "unlocking" effects. Revenue estimates based on a presumption of no such response (sometimes called static revenue estimates) would therefore substantially overstate the actual reduction in tax payments anticipated by the analysts. In fact, Treasury analysts concluded that the earlier versions of proposals to cut the tax rate on capital gains advocated by the Bush administration would produce revenue *gains*, and the congressional analysts also estimated that the behavioral response would substantially offset the static revenue loss.

The potential intertwining of the political and analytical in the present state of distributional information is dramatically illustrated by the burden-table treatment of this policy issue. Because the Treasury's burden tables were based, according to their standard practice, on tax liabilities, the capital gains proposal implied an increase in tax burdens on high-income people rather than the reduction in liabilities that would be implied with no behavioral response. By contrast, the burden tables made available by the Joint Committee on Taxation showed the *static* revenue effects, based on the view that the implied gains for those who realized capital gains gave a better measure of the change in their tax burdens. Although there is a good argument, discussed in detail in this volume, for the JCT procedure, it is understandable that the niceties of the technical details were lost on the infuriated advocates of the policy change.

What Is the Appropriate Reach of Behavioral Analysis?

Policy makers realize that tax policy often has effects far beyond whose tax liabilities are immediately affected. That is why they are concerned about the influence of the tax system on economic growth. Perhaps the broadest and most important behavioral response to tax policy is that of the entire economy. The problem of taking into account dynamic feedback effects of tax policy changes on aggregate revenue has been much discussed and disputed. The distributional consequences of feedback phenomena could be equally important. The capital gains debate provides a good example. Advocates of cutting the rate of tax on capital gains claimed beneficial effects on rank-and-file workers. Such effects are disparaged by skeptics as trickle-down economics. The fact that incorporating general equilibrium feedback effects, whether revenues or the distribution of welfare, into analysis to be used in the political process raises serious problems does not make the phenomenon unimportant.

An infinite research agenda is implicit in the problems discussed above. The objective of this volume, however, is finite—to assess the state of distributional analysis in the policy process today and to suggest improvements that might be implemented in the reasonably near future. Improvements are needed both in the analytical techniques and in the sophistication of the user community, so one principal objective is to set forth a clear statement of what distributional analysis does *and does not* tell us.

In putting together this volume I have divided the material, into three parts.

What Is Wrong with Distributional Analysis— A Policy Maker's Perspective

Michael Graetz's extended essay on the uses of distributional analysis in the making of tax policy is an ideal introduction to the subject. Graetz was the deputy assistant secretary of the Treasury for tax policy in the Bush administration. He writes as a survivor of the notorious

5

"budget summit" that led ultimately to the Omnibus Budget Resolution Act of 1990, an unprecedented, protracted negotiation between executive and legislative branches, in which burden tables played a critical role.

Graetz's piece should be read as his personal perspective on the issues. Not everyone will agree with his analysis or criticisms. But he covers an enormous amount of ground and articulates clearly numerous problems that need to be addressed in the current practice of distributional analysis in the making of tax policy. Graetz takes particular issue with the attempt by the JCT, mentioned above, to present figures on the changes in the burden of taxes rather than on changes in taxes paid. A prominent example of this distinction has been mentioned above: the difference between (a) the amount of taxes saved as a consequence of reducing the rate on capital gains (the projected amount saved was actually negative for some versions of the proposal—that is, taxpayers would send more money to the government with a lower rate of tax) and (b) the change in burden on the taxpayers involved, which was obviously a reduction. In Graetz's view, the object of the game is to influence the distribution of after-tax income, what people have left over to pay for things they want (other than government). If, as he assumes, people's pretax income is determined elsewhere, then we have to determine the amount of taxes people actually pay. We can then work backward to the distribution of after-tax incomes.

As has been discussed above, economists think that they know how to sort this one out. What ought to be measured is the impact of the tax-law change on the total value obtained by the individual from the economic system, which is less of an abstraction than it seems. It translates into something like the maximum amount a person would pay to see the change made (a reduction in rates) or the minimum amount a person would have to be paid to accept the change willingly (an increase in rates). For the capital-gains–rate cut, the amount that direct beneficiaries would pay obviously must at least equal the tax savings they would enjoy if they did not change their realization behavior. This is the JCT measure. It would actually be an understatement, since taxpayers value the opportunity that the lower rate provides to realize gains more often or earlier.

The growth-inducing benefits claimed for the capital-gains–tax cut implies that many others besides the taxpayers directly involved would benefit from—and in principle be willing to pay for—the tax-rate cut. Considerations such as these lend support to Graetz's contention that whatever the theoretical merits of one approach or another, many fine distinctions are lost on the tax policy makers who compose the audience for burden tables. From this catalog of shortcomings in the present practice of distributional analysis and of the burden-table device, Graetz draws the radical conclusion that we would be better served if this practice and device were banned from the room when the tax policy sausage is actually being prepared. The tool is too crude, and it constrains policy in ways that thoughtful legislators would not accept if they knew what was really involved.

The Current State of the Art

To provide some factual foundation for the discussion of the practices of the official agencies, we were delighted to be able to enlist senior members of the three key agency staffs to collaborate in explaining and discussing their methods. A chapter by Glenn Hubbard frames the presentations by the agency authors. Like Graetz, Hubbard brought recent executive branch experience to bear, having served, like Graetz, as the deputy assistant secretary of the Treasury for tax policy in the Bush administration, on the economic side. As the economist-official with the care and keeping of the Office of Tax Analysis in his portfolio during the political struggle over capital-gains revisions, Hubbard also had an exceptional opportunity to learn about the uses of burden tables in the heat of political battles. In addition to an overview of the three agency approaches to distributional analysis, Hubbard offers some suggestions for improvement.

To capitalize on the opportunity for comparison of their different approaches, the agency authors agreed to include analyses of a common legislative proposal. (In the event, that turned out to be the Omnibus Budget Reconciliation Act of 1993.) As a proponent of changes in the methods, I am happy to claim credit for instigating the extraordinarily enlightening expositions by James R. Nunns, of the Office of Tax Policy in the U.S. Treasury; Richard Kasten, of the Congressional Budget Office, and Eric Toder, formerly with the CBO and now at Treasury; and Thomas Barthold, of the Joint Committee on Taxation. Many who attended the AEI conference described these presentations and their ensuing discussions as the highlight events. I expect that many will refer to the versions published here as valuable references.

Advances in Distributional Analysis

A major objective of this volume is to identify avenues for improvement of the treatment of distributional issues in the tax policy process. As it happens, an important evolutionary step was taken in the standard approaches of the official agencies shortly before the AEI conference: the JCT released a pamphlet that described the distributional analysis procedures it would follow in the future.

Two officials were particularly important in developing the revised methods and in making the details available to the public: Harry L. Gutman and Alan Auerbach, respectively chief and deputy chief of staff of the Joint Committee. Economist Auerbach, now at the University of California, Berkeley, contributed the chapter that begins this section. His essay puts the JCT efforts in the perspective of a wide range of economic analytical problems, including the often contentious one of estimating revenue, as well as that of distributional analysis. He offers an excellent introduction to the broader objective of part three, "Advances in Distributional Analysis."

The JCT pamphlet is itself the subject of the first chapter in part three. In part, the pamphlet provided a clarifying discussion of methods already in use (for example, the practice of using static behavior as the basis for estimating burdens). An important departure from past practice, of particular interest to me, was the proposed treatment of taxes based on consumption and economically equivalent taxes that might not obviously be based on consumption—for example, a tax on corporate cash flow. In taking a fresh look at the economic analysis—associating the burden with the act of earning, rather than the act of spending—and at the adequacy of the data base used, the JCT took a significant stride toward resolving one of the sources of my frustration.

A summary of the innovations contained in the JCT pamphlet is provided here by Thomas Barthold, JCT staff, and William Jack, formerly at the JCT and now at the International Monetary Fund. In his commentary, Edgar Browning of Texas A&M University welcomes the advances in the JCT approach but offers several criticisms that suggest areas for further improvement. Of particular interest is his argument that the JCT errs in treating the static-revenue estimate as an overstatement of the burdens of tax increases (and an understatement of the gain from tax cuts) in the critically important case of taxes on labor supply.

Browning's argument is simple: the common assumption that the labor supply is insensitive to the wage makes economic sense if the substitution effect of a wage cut (lowering the incentive to work) is exactly balanced by the income effect—whereby the worker, in effect, adds to work effort to make up the loss. An increase in the tax rate on earnings in this setting will result in no change in labor supply, so the static-revenue estimate will be equal to the actual revenue change. But the worker would be better off if simply required to pay the fixed amount of extra revenue, while keeping constant the amount earned from extra work. The burden thus exceeds the revenue. Browning shows that the difference can be large; under plausible circumstances, the burden can be twice the amount of the static-revenue estimate.

Browning applauds the innovations in the JCT approach to consumption taxes. But here, too, he has some observations about the way to think about the effect of consumption taxes on recipients of transfer payments. He argues that it is most plausible to assume that the recipients are unaffected by changes in consumption taxes. The appropriate treatment of transfer payments in the income used to classify households in the burden tables (most transfer payments are left out of the income "classifier") also receives provocative commentary in Browning's contribution.

A theme emphasized in this volume is the need and potential for considering dimensions of the distribution of burdens other than those incorporated in the usual burden tables. Three chapters explore the extension of the standard tools. The authors each bring their own frameworks, often conceived for the world of advanced scholarship, into the realm of the practical as a tool for day-to-day policy making.

A dimension of distribution seriously absent from burden tables is that across generations. It is extraordinarily little recognized that a tax burden avoided through deficit financing today does not disappear, but must show up sometime in the future. Present-day burden tables would permit us the illusion that a cut in income-tax rates reduces the tax burdens of all income classes, as though no one would ever have to pick up the tab! Alan J. Auerbach, Jagadeesh Gokhale, and Laurence J. Kotlikoff have developed generational accounting to quantify the distribution of burdens among generations, including the burden passed forward. In their chapter, they apply generational accounting to recent deficit-reduction and proposed health-care legislation, demonstrating the practical promise of this tool, which is now in an advanced developmental stage. Jane G. Gravelle, of the Congressional Research Service, and Carolyn L. Weaver, of the American Enterprise Institute, offer wise commentary.

Even if they are not sure of the responses, policy makers should have available on a regular basis the implications of their decisions for the incentives at various margins, especially the margin between more and less work. An income tax affects this margin in an apparently obvious way, but *apparently* is the operant term. Complex provisions of the income tax, such as the phasing down of itemized deductions at higher income, result in hidden changes in marginal incentives. More important, nontax programs can have strong marginal incentive effects—for example, the income-related standard for eligibility for Medicare—and the provisions in question may interact with one another or with income-tax provisions in ways that are hard to discern.

The chapter by Andrew B. Lyon of the University of Maryland provides a remarkable compilation and display of information on the distribution of marginal tax rates. Some version of his figures and tables would clearly qualify as useful additions to the regular kit of tools used by the makers of tax and transfer policy. Gary Burtless of the Brookings Institution and C. Eugene Steuerle, former deputy assistant secretary of the Treasury for tax policy and now of the Urban Institute, both bring their wisdom and experience to bear in thoughtful comments. Among their important points is the need to be modest in our claims about behavioral effects and to stress the uncontroversial, factual nature of the incentives built into tax and transfer systems. We may not know with confidence how people react to marginal tax rates, and policy makers may not be convinced by our professional estimates. We can, however, calculate accurately. It would serve the interest of good policy, as a part of the routine analysis of major changes, to provide reports that make their effects on incentive structure clear and explicit, as Lyon has done in his chapter.

The authors of the earlier chapters have noted, variously, the desirability of considering a long-term or lifetime measure of individual or household economic circumstances; of looking simultaneously at tax and at transfer programs; of looking at the state, local, and federal levels; of incorporating future as well as living generations in the analysis; of using a measure of ability to pay that does not incorporate taste factors (as a measure of income incorporates a person's willingness to work); of incorporating deadweight loss along with actual tax payments in the measure of burden; and of recognizing that tax rules affect people's well-being by the rules' impact on the prices people pay and the wages they receive, as well as by the direct liabilities the taxes impose. Economists know that each of these elements is important, in principle. In their recent work, Don Fullerton and Diane Rogers have tackled almost the entire agenda. For this volume they have prepared a description of their approach, together with an assessment of the potential for using it in day-to-day policy analysis.

Among the innovations I find attractive in their approach is the use of estimated lifetime earnings profiles as the basis for classifying individuals and married couples, with the ability to pay being measured by opportunity—that is, independent of the amount a person chooses to work, given the earnings profile or, as the authors would say, inclusive of the value of leisure. It is an ambitious exercise, and not surprisingly the authors need to simplify some features of the tax and transfer rules, of the sort highlighted by Lyon, and of the sustainability of the system through time, of the sort highlighted by Auerbach, Gokhale, and Kotlikoff. Fullerton and Rogers recognize, further, that the data demands and the analytical sophistication of their methods make it difficult to reproduce and explain them to policy makers. Other qualifications and concerns are articulated by Gilbert E. Metcalf, of Tufts University, in his insightful commentary.

Readers will find much in this volume with which to agree and some with which to disagree. But I am sure all will recognize that the authors have done a tremendous service in articulating the challenges and identifying realistic directions for advancing distributional analysis for making policy. I am much more sanguine about the prospects for distributional analysis after reading these chapters than I was when I set out to organize the conference.

PART ONE

What Is Wrong
with Distributional Analysis

2
Distributional Tables, Tax Legislation, and the Illusion of Precision

Michael J. Graetz

Although their meaning and contours have long been controversial, the general criteria for evaluating changes in tax law enjoy both stability and consensus. At least since Adam Smith, there has been virtually universal agreement that the nation's tax law should be fair, economically efficient, and simple to comply with and to administer. Tax law changes, therefore, should be designed to make the law more equitable, easier to comply with, and more conducive to economic growth, as well as to reduce the law's interference with private economic decision making. To be sure, precisely what the criteria imply for policy making is controversial. Fairness, is often said to require that persons with equal ability to pay taxes should pay equal amounts of tax and that persons with greater ability to pay should pay more. But disputes have long raged over the traits relevant to evaluate whether people's circumstances are appropriately similar to warrant similar treatment and over the standards for evaluating peoples' relative abilities to pay.

Nonetheless, a "fair" distribution of the tax burden among people at different levels of income has long been regarded as a necessary attribute of a just tax system, and its assessment is essential to evaluate how a nation's tax law—or proposed changes in it—measure up. Even

I want to thank William Andrews, David Bradford, Daniel Halperin, Louis Kaplow, Alvin Klevorick, Jeff Lehman, Reed Shuldiner, Alvin Warren, and participants in conferences and workshops at the American Enterprise Institute, the Harvard Law School, the University of Pennsylvania Law School, and Yale Law School for helpful comments. I also want to thank José Esteves for producing the graphs contained herein and Anand Raman for research assistance. An expanded version of this essay, including a discussion of revenue estimating, appears in the *Columbia Law Review*, as "Paint-by-Numbers Tax Lawmaking," in volume 95, pages 609–682.

tax policy analysts who regard the size of the economic pie as far more important than the way it is shared—including those who elevate economic efficiency over redistribution—do not argue that the distribution of tax burdens has no relevance. Likewise, answers to questions regarding the economic effects of proposed or enacted tax legislation are routinely disputed. Even the need to finance budget expenditures with revenues—a seemingly straightforward imperative—proves controversial in execution. The pursuit of simplicity is frequently a bystander. Conflict among these purposes is inevitable—conflict that demands and is reflected in inevitable political compromise. Trade-offs among these goals are the stuff of tax legislation.

As an example, in 1981, horizontal equity—and some contend vertical equity—was put aside in a quest for economic growth.[1] The 1986 tax reform act was motivated by an effort to restore and improve horizontal equity and to reduce the tax law's interference with economic decision making in private markets.[2] In combination, these two acts reduced the marginal tax rate at the top of the income scale from 70 percent to 28 percent. Democrats argued subsequently that Republican tax policy of the 1980s favored the rich and disadvantaged the middle class. This political attack criticized "trickle-down" economics and promised cuts to the "excessive" tax burdens on the middle class and increases in the "inadequate" taxes on the rich. These arguments became a central theme in the negotiations leading to the budget act of 1990, in the 1990 midterm elections, and in President Clinton's 1992 campaign. They also played an important role in the enactment of the 1993 budget act, which raised the top rate to 40 percent and barely passed Congress without one Republican vote.

Perhaps most important to tax policy makers, the public seems responsive to the perceived fairness of taxes—particularly of their own tax burdens, but also the burdens of others.[3] As a practical matter, tax compliance may decline if taxes are perceived by the public to be unfair. Press reports, congressional staff studies, and academic studies describing recent shifts in the nation's distribution of income and wealth in favor of the very wealthy, coupled with the public's general antitax attitude, have heightened the concerns of both the public and their representatives with issues of tax distribution. Public interest in

1. Eugene Steuerle, *The Tax Decade—How Taxes Came to Dominate the Public Agenda* (Washington, D.C.: Urban Institute, 1991), p. 107.

2. Michael J. Graetz, "The Truth about Tax Reform," *University of Florida Law Review* 40 (1988): 629–33.

3. Steven M. Sheffrin, "What Does the Public Believe about Tax Fairness?" *National Tax Journal* 46 (1993): 301.

distributional questions may explain why politicians of all political stripes seem to want to argue that their policies are progressive, thereby confirming the 1976 observation of conservative Treasury Secretary William Simon: "There appears to be a widespread consensus that an element of progression is desirable in the tax structure."[4]

Budgetary pressures have also driven recent tax legislation. Congress's concern with federal budgetary deficits has increased dramatically over the past decade. The 1986 act was constrained to be both revenue- and distributionally "neutral," thereby neither increasing nor reducing anticipated total revenues nor shifting the tax burden across differing levels of income.[5] In writing the 1986 act, revenue and distributional data were used creatively by both congressional staff and decision makers to constrain and guide tax policy making toward substantive outcomes based on agreed normative goals and widely shared legislative directions.[6] In contrast, since 1986, virtually all significant tax legislation has been a revenue-raising part of Omnibus Budget Reconciliation Act legislation, with the principal mission of deficit containment. In both 1990 and 1993, specific deficit goals—reductions in projected five-year budget deficits by a total of $500 billion in each case—dominated the policy-making process. And on both occasions, Democrats insisted that tax increases were required to increase the progressivity of the federal tax system. Indeed, in 1993, President Clinton demanded and a Democratic majority in Congress agreed that at least 70 percent of tax increases be levied on people with incomes of at least $100,000. Achieving specific revenue and distributional numbers have themselves become policy goals.

The political focus on traditional tax policy–making criteria has been subordinated in recent legislation to reflect this overriding focus of ensuring specific annual revenue effects of proposed tax policy changes over the budget period (generally five years, but under the 1993 budget act, ten years in some cases). In the 1993 act, tax-rate increases were made retroactive to the beginning of 1993 (with deferred payments allowed for three years) solely to satisfy five-year revenue targets. In addition, sizable penalties on marriage were enacted for high-income taxpayers in 1993 solely to conform to a specific combination of revenue and distributional targets, given the president's decision not to raise the top income-tax rate above 40 percent.

This increased reliance on distributional tables and revenue estimates as outcome-determinative factors in tax legislation presents two

---

4. William Simon, secretary of the Treasury, to Mrs. Llewellyn Lowe, Treasury document 76-25, reprinted in *Tax Notes* (December 27, 1976): 11.

5. Graetz, "The Truth about Tax Reform," pp. 623–25.

6. See, for example, Steuerle, *The Tax Decade*.

different problems. Although it is often important to know the likely effect of proposed tax legislation on total federal finances, with regard to revenue effects policy makers are often asking the wrong question, primarily because they have bound themselves to do so by imposing statutory budgetary requirements that turn on annual revenue effects over a five- or ten-year period. In contrast, the basic distributional question being addressed is unquestionably a proper one. In changing a tax system whose history—indeed whose constitutional status—is grounded in notions of ability to pay, it is important for policy makers to attempt to know the distributional consequences of proposed changes. The basis for congressional evaluation and decision making regarding distributional issues, however, is also seriously flawed.

Congressional decision making regarding both the revenue and distributional questions reveals a unitary weakness in the current tax-legislative process: congressional decision makers routinely suffer from what I term illusions of precision. Congress today seems to want tax policy making to turn on simple numerical answers, reminiscent of the supercomputer Deep Thought who, in the science fiction classic *The Hitchhiker's Guide to the Galaxy*, revealed that the "answer to the Great Question of Life, the Universe and Everything [was] 42."[7] Armed with mathematical answers to both revenue and distributional questions, tax policy makers routinely eschew the difficulties of exercising judgment to strike an appropriate balance among ambiguous and often conflicting normative goals, putting aside in the process the massive empirical uncertainties they inevitably face. Instead, they constrain themselves to write laws that conform to misleading or wrongheaded mathematical straitjackets.

This chapter deals in some detail with one kind of such numbers— distributional numbers—and how they are used and misused in the tax legislative process.[8] The current practice of fashioning tax legisla-

7. Douglas Adams, *The Hitchhiker's Guide to the Galaxy*, in *The Hitchhiker's Trilogy* (New York: Crown, 1983), p. 112.

8. Tax policy making is not unique in the political or legislative process in its misuse of numerical constructs. It has become well known, for example, that the consumer price index (CPI) tends to overstate the impact of inflation on purchasing power, but inflation adjustments tied to CPI changes can nevertheless be found in much legislation, including social security benefits, welfare payments, and budget rules. Similarly, the main advantage of the current measure of the "poverty level" is its consistency over time; it probably was not a good measure of poverty when first constructed in the 1940s and surely is inadequate and misleading today. Yet, legislation is routinely advanced targeting subsidies to some percentage of this "poverty level." In 1994, for example, Democrats and Republicans both linked government subsidies for health in-

tion to achieve a particular result in a distribution table creates the illusion of precision when such precision is impossible. In reaching this conclusion, I do not mean to embrace an easy attack on the theoretical difficulties and limitations of data in order to conclude that nothing of any import can or should be said. That would be palpably false. There is much we know about the likely winners and losers from changes. Decision makers need such information and are entitled to share in this knowledge. But current illusions of precision should be abandoned.

The tax policy–making process would be far better served by abandoning altogether the current practice of staffs routinely constructing distributional tables for Congress and the administration to consider *while legislation is proceeding through the Congress*. Instead, decision makers should be provided general qualitative information about how the proposed amendments to the law will likely affect the size and distribution of people's after-tax incomes. Quantitative estimates of the effects of tax legislation on the distribution of taxes should be periodically produced by the relevant tax staffs as background information for decision makers and should take into account the variations in approaches to specific issues that I discuss here in detail. In the conclusion to this chapter, I provide examples of the kinds of information that should be presented to decision makers and describe why I believe such a change would improve the tax decision–making process.

The Relevant Staffs

Policy makers receive two sets of tables that have been outcome-determinative in the legislative process: revenue tables, which estimate anticipated annual-revenue effects of each proposed change over the following five or ten years, and distributional tables, which purport to reflect the anticipated distribution among income classes of proposed changes in the tax law. The computer revolution permits new tables reflecting new policy options to be generated in a matter of hours. When different political parties are in control at the White House and the Congress, the political contest over the relevant facts sometimes produces dueling tables from the administration and congressional staffs. In recent years, as legislation has progressed through the law-

---

surance to the relationship of a family's income to the poverty level. Likewise, each year the Internal Revenue Service publishes the amount of the so-called tax gap now estimated to be more than $100 billion—the amount of underreported taxes from legal sources of income. One cannot help but wonder if the IRS knows with such precision how much in taxes is being underreported, why it does not simply collect some of this money.

making process, these distributional tables have become Congress's basis for evaluating the vertical equity of proposed legislation.

Generally, politicians get their tax-distributional information from three staffs of experts: the staff of the Joint Committee on Taxation (JCT), the Congressional Budget Office (CBO), and the Treasury's Office of Tax Analysis (OTA). JCT is the official scorekeeper for the Congress for revenue estimates, and it also provides the tax-writing committees with tables reflecting its estimates of distributional changes of pending legislation.

In 1974, budget committees were established in both the House and Senate, and the Congressional Budget Office was created to serve the new budget committees. CBO is the official scorekeeper for the Congress on spending and technical budget issues, such as the federal budgetary treatment of various health reform proposals, and it often publishes analyses of recently enacted tax legislation or issues pending before the Congress. CBO is responsible for estimating federal government spending, changes in spending in connection with appropriations and budget legislation, and total annual receipts of the federal government for each year of the five- or ten-year budget period. It does not, however, estimate the revenue consequences of specific legislative tax proposals, nor does it normally produce distributional tables for members of Congress to consider during legislative deliberations. In connection with the 1990 budget act negotiations, however, CBO did produce distributional tables of legislative proposals, presumably at the request of the Democratic congressional leadership or chairmen of the House and Senate budget committees. CBO often produces distributional analyses of legislation subsequent to enactment.

In combination, JCT and CBO estimates of spending, receipts, and revenues are critical in the legislative process, since under rules of both the House and the Senate these estimates determine whether proposed legislation is potentially subject to a point of order. If a budget point of order applies, supermajority votes—for example, sixty of the one hundred senators—are necessary to waive or override the point of order and take up the legislation on its merits.

At least since the beginning of the federal income tax in 1913, the secretary of the Treasury has had at least one economist whose principal function was to provide analysis and advice on tax-policy matters. Over time, the responsibility for tax-policy advice within the Treasury has come to reside in the Office of the Assistant Secretary for Tax Policy. The economists of this office are responsible for analyses of the economic aspects of tax-policy proposals. They make up the Treasury's Office of Tax Analysis, which reports to the secretary of Treasury through the assistant secretary for tax policy. OTA is the administration's official estimator of total budget receipts and anticipated revenue effects of proposed legislative changes. OTA also routinely provides the administration's decision makers with distributional and analytical analyses of tax proposals and legislation. Sometimes OTA's distributional tables are used by members of Congress during the formulation of legislation, but the JCT tables have dominated the legislative process in recent years. OTA's revenue estimates, however, play a critical role in the legislative process, since under the 1990 and 1993 Budget Acts the administration's official revenue estimates—not those of CBO or JCT—determine whether automatic spending reductions (so-called sequestration) take effect.

The Office of Management and Budget (OMB) is the administration's counterpart to CBO. OMB is responsible for estimating spending and is nominally responsible for estimating total receipts and revenue effects of legislation, but the substance of these latter two tasks is assigned to OTA. OMB simply takes OTA estimates of receipts and revenues and incorporates them into OMB official publications and estimates. Unlike CBO, OMB has not and does not currently perform its own analyses of tax legislation or tax policy proposals.

As this brief review suggests, both OTA and JCT revenue estimates are critical in the legislative process, while JCT distributional tables have recently been most significant. In an important public service, JCT has recently published lengthy pamphlets detailing the methodology it uses in producing distributional tables and in making revenue estimates.[9] As a typical example, table 2–1 is from the JCT Summary of the Omnibus Budget Reconciliation Act of 1993 and reflects JCT's estimates of the distributional effects of that legislation. These data are often reconfigured, explained, and sometimes contested by other congressional staffs, the media, and private analysts. Recently, the JCT revised certain important aspects of its standard distributional analyses.[10] Staff members from both OTA and CBO have also outlined their (somewhat different) methodologies.[11] Likewise, private and aca-

---

9. Joint Committee on Taxation, *Methodology and Issues in Measuring Changes in the Distribution of Tax Burdens* (Washington, D.C.: Superintendent of Documents, JCS-7-93, 1993). See also JCT, *Discussion of Revenue Estimation Methodology and Process* (Washington, D.C.: Superintendent of Documents, JCS-14-92, 1992), and *Explanation of Methodology Used to Estimate Proposals Affecting the Taxation of Income from Capital Gains* (Washington, D.C.: Superintendent of Documents, JCS-12-90, 1990).

10. Joint Committee on Taxation, *Methodology and Issues*, 1993; and Thomas A. Barthold, "How Should We Measure Distribution," *National Tax Journal* 46 (1993): 291.

11. Susan C. Nelson, "Family Economic Income and Other Income Concepts Used in Analyzing Tax Reform," in Office of Tax Analysis, Department of Trea-

TABLE 2–1
Distributional Effects of the Revenue Provisions in the 1993 OBRA

Expanded Income Class (dollars)	Present-Law Federal Taxes (billions of $)	Present-Law Average Tax Rate (percent)	Proposed Change in Tax Burden (millions of $)	Burden Change as a Share of Income (percent)
Less than 10,000	9	10.4	− 1.152	− 1.28
10,000 to 20,000	39	11.9	− 993	− 0.30
20,000 to 30,000	72	17.0	92	0.02
30,000 to 40,000	86	19.1	949	0.21
40,000 to 50,000	93	20.9	1,271	0.29
50,000 to 75,000	201	22.3	3,517	0.39
75,000 to 100,000	120	24.6	2,653	0.54
100,000 to 200,000	142	26.6	4,598	0.86
200,000 and over	168	30.2	29,683	5.39
Total, all taxpayers	930	22.1	40,800	0.97

NOTE: Includes all revenue provisions except individual and corporate estimates tax changes, information reporting for discharge of indebtedness, targeted jobs credit, capital gains incentives, provisions affecting qualified pension plans, mortgage revenue bonds, low-income housing credit, luxury tax provisions, excise tax on diesel fuel used on noncommercial motorboats, empowerment zones and enterprise communities, vaccine excise tax, GSO and FUTA extensions, transfer of Federal Reserve funds, deduction disallowance for certain health plans, orphan drug credit, and diesel fuel compliance.
SOURCE: Joint Committee on Taxation, August 3, 1993.

demic economists have demonstrated great interest in the distribution of taxes.[12]

Distributional Tables

The distributional data produced by these three government staffs are of two general types, only one of which is problematic. First, each staff

---

sury, *Compendium of Tax Research* (Washington, D.C.: Superintendent of Documents, 1987); and Richard A. Kasten "CBO's Method for Simulating the Distribution of Combined Federal Taxes Using Census, Tax Return, and Expenditure Micro-Data," Manuscript prepared for 46th Annual Federation of Tax Administrators, Cincinnati, Ohio, October 27–30, 1991 (Lexis: 91 State Tax Notes, 229-15).

12. Don Fullerton and Diane Lim Rogers, *Who Bears the Lifetime Tax Burden?* (Washington, D.C.: Brookings Institution, 1993). See also Joseph A. Pechman,

from time to time publishes distributional data as part of an analysis of various kinds of tax issues. CBO, for example, frequently publishes analyses of the distributional impact of recently enacted tax legislation, of the tax system as a whole, or of specific tax provisions. Its analyses of the revenue act of 1993 and of the exclusion from income of employer-provided health benefits offer two recent examples. Likewise, OTA annually publishes an analysis of taxes paid by higher-income taxpayers. While these documents may have more force in the legislative arena than private or academic analyses of distributional issues, they are essentially designed to serve similar functions—that is, to provide continuing information and analysis of significant tax policy issues.

A second and more problematic use of distributional tables is that made by policy makers during legislative drafting and deliberation. When tax legislation is being considered by the committees, distributional tables, such as the one set forth above as table 2–1, are reviewed by policy makers when deliberating and deciding the shape and detail of legislation being considered. As tentative decisions are made, new distributional tables reflecting the tentative new decisions are often produced, typically by JCT but sometimes by OTA as well. To serve this function, these tables must be produced and revised quickly, often in a matter of hours. Members of Congress are not especially responsive to staff requests for additional time for analysis. As I will describe subsequently, in both 1990 and 1993 important legislative decisions were taken to achieve certain results in the JCT's distributional tables (as well as specific revenue targets), and the 1986 Tax Reform Act was constrained to be distributionally (as well as revenue-) neutral.[13] This

---

Who Paid the Taxes, 1966–1985 (Washington, D.C.: Brookings Institution, 1985); and Joseph A. Pechman and B. A. Okner, *Who Bears the Tax Burden?* (Washington, D.C.: Brookings Institution, 1974).

13. In the presence of ambiguity, politicians will often also want to know how most effectively to respond to factual claims by their political adversaries. Given the nature of my enterprise here, I can simply assume that each staff regards its mission in each of these contexts as providing the best information possible to the politicians who have decision making responsibilities. I can also simply assume here that political decision makers want to be as well informed as possible to decide whether to support or to oppose alternative policies. Assuming a political actor who wants the best information available seems the best way to frame the issues to be discussed in this chapter, although we are not obliged to be Pollyannish in evaluating the judgments I offer here. We all know that there are times when immediate political advantage is of greater import to a politician than "good" policy, although we might have differing views about how frequent are those occasions. We can also admit that there

means that as legislation is being crafted, changes are made in the specifics of the legislation or proposals are added or dropped to make the distributional tables "come out right." As Mickey Kaus has put it, "distributional charts. . . . have elevated the 'details of the counting-house' into the sine qua non of justice and 'fairness.' "[14]

Given the limits of time, inadequacies of data, and important theoretical conundrums, what kind of data should be provided by the staffs to best inform the decision makers? Are the distributional tables of the sort now routinely being provided the most appropriate kind of information? Should the politicians' distributional questions be answered in the manner that economists or moral philosophers regard as theoretically the best? In these circumstances, where representatives selected through democratic processes are imposing social obligations on the citizenry, how, if at all, should the public's intuitions and ability to understand complex information constrain the process? Ultimately the question I address here is, What distributional information should be provided to decision makers in the tax policy–making process in order to enable them to make well-informed choices? If this chapter does nothing more, it proves that question to be difficult enough.

I shall approach this issue by examining limitations inherent in the staffs' ability to provide precise, noncontroversial answers to distributional questions. To begin this inquiry, I briefly examine a somewhat old-fashioned theoretical economic consensus about how best to illuminate distributional issues and to illustrate some aspects of distribution that are buried in seemingly precise summary measures. For the uninitiated, this should put more flesh on the distributional issue itself. I next explore some significant areas where the different staffs disagree over answers to specific questions necessary to construct distributional tables. Then I describe areas of staff agreement where the consensus hides potentially important information.

Impossible Goals and Impractical Tasks

Thoughtful economists have long known that it is impossible to assess precisely the effects of government policies on the distribution of in-

---

may be moments when the purveyors of the information might be pursuing their own policy agendas, rather than simply serving to best inform the decision maker. But let us put aside for now questions of potential misuse of information or abuse of position.

14. Mickey Kaus, *The End of Equality* (New York: HarperCollins, 1993), p. 22.

come and wealth. In his excellent public finance treatise, Carl Shoup describes the problem:

> To say, for example, that households with before-tax incomes between $2,000 and $5,000 pay 12 percent of that income in taxes, directly and indirectly, is to make a statement that is without significance because it is conceptually invalid. It is conceptually invalid because it postulates, for implicit comparison, a state of affairs in which there are no taxes whatever, and no government borrowing or creation of new money, hence impliedly no government services, not even of the minimum type and amount necessary to assure existence of the society. . . . [This] objection is conclusive.[15]

Shoup's basic point is quite telling: the most interesting questions—the total effects of government action (or even of one level of government, say the federal government) on the distribution of income—are impossible to evaluate, even in principle. This is because the point for comparison, namely, the distribution of income absent any government, is unknowable, indeed unimaginable. But attempting to quantify this impossible answer is the daily bread of the tax-policy staffs of the Congress and the Treasury. The first two columns of the standard distributional tables prepared routinely by CBO, JCT, and OTA purport to show the amount of taxes and average tax rates paid currently by people at different levels of income (see table 2–1, above). Indeed, virtually everyone who analyzes the distribution of tax burdens and estimates the effects of proposed changes begins at this same "conceptually invalid" place—with an estimate of the distribution of the existing tax burden. The fundamental questions that are raised by these estimates are simply never asked; the extent to which government policies have affected the amount of income earned by the people who are being evaluated in such tables is buried, as it must be. This means that the *least controversial* aspect of the table—the snapshot of conditions as they supposedly exist, before any policy changes are considered—is itself constructed on quicksand.

It is neither conceptually invalid nor without meaning to inquire whether a change in tax (or other government) policy is likely to make the distribution of after-tax income or wealth more equal or more unequal.[16] To the contrary, this question is frequently essential and often answerable, at least generally, with much confidence. It should not be controversial to say that a shift from a progressive personal-income tax to a flat-rate consumption tax would make the after-tax distribution of

15. Carl S. Shoup, *Public Finance* (Chicago: Aldine, 1969), pp. 577–78.
16. Ibid., pp. 578–79.

income more unequal. But the way in which answers to such questions are presented to decision makers for evaluating changes in policy is troublesome.

Where Has Gini Gone?

Toward the beginning of this century, and for a long while thereafter, there was little dispute within the economics profession about the proper way—at least in theory—to measure the distributional effects of changes in the tax law: the magnitude of each unit's after-tax income would be determined before and after the revision of the tax law and compared. To determine whether a tax change increases or reduces income inequality and to depict these effects graphically, one would typically construct two Lorenz curves,[17] one before the change, the other after—and then compare their Gini coefficients.[18]

A Lorenz curve arranges the population from the poorest to the richest along the horizontal axis and the percentages of income enjoyed by various percentages of the population along the vertical axis. Zero percent of the population will always be shown as having 0 percent of the income, and 100 percent of the population will always have 100 percent of the income. In this construction, if everyone has the same income, the Lorenz curve will be a diagonal straight line. Whenever the poor have proportionally less income than the rich, the common state of affairs, the Lorenz curve stretches below the diagonal, with its slope typically rising as one moves from poorer to richer segments of the population. Figure 2–1 depicts a typical Lorenz curve.

If the Lorenz curve after a tax revision lies entirely between the diagonal and the preenactment Lorenz curve, the tax change will have made the distribution of income relatively more equal. The introduction of an effective progressive income tax, which distributes taxes more unequally than pretax incomes by imposing a higher share of taxes as pretax income rises, would result in a more equal distribution of posttax than pretax income, presumably for every segment of the population (assuming that the tax does not result in a reorganization of the orderings of pretax income levels). Such an outcome is shown in figure 2–2. In contrast, a proportional income tax should preserve relative differences in pretax income, resulting in an unchanged Lorenz curve and, on this criterion at least, would be distributionally neutral.

Of course, comparing Lorenz curves tells nothing about absolute levels of income, only relative shares. There is no way to tell from these

17. M. O. Lorenz "Methods for Measuring Concentration of Wealth," *Journal of the American Statistical Association*, vol. 9 (1905).

18. C. Gini, *Variabilitá e Mutabilitá* (Bologna: 1912).

FIGURE 2–1
LORENZ CURVE OF RELATIVE WEALTH

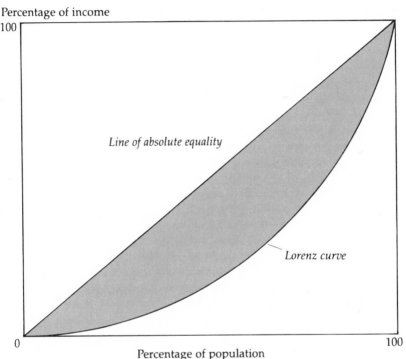

Percentage of income

Line of absolute equality

Lorenz curve

Percentage of population

SOURCE: Author.

curves alone how much lower (or higher) the levels of income are before and after the tax change. Moreover, a universally equality-enhanc-
ing result of the sort depicted in figure 2–2 is by no means inevitable
from a change in policy, and if the Lorenz curve after the change
crosses the one before the change, simply eyeballing the graphs will
tell little. Some index number is needed to identify whether relative
inequality has been increased or decreased. This is where Gini came
in. A Gini coefficient quantifies how far an income distribution is from
the diagonal (the equal distribution of incomes) by measuring the area
between the diagonal and a given Lorenz curve as a fraction of the total
area under the diagonal. This fraction will always be between zero and
one, with zero representing an equal distribution (a Lorenz curve along
the diagonal) and one representing maximum inequality. Lower Gini
coefficients signal more equal distributions of income. Since a Gini coefficient can always be calculated for any Lorenz curve, Gini permits a
complete ranking of income distributions, regardless of the shapes or

FIGURE 2–2

LORENZ CURVE AFTER A TAX REVISION

Percentage of income

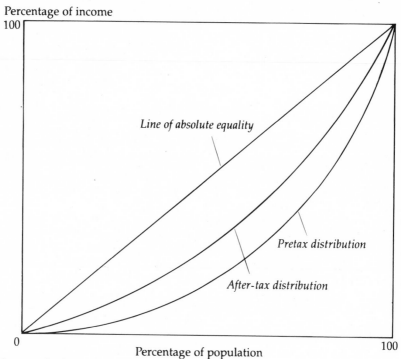

SOURCE: Author.

intersections of the Lorenz curves being compared. This comprehensive ordering quality is useful and no doubt accounts for some substantial measure of Gini's longstanding popularity. Any transfer from a richer to a poorer person will always reduce the value of the Gini coefficient. Moreover, the Gini coefficient will remain unchanged if everyone's income is lowered (or raised) in the same proportion. Thus a progressive income tax would lower the Gini coefficient, and a proportional income tax would leave it unchanged.[19]

19. Gini coefficients and other measures of income inequality can be used in a variety of ways. The text, for example, discusses Lorenz curves and Gini coefficients in comparing pretax and posttax Ginis and also in comparing posttax Ginis before and after a change in the tax law. Changes in tax laws may produce changes in pretax incomes, which, in principle at least, might be captured by comparing pretax Ginis before and after the change, although observed changes in pretax income may be attributable to a variety of other

The ethical and normative force of the Gini coefficient, however, has been questioned.[20] Although transfers from richer to poorer people will always reduce the Gini coefficient, changes in Gini coefficients turn on the number of people between the income levels of the redistribution without regard to the differing levels of income. Weights are given to people based solely on peoples' rank ordering by income level.[21] The important point of these criticisms has been to expand the numbers and kinds of measures of inequality in the literature,[22] to demonstrate the normative complexity of the concept of inequality, and to suggest the controversy—or, on the contrary, the closed-mindedness—of relying on any single measure of inequality.[23] Nevertheless, economic treatments of income distribution issues continue to accord Gini a prominent place.[24]

---

factors. Relatively greater incomes to educated people clearly made the pretax distribution of income more unequal during the 1980s. Changes in tax law also might change the relationship of pretax and posttax income curves. Quantifying this effect is somewhat more difficult; one way to do so would be to examine the *difference* between pretax minus posttax Ginis before the change and pretax minus posttax Ginis after the change. Keeping all this straight requires close scrutiny, and politicians often blur the various elements. Throughout the 1980s, Republicans often pointed to the increased share of income taxes paid by higher-income taxpayers during the period following the 1981 tax act, but this could have occurred as a result of higher shares of pretax income, even if the tax law had become less progressive. The relative shares of pretax income might or might not have been connected to the tax change. Some would argue that pretax incomes of upper-income taxpayers grew because people responded to lower tax rates by working harder and forgoing tax-sheltered income. Others would contend that higher returns to education prompted the increase and that upper-income people received more pay for the same work as the economy became more global and less regulated.

20. A. Sen, *On Economic Inequality* (Oxford: Oxford University Press, 1973), pp. 31–39; and A. B. Atkinson, "On the Measurement of Inequality," *Journal of Economic Theory*, vol. 2 (1970).

21. Sen, *On Economic Inequality*, pp. 32–34.

22. Atkinson, "On the Measurement of Inequality."

23. Sen, *On Economic Inequality*, pp. 31–39.

24. See, for example, Richard J. Aronson and Peter J. Lambert, "Decomposing the Gini Coefficient to Reveal the Vertical, Horizontal and Re-ranking Effects of Income Taxation," *National Tax Journal* 47 (1994): 273; Alissa Goodman and Steve Webb, "For Richer, for Poorer: The Changing Distribution of Income in the United Kingdom 1961–1991," Institute for Fiscal Studies, Commentary 42, London, 1994; and Peter J. Lambert, *The Distribution and Redistribution of Income: A Mathematical Analysis* (New York: Manchester University Press, 1993).

I have been unable to find any occasion on which OTA or JCT has published Gini coefficients for proposed or enacted tax laws. Perhaps they have rejected this idea because of the difficulties with Gini noted above. Another potential reason—that neither the populace nor their elected representatives would have any idea what a Gini coefficient is or means—although possible, seems unlikely. These staffs' regular business is translating difficult and obscure legal and economic concepts to make them understandable to politicians, and Gini coefficients or other such measures of the effects of tax changes on the aftertax distribution of income do not seem to pose any unique problems in this regard. Indeed the CBO has published studies on the changes over time in the aftertax distribution of income, including estimates of Gini coefficients to evaluate the relative progressivity of legislation of 1977, 1981, and 1984, but this is not its standard procedure for distributing tax changes.[25] In its 1992 *Economic Report of the President*, the Council of Economic Advisers, while emphasizing that they present an incomplete picture, also set forth Gini coefficients of U.S. family income for the period 1947–1991, which showed relatively gradual increases in Gini—less equality of incomes—during the period 1968–1990.[26] Such shifts in the distribution of income over time are, of course, only partly caused by changes in the tax law; market forces and other government actions may be far more important.

It is well beyond my task here to rehearse or comment on the debates that have occurred. Rather my purposes have been two: first, to introduce uninitiated readers to the subject of Lorenz curves and Gini coefficient, to begin to illustrate the issues and difficulties that can lie behind what may appear to be precise comparisons of different income distributions. Each of the measures used makes controversial choices about what information to include and about how to depict comparisons or changes over time. Second, this discussion demonstrates that the effects of the relevant government policies on the distribution of after-tax income have historically been of concern to economists and others who have long analyzed income-distributional issues outside the legislative arena. Ultimately it is the impact of legislation on the distribution of aftertax incomes that should be of concern in analyzing distributional consequences of legislative changes.

Regardless of the difficulties with the precise mechanisms for quantifying and comparing different policy proposals, the focus on aftertax incomes, which is fundamental to the construction of Lorenz

25. Congressional Budget Office, *The Changing Distribution of Federal Taxes: 1975–1990* (Washington, D.C.: Superintendent of Documents, 1987).

26. Council of Economic Advisers, *The Economic Report of the President* (Washington, D.C.: Superintendent of Documents, 1992).

curves (and Gini coefficients and other inequality measures based on them), remains an extremely useful baseline for evaluating the questions I raise here. Indeed, in my opinion, the impact of policy proposals or legislative changes on the distribution of aftertax incomes is at bottom the distributional question that policy makers are and should be concerned with. As will become clear in the following section, however, distributional tables, particularly of the JCT, often stray rather far from even attempting to answer this question. But I am confident that policy makers often are not aware that the distributional tables they are using address quite a different question.

Staff Disagreements in Constructing Distributional Tables

There are several areas of disagreement in constructing distributional tables. I shall discuss five below: distributing changes in taxes versus changes in burden, measuring income, units of analysis, relevant time horizon, and tax-incidence assumptions.

Distributing Changes in Taxes versus Changes in Burden. Since virtually every normative measure (including Gini coefficients) of changes in income distributions expected from or caused by changes in government policies is based on comparisons of after-tax incomes, it is only natural to assume that distributional tables reflect the staffs' best estimates of who will bear tax (revenue) increases or pay reduced taxes attributable to tax-law changes. Although this generally is true for OTA, JCT distributes the changes in tax revenue that would result if no one changed behavior in response to the change in the tax law, rather than its estimates of the changes in taxes it expects to result from the changes in law.

To understand the JCT methodology—which has recently been and may well continue to be of great importance in the political process—it is necessary to understand how the JCT distributional analysis differs from its estimates of revenue effects of tax changes.[27] In estimating the revenue effects of tax changes, JCT takes into account its predictions of the behavioral responses of people affected by the tax (including consumers, producers, and suppliers of capital and labor). It holds constant, however, major macroeconomic variables (such as the level of GDP, aggregate cash and noncash wages, corporate profits, interest rates, and assumptions of inflation). The relevant macroeconomic variables are given to JCT by CBO, which uses them in its general-budget estimates. OTA follows the same practice for revenue

---

27. Joint Committee on Taxation, *Methodology and Issues.*

estimates, except that the macroeconomic variables are supplied by the so-called troika (the Council of Economic Advisers, the Office of Management and Budget, and Treasury's assistant secretary for economic policy). Thus, for example, in estimating the revenue effects of the income-tax rate increases enacted in 1993, JCT took into account likely shifts of investments of high-income people to purchases of tax-exempt bonds or to other tax-favored investments by substituting low-dividend, high-capital gain stocks for high-dividend stocks. It did not take into account the macroeconomic impact on GDP or total wages.[28] Likewise, in estimating the revenue effects from President Clinton's 1994 proposal for a $1 increase in the tobacco tax, the JCT and OTA took into account their estimates of how many people would quit or reduce smoking in response to the tax increase. It is useful to think of these revenue calculations as occurring in two stages: JCT and OTA first estimate the revenue gain or loss that would occur if behavior were unchanged—the cognoscenti call this the static revenue change—and then estimate any offset to the static-revenue estimate attributable to peoples' behavioral responses. Revenue estimates take into account both these aspects of proposed or enacted tax changes.

In constructing their distributional tables, however, JCT and CBO are interested in the distribution of changes in economic well-being (which they label "tax burdens") rather than changes in taxes paid and use only the static-revenue change in measuring the change in tax burdens to be distributed across income classes. The JCT only distributes the static-revenue line in estimating changes in economic burden. It regards its policy of ignoring behavioral effects as necessary "to present meaningful estimates of the change in well-being."[29] Thus, voluntary behavioral shifts and any additional taxes which accompany them are ignored by JCT in producing tables reflecting changes in the economic burdens of taxation. The JCT decision to use the static-revenue estimate as a measure of the changes in economic burden is based on a straightforward argument.

To the extent that increases in the actual taxes paid are attributable to behavioral changes, such as a voluntary increase in the behavior that is to be taxed, the voluntary increases in the taxed behavior must have been at least equaled or exceeded by some other benefit; otherwise, the change in behavior would not have occurred. In the case of decreases in tax rates, voluntary increases in the behavior subject to the tax reduction are therefore ignored. Likewise, in the case of an increase in tax rates, offsetting reductions in revenue attributable to behavioral re-

---

28. Joint Committee on Taxation, *Discussion of Revenue Estimation Methodology*.

29. Joint Committee on Taxation, *Methodology and Issues*, pp. 28–29.

sponses reflect changes that taxpayers would have preferred not to have made, absent the tax increase. This means that in such cases the static-revenue estimate overstates the change in burden, and the dynamic-revenue change understates the burden. As the JCT explicitly acknowledges, the decision to estimate burdens using the static-revenue estimate has certain systematic effects: it "overestimates the loss of economic well-being due to a tax increase, and understates the progressive improvement in economic well-being due to a tax reduction."[30] In other words, when tax decreases are translated into economists' measures of "welfare gains and losses," the static-revenue loss represents a minimum of the welfare gain because the behavioral changes that are ignored would occur only if they also added to the person's welfare. In contrast, static-revenue gains from tax increases typically reflect the maximum welfare loss, because people's behavioral responses will be undertaken for the purpose of reducing the welfare losses that would otherwise occur. If one regards the key distributional question as the effect of the tax change on the distribution of after-tax income, the JCT's practice of distributing static-revenue change overstates the burden of tax increases and understates the effect of tax reductions.[31] The JCT distribution methodology is intended as an easy, feasible approximation of changes in economic well-being. In some cases, a proper measurement of burdens will equate to changes in after-tax income, but in other instances, the benefits that occur will be in psychological well-being—so-called psychic income—or some other nonmonetary benefit that will not be connected to after-tax income.

In contrast to both JCT and CBO, OTA's distribution tables reflect for each income class its best estimates of the actual changes in revenues expected to result from the change in law, taking into account both the static-revenue estimate and predicted behavioral responses. OTA therefore is measuring changes in actual taxes paid, and if this information is combined with changes in pretax income, a straightforward determination of changes in after-tax income becomes possible.

This difference in methodology between JCT and OTA is extremely important but not well understood by policy makers. While distributing changes in burden rather than changes in taxes has been a long-standing practice of JCT, at least with respect to changes in capital gains taxes, it has only recently described and defended this process. In 1993 JCT also changed the heading on its tax-distributional

---

30. Ibid.

31. Each of the observations in this paragraph assumes no changes in macroeconomic variables or, following JCT and OTA common practice, ignores such changes.

tables, so that instead of showing "changes in taxes," columns 3 and 4 of the tables now show "changes in tax burden." The first two columns of the JCT table, which show the existing prechange state of affairs, show the distribution of taxes, not an estimate of the distribution of the burden of existing taxes. This means that the JCT table contains a mixture of apples and oranges, although the juxtaposition of the figures implies that the columns should be compared.

Thus, in distributing the tax-rate increases of the 1993 legislation, the JCT distributional table (table 2–1) reflects the increase in taxes that would be paid by high-income taxpayers if the tax-rate increase induced *no* behavioral response. To the extent that taxpayers avoid paying additional taxes attributable to the rate increase by shifting their investment portfolios, for example, toward tax-exempt bonds, or by substituting leisure or nonmarket work for taxable income, the increase in tax progressivity will be less than policy makers would naturally be led to expect based on the JCT tables. In other words, if it were possible to look at the effect of the tax-rate increase as it would be looked at retrospectively, say in the year after enactment, the JCT would, *ceteris paribus*, always show a smaller increase in actual taxes paid than the increased tax burden depicted by its distributional tables. As suggested above, this means that a JCT distributional table for years following enactment will show a distribution of existing taxes (columns 1 and 2 of table 2–1) that is inherently (and always) inconsistent with its methodology for distributing the burden of proposed or enacted tax changes (columns 3 and 4 of table 2–1). Although the JCT is estimating changes in burdens, rather than changes in after-tax income, it does not (and cannot) measure existing burdens, only existing taxes paid.

To understand further the implications of this decision, let us look more closely at a few specific cases that recently have been important in the policy-making arena—reductions in capital gains taxes and increases in tobacco taxes—and briefly consider a recent proposal for a high tax on certain kinds of ammunition. First, during George Bush's repeated efforts between 1989 and 1992 to reintroduce a lower tax rate for capital gains, the tax policy community focused considerable attention on differences in revenue estimates between OTA and JCT. Beginning with the 1990 budget act, however, differences in their *distributional* methodologies became even more important than differing revenue estimates to the politics of capital-gains tax cuts. The capital gains distributions of JCT and OTA differ for a number of reasons, including the fact that Treasury's measure of "family economic income" includes capital gains as they accrue, while JCT's "expanded income" includes gains only when realized. But differences in defining the income classes have relatively minor consequences (see text, below). Of far greater, indeed critical, importance is JCT's policy of distributing the burden—or static-revenue estimate—rather than its estimate of the change in tax liabilities after taking behavioral changes into account. In contrast, OTA's tables distribute its estimates of changes in actual taxes paid.

In the case of capital-gains tax reductions, this practice means that JCT's distribution omits any effect of increased realizations of capital gains attributable to the reduction of capital gains rates, and its distribution tables depict a total reduction in tax burden four to six times greater than JCT's own estimates of the reductions in tax collections created by the capital-gains tax cut. Since the great bulk of tax savings from a capital-gains rate reduction accrues to the upper-income taxpayers, any offsetting tax increase on those taxpayers to achieve "distributional neutrality" in JCT's tables—whether through base broadening or rate increases—would have be four to six times as great as the JCT's projected revenue loss of a capital-gains tax reduction. This effect is made clear by the JCT pamphlet on capital gains discussing the capital-gains tax reduction proposed in President Bush's fiscal year 1991 budget. JCT estimated a total revenue loss of $11.4 billion during the period 1990–1995, with the greatest revenue loss in any one year totaling $4.3 billion (in 1992 and 1994).[32] In its distributional table, however, JCT distributes a one-year tax reduction of $15.9 billion to upper-income individuals—its static-revenue loss, an amount about four times greater than its largest estimated revenue loss for any year.[33] Figure 2–3 shows the distribution of JCT's estimated revenue loss—the expected change in actual taxes—compared with its own distribution of the reduction in tax burden.

These distributions show the alternative revenue increases necessary in each income class to offset a capital-gains tax reduction and to achieve distributional neutrality in a distributional table, depending on whether the actual (estimated) change in taxes or the (estimated) static effect only is distributed. JCT's methodology for distributing capital gains had not changed, although for some reason the capital-gains cuts of the 1993 act are omitted from JCT's distribution table.[34]

If the capital-gains proposal were adopted and JCT's prediction of revenues proved exactly accurate, its distributions of "existing federal taxes" in subsequent years would reflect only the actual change in tax revenues in each income class. Thus, JCT's methodology of distributing tax proposals is not consistent with its methodology for distributing existing federal taxes, and a capital-gains tax cut would appear to distribute very differently looking forward and backward.

---

32. Joint Committee on Taxation, *Explanation of Methodology*, pp. 3, 10.

33. Ibid., p. 46.

34. Joint Committee on Taxation, *Methodology and Issues*, p. 29, table 1, supra, n. 4.

FIGURE 2–3

DISTRIBUTIONAL EFFECT OF THE ADMINISTRATION'S CAPITAL GAINS PROPOSAL
ON INCOMES OF LESS THAN $10,000 TO INCOMES OF MORE THAN $200,000
(1990 income levels)

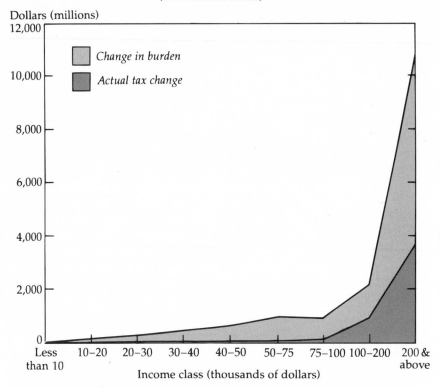

SOURCE: JCT, *Explanation of Methodology.*

Moreover, the JCT's use of static-revenue losses as a proxy for distributing changes in tax burdens creates incentives and opportunities
for political gamesmanship. In the 1990 budget summit agreement, the
multiplier effect from JCT's methodology for distribution of capital
gains was avoided by substituting a proposal equivalent in present
value terms to a capital-gains reduction on corporate stock—an immediate deduction for a portion of the cost of purchasing corporate
stock.[35] This difference demonstrates the inadequacy of using the static

35. For a demonstration that immediate deduction of the cost of an asset is
equivalent in present value to exempting the gain, see Graetz, *Federal Income
Taxation: Principles and Policies*, 2d. ed. (Foundation Press, 1988), pp. 386–89.
There were other important differences in the capital gains and immediate

MICHAEL J. GRAETZ

revenue loss as a proxy for welfare loss. While the welfare effects of two changes such as these should be identical, the effects depicted in the JCT's distributional tables were strikingly different. As a result, the tax increases necessary to neutralize the distribution effects of the immediate deduction form of tax cut were one-fifth the size of the tax increases necessary to neutralize the capital-gains rate cut.

Likewise, the potential regressivity of proposals for increased tobacco taxes concerned members of Congress in both 1990, when these taxes were most recently raised, and again in 1994, when legislators considered a tobacco-tax increase proposed to finance in part President Clinton's health-care reform proposals. In distributing the burden of these tax proposals to income classes, JCT distributed the static-revenue loss—the increased taxes that would be paid if no one stopped or reduced smoking in response to the change in taxes—even though this reduction in smoking is the behavioral response that proponents of this particular tax increase are attempting to induce. Politicians not intimately familiar with JCT methodology would naturally assume after looking at JCT's distributional tables that the burden of such a tobacco-tax increase is far more regressive than JCT estimates. Again, to offset such a tax increase to achieve distributional neutrality in JCT's tables, a far larger tax reduction would have to be enacted for the income levels burdened by the tobacco-tax increase. And once again, the distributional consequences of such changes would look quite different retrospectively; a change shown as distributionally neutral when viewed prospectively would be reflected as a total tax reduction when viewed after subsequent distributions of existing taxes.

For a related example, consider Senator Daniel Patrick Moynihan's 1994 proposal for a massive tax increase on certain forms of ammunition. Senator Moynihan clearly intended to increase the price of such ammunition so that virtually no one would purchase it. A reasonable revenue estimate of the tax increase would be approximately zero, but unless the JCT abandoned its standard practice, its distributional table of the increased ammunition taxes attributable to the rate increase, ignoring behavior—distribution of the static line—would show a large tax increase for a handful of people. This seems to be an example of a

---

deduction proposals that affected the magnitude of the revenue losses of the two proposals. The capital-gains proposal was retroactive, for example, and the immediate deduction was not, but the basic point of the text also held in a comparison with a prospective capital-gains proposal. The static-revenue loss from an immediate deduction did not take into account stock purchases stimulated by the new tax incentive and therefore produced far smaller effects in the distributional tables.

37

case in which the JCT staff pamphlet suggests it would probably "exercise its judgment and adjust the burden from the static revenue estimate." Whether the proposed tobacco-tax increase would fall into that category or not is a mystery. Moreover, policy makers are not likely to know when such adjustments are made or what their size is.

In my view, the JCT staff decision to attempt to estimate changes in burdens rather than changes in taxes is a disservice to the political process. First, there will often be no reason to believe that the static-revenue estimate is a good measure of burden. Some people would quit smoking, for example, in response to a $.20 increase in the cigarette tax, just as they would in response to a $1 increase. For these people, even under the JCT reasoning, a $.20 tax increase is the correct measure of their burden, not a $1 tax increase. This point holds true for all people who are inframarginal and would quit smoking in response to a tax increase smaller than the one proposed.

Second, if one believes that the appropriate distributional question relates to the changes in after-tax incomes that result from the change in the tax law (see the discussion of Lorenz curves and Gini coefficients), the static-revenue loss is totally disconnected from that measure.

Third, the JCT tables are constructed in a manner that will always produce different results looking forward and looking backward, even if all the important variables turn out to be exactly as the JCT estimates they will be. If one expects policy makers to look both forward at distributional effects of proposed changes and backward at the distribution of taxes after the change, one will find that the JCT staff predictions never match experience. Furthermore, the first two columns of the JCT table depict distributions of existing taxes, and columns 3 and 4 show distributions of changes in burdens. Thus JCT's decision to distribute burdens seems inevitably to add confusion to the policy process.

Fourth, even if one believes that the static-revenue loss is a better measure of welfare loss or economic burden than the actual tax increases that will occur, the JCT's decision to distribute the static-revenue loss remains troubling. The effort to measure welfare loss does not seem to be answering the question that political decision makers are asking. Inevitably, notwithstanding the JCT's admirable recent publication of its methodology and its new willingness to discuss this issue publicly, JCT tax-distribution tables will be understood by political decision makers and the public at large as estimates of the distribution of the change in taxes that the changes in law are expected to produce. Of course, this objection might be dismissed as tautological. If the question the policy maker is asking—or thinks he is asking—relates to the distribution of the changes in the taxes that actually will be paid, any answer that departs from this measure obviously is inappropriate and has the potential for mischief in the political process. Different people may reach opposite judgments about the question being asked, but—having tried on a number of occasions in 1990 to have policy makers of both political parties comprehend the JCT's methodology—I am confident about the potential for misunderstandings.

Finally, further confusion results from the fact that the Treasury and congressional staffs have reached differing judgments on this matter. When tax changes are not expected to induce substantial changes in behavior, the estimated static-revenue change will not differ significantly from the revenue estimate itself, and OTA and JCT tables will look similar. Tables reflecting increased personal exemptions or limitations on deductions for state-income taxes will look very similar, whether produced by OTA or JCT. However, there will be important differences between the estimates shown by OTA in distributing actual taxes and those of the JCT in distributing static-revenue losses in every instance where the expected behavioral responses to a tax change are large. Tables grouping large numbers of proposed changes will often include proposals of both sorts. Multiple presentations of such information may have advantages and disadvantages. They will demonstrate a wide range of answers for policy makers, and when the political masters of the Treasury and Congress are members of the same party, this may be useful. But when the party controlling the executive and the majority in Congress are different, each staff will be accused of manipulating data for political purposes or caving in to please their political masters. Surely this undermines the reliability of the tax policy–making process. Multiple presentations by the same staff would avoid this problem and probably should be encouraged.

Although OTA's practice of distributing estimated changes in taxes generally produces a better estimate of the effects of tax changes on aftertax income and thus seems preferable to JCT's practice of distributing static-revenue changes (as a proxy for welfare or burden changes), there are occasions when the distribution of estimated revenue changes itself can be misleading. OTA estimated, for example, that President Bush's proposed exclusions from income of a portion of capital gains would increase federal revenues in both the short and the long term by inducing sufficient additional realizations of capital gains so that taxes assessed on these additional realizations were predicted to more than offset the taxes lost because of the exclusion of a portion of gains. OTA distribution tables therefore showed a tax increase for the upper-income classes in circumstances where these people would clearly benefit, not suffer, from a capital-gains tax cut. Obviously, the idea that these income groups "deserve" some additional tax reduction to offset this increase in taxes is absurd. The existence of such anomalies offers further evidence of the dangers of decision makers' simply relying on the numerical answers provided by distributional tables to determine the effects of their policies, rather than directly addressing the question of what kinds of offsetting changes, if any, are necessary to achieve results that can be agreed on as fair.

Thus, both staffs' methodologies may have significant shortcomings when assessing certain types of policy changes. Yet relying on the staffs to make ad hoc adjustments to their standard methodologies when appropriate to achieve reasonable results would give extraordinary discretionary power to the staff and would create significant potential for mischief. In contrast, there is little disagreement about the general distributional consequences of the kinds of tax changes I have discussed here. It would be quite easy for JCT and Treasury staff to describe in narrative form the general effects on people at different income levels of tax changes such as these. The process of quantifying the effects of such changes, however, inevitably introduces distortions.

The Measurement of Income. Although all three relevant tax staffs use an annual measure of income rather than a lifetime measure (an issue that is discussed below), there is nevertheless considerable divergence in how the staffs measure annual income. JCT uses a concept of expanded income, which adds to adjusted gross income for federal income tax purposes estimates of certain cash receipts not included in adjusted gross income. JCT includes tax-exempt interest and workers' compensation payments, certain federal entitlement benefits under social security and Medicare, and certain excluded employer-paid fringe benefits, such as for health and life insurance; but it does not permit certain deductions disallowed under the minimum tax (for example, state and local taxes), and it makes an adjustment relating to corporate taxes. Under this measure of expanded income, JCT includes capital gains only when they are realized through the sales of assets, and it includes retirement income when it is actually received rather than when contributions are made by individuals or employers to retirement plans or when income is earned by such plans for their beneficiaries.

OTA classifies taxpayers by a different measure of income. OTA attempts to measure income by including accruals of capital gains and losses, without regard to whether they are realized for tax purposes; by imputing to individuals income as earned in pension funds and inside interest buildup on life insurance; by adding a much greater range of nontaxable government transfer payments, including AFDC; and by including imputed rent on owner-occupied housing.

OTA attempts to adjust its estimates of accrued capital gains for inflation, an adjustment not made by either of the two other staffs, and apparently none of the staffs adjust interest income or expenses for inflation. Whenever inflation occurs, interest income is generally overstated, as are interest deductions in comparison with inflation-adjusted real incomes. These misstatements distort the ability to compare the relationship of taxes to real income, among different taxpayers (depending, for example, on their borrowing and lending practices) and among the same taxpayers across years (taxpayers with identical real incomes typically have different nominal incomes in different years).

Most economists would agree that Treasury's broader measure of economic income is theoretically more appropriate, but the data available to the JCT are more reliable. Indeed, the JCT describes its income concept as "a considered compromise between theory, ease of implementation, and understandability."[36] As is well recognized within the tax professional community, many alternative measures of income might be used by these staffs. Indeed, CBO uses a third measure, which is based on cash receipts and closely linked to the federal income tax definition of income. CBO ignores noncash income, accrued but unrealized changes in family wealth, and imputed income.[37] Thus, CBO's measure of income is closer to JCT's definition than to OTA's. Figure 2–4 shows the different estimates of effective tax rates of pre-1993 tax law under the three staffs' different income and classification measures.

Obviously, the trade-off between greater theoretical purity and more reliable data is a judgment that different staffs can be expected to make differently, and, indeed, that the same staff might make differently at different times. JCT emphasizes the importance of understandability in choosing an income measure, although there is considerable irony in this choice, given its decision to measure changes in economic burden rather than in tax changes. People will probably have different judgments about the importance of public understandability as a criterion for constructing distributional tables. Consider, for example, OTA's decision to include imputed rent on owner-occupied housing as income. Tax-policy experts will recognize such imputed rent to be income in theory, and people readily understand that taxpayers who

36. Joint Committee on Taxation, *Explanation of Methodology*, p. 16.
37. Richard A. Kasten, "CBO's Methodology for Simulating the Distribution of Combined Federal Taxes Using Census, Tax Return and Expenditure Microdata," *State Tax Notes*, November 19, 1991.

FIGURE 2–4

EFFECTIVE FEDERAL TAX RATES FOR INCOMES UP TO $200,000 AND OVER

Percent

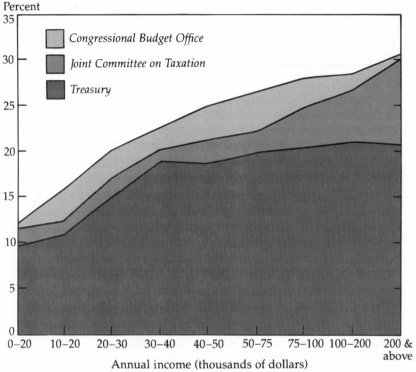

NOTES: Numbers are given as a percentage of pretax income. OTA numbers are at 1994 income levels. JCT and CBO are at 1993 income levels.
SOURCES: Office of Tax Analysis, February 1993; Joint Committee on Taxation, 1993, table 2; Congressional Budget Office memorandum, February 11, 1993.

own their own homes generally are wealthier than those who do not. If distribution tables were constructed with respect to wealth, an adjustment for owner-occupied housing would be important and straightforward, and several of OTA's adjustments can be understood as ways to take differences in wealth into account through the income measure. The concept of imputed income, however, is not comprehensible to the public. Most people do not view imputed rent as income. Consider the following quotation from David Brinkley:

> Finally, a few words about federal taxes and what some of the great minds in the U.S. Treasury are thinking about.
> The Treasury likes to calculate the American people's ability to pay taxes based not on how much money we have, but

on how much we might have or could have had. For example, a family that owns a house and lives in it, the Treasury figures that if the family didn't own the house and rented it from somebody else, the rent would be $500 a month. So it would add that amount, $6,000 a year, to the family's so-called imputed income. Imputed income is income you might have had, but don't. They don't tax you on that amount.

The IRS does not play this silly game. Instead the Treasury calculates how much they could take away from us if they decided to. If that were the system, consider the possibilities. How about being taxed on Ed McMahon's $10 million magazine lottery? You didn't win it, you say? But you could have. The Treasury must have something better to do. If not, there is a good place for Clinton to cut some spending.

For all of us at ABC News, until next week, thank you.[38]

Politicians (and the public generally) would no doubt have reactions similar to Brinkley's. The important question here is the trade-off between the benefits of greater theoretical precision and the costs of public bewilderment or distrust. Obviously, the different tax staffs have reached different judgments as to which aim should prevail.

The Unit of Analysis—Families, Couples, Individuals, or Households. In showing the distribution of existing taxes and proposals for change, it is important to determine whether and how to aggregate members of a family or household. Treating each individual separately would clearly be a poor choice; it would, for example, generally treat nonworking spouses who have no independent income as having zero or low income, without regard to the money earned by a working spouse on behalf of the family, and it would do the same with young children. Nevertheless, the individual is routinely the unit of analysis in widely used per capita income statistics. In principle, since a family or household's aggregate income is typically shared for living expenses, the family or household is the appropriate unit for use in distributional tables. For many people, the unit "family" and the unit "household" are interchangeable and would generally serve to aggregate income of parents and dependent children, while ignoring variations in patterns of sharing income.

When a nuclear family has split apart, however, aggregation of all family income does not seem appropriate. Some adjustment is necessary to account for alimony or child-support payments. In practice, the allocation of these payments in distributional tables will turn on their

---

38. "This Week with David Brinkley," Washington, D.C.: ABC News, February 28, 1993.

statutory-tax treatment, which, for all practical purposes, is essentially elective. Even when the family stays together, questions remain, such as the age at which a child is treated as moving outside the family unit and regarded as a separate unit for distributional analysis. Similar questions occur when there are dependents in the household who are not children—for example, grandparents residing in the parents' home. I do not treat these questions in any detail here.

Surprisingly, given the general theoretical consensus that the family or household is the appropriate unit for analysis, each staff follows a different approach in classifying taxpayers. The JCT staff, in light of the difficulty of constructing family or household income from data available on tax returns, stays close to information available from tax returns and classifies taxpayers based on tax filing status. JCT thus generally does not include minor children with their parents; JCT generally ignores dependents in constructing distributional tables.[39] Because the JCT takes no account of dependents who file separate returns, their methodology eliminates nearly 15 percent of returns filed. JCT expects to aggregate family income in the future when the quality of tax data improves through better social security number matching.[40]

In contrast, OTA and CBO apparently regard the theoretical advantages of using family or household units as outweighing the disadvantages of having to impute incomes among different tax returns. Thus, despite the shortcomings of the data available to them, both OTA and CBO use statistical analyses to estimate total family income and use families as their basis for analysis. There are also a variety of potential approaches in the weighting of family units in determining the division of income.[41] For example, OTA uses the family as the unit of

---

39. Joint Committee on Taxation, *Explanation of Methodology*, p. 13, nn. 16 and 97.

40. Ibid.

41. This issue is well demonstrated in the following example from Atkinson, 1983, pp. 52–53 (expressed in dollars rather than in British pounds):

> The choice of weights may make a significant difference. Some of the effects may be seen from the simple example of a hypothetical, male-dominated society where there are 20 men each with a wealth of $20,000, 80 men with $7500, and 100 women with no wealth. All the 20 rich men are married, as are 40 of the 80 men with $7500, leaving 40 single men and 40 single women. On an individual basis (commonly employed in wealth statistics, since they are often based on records of estates at death), the top 10 percent (20 out of 200) own 40 percent of the wealth ($400,000 out of $1 million). Suppose now that we consider the total wealth of the family (Y), and first treat all families, or single individuals, as one unit. . . . There are 140 such families,

analysis and attempts to aggregate the income of parents and their children. CBO uses a methodology common in social scientists' analysis of poverty and applies an income-equivalent scale to standardize families' and households' incomes, based on their differing sizes.

The need to allocate income of entities to individuals or families also causes some difficulties. For example, how does one allocate to the tax returns of families, individuals, or couples the income (and attendant taxes) of a trust that is accumulating income, the subsequent distribution of which is at the discretion of a trustee? Likewise, after a family member's death, income can be taxed to an estate over a period of years awaiting final determination of how the income is to be distributed; this also causes difficulties in allocating income to the appropriate income class. Related issues arise in allocating corporate income and, to a lesser extent, partnership income.

Once the staff determines the family unit and measure of income to be used in constructing distributional tables, people can be allocated to various income classes. Table 2–1 groups people into nine income categories. Distinctions among families in the same income class are not captured in the distributional table. If Congress were sufficiently concerned about the regressive impact of a tobacco-tax increase to enact an offsetting tax reduction so that the distributional table would show no change for people in a particular income class, say in the $20,000 to $30,000 class, there is no reason to assume that the families or couples who would be subjected to the tax increase are the same as the families or couples who would benefit from the tax reduction. All that a distributional table can show is the total impact on all the families or couples within the same income classification. This rather obvious and important point often seems to be lost to policy makers.

The Relevant Time Horizon. Different treatment by the different staffs also occurs with the time horizon over which changes in the tax law are evaluated in order to estimate their distributional impact. OTA—

so that 40 percent of wealth is owned by 14.3 percent (20 out of 140) of families. On the other hand, suppose that we treat a married couple as two units, each greater than $1 million (it rises in fact to $1.7 million), which may upset the accountants but is logically quite correct. The 20 rich couples account for 20 percent of the effective population, and benefit from 47.1 percent ($800,000 out of $1.7 million) of the total equivalent wealth. However, if we treat a couple as two units, but only allocate each a benefit of $Y/2$ . . . then the top 20 percent has 40 percent of total wealth (which in this case remains at $1 million). The reader should consider other possible variations, including the cases where some of the wealthy are not married and where women possess wealth. [Sexism in original.]

like the JCT, before May 1, 1992—assesses the distributional consequences of a set of legislative changes with respect to a single taxable year in which all the changes are fully phased in. JCT, however, now rejects this treatment on the ground that it is distorting, for example, with respect to all temporary provisions, particularly those that expire within the budget horizon. Therefore, JCT now generally uses a rough five-year average impact of the tax changes on the ground that the five-year budget period—prescribed by law as the relevant period for revenue estimating—is the appropriate time horizon to legislators.[42]

The JCT contends that the correct approach would be to calculate the present value of the burden of a tax change in each future year into the indefinite future and apply an appropriate discount rate to this stream of annual burdens.[43] However, the frequency—indeed the likelihood—of changes in both the law and discount rates in the future makes it questionable whether this approach *is* indeed correct.

As with the differing choices about units for classifying people, again there are arguments on behalf of each of the staffs' judgments. In some cases, important differences in distributional tables will result from these different time horizons. Moreover, each staff ignores wealth effects that may be important because of changes in the values of existing assets that occur because of transitions from existing to new law.

Tax-Incidence Assumptions. Probably the greatest gulf between what experts know about taxes and what the public and most politicians believe concerns the economic burden, or incidence, of a tax—often quite different from its statutory burden. In particular, taxes imposed on and paid by business entities must ultimately be borne by people— the business's owners, its employees, its customers, or some combination of these people and perhaps others. The public, however, fails to appreciate tax shifting, even when economists are unified in their view about which group of taxpayers will ultimately bear the burden of the tax. For example, there is essentially no dispute in the economic literature that virtually the entirety of a payroll tax will be borne by employees in the form of lower wages, regardless of whether the Treasury collects the tax from employers or employees. Despite the economic consensus, workers clearly seem to prefer taxes on employers rather than on themselves, and it would be wrong to fault them as completely naive. In the short run, the incidence may well be different depending on whether the tax is imposed on employers or on employees, because employers may be prohibited by contract, habit, or economic condi-

---

42. Joint Committee on Taxation, *Methodology and Issues*, pp. 31–36.
43. Ibid.

tions from immediately shifting to employees the burden of the tax by lowering wages. This short-term advantage, however, may serve to make employees myopic about long-term consequences of payroll taxes and may thereby substantially affect the politics of these taxes.

With other taxes, economists frequently disagree about the shifting of the tax burden. The question of who bears the true burden of the corporate income tax has long been controversial among economists. Moreover, the economic incidence of a tax may depend far more on its details than the economic literature usually suggests. For example, the appropriate incidence assumptions about corporate income taxes may depend on the details of corporate tax law, in particular on the rules for the recovery of capital expenditure. Liberal capital expenditure allowances may have the effect of shifting the corporate tax burden from owners of capital to labor.[44] Given the wide variations in burdens of different corporations under the 1984 corporate income tax (the tax under examination), depending on the companies' capital structure as well as their industry, Fullerton and Rogers suggest that corporate income tax should be analyzed not in the traditional manner of corporate income taxes but, rather, similarly to variable excise taxes on different types of consumption.[45] Today's corporate income tax is considerably more neutral across industries than that of a decade ago, but there may still be enough variations to induce excise-type tax effects.

Until recently, JCT did not distribute corporate income tax changes at all, on the ground that the incidence of the tax was too uncertain. JCT's refusal to distribute corporate tax changes had enormous practical consequences for policy makers relying on distributional tables as a basis for their political decisions. Not distributing corporate income taxes created political incentives for policy makers to locate tax-reducing provisions at the corporate level (where they would not reduce progressivity in the distributional tables) and tax increases at the shareholder level (where they would increase progressivity in the distributional tables). In the 1990 budget negotiations, for example, it was not possible to offset regressive distributional burdens of selected excise taxes on the middle class through corporate tax changes, and President Bush would not agree to significant individual-income tax–rate increases. In addition, under this distributional methodology, economically similar policies would be treated differently in the distributional tables; for example, integration of the corporation income tax in the form of a dividend exclusion or shareholder credit for individuals would show up as a substantial tax reduction for high-

---

44. Don Fullerton and Diane Lim Rogers, *Who Bears the Lifetime Tax Burden?*
45. Ibid., pp. 76–91.

income individuals, while corporate tax integration through a deduction for corporate dividends would be ignored in the tables.

Since 1992, JCT has allocated both corporate income and related corporate taxes to owners of capital generally. OTA uses a similar incidence assumption. In contrast, the CBO has used three corporate-tax incidence variations in recent years, sometimes treating the tax as borne by owners of capital, sometimes treating the tax as borne by labor (which the CBO says is more appropriate in an open economy with global capital markets),[46] and sometimes allocating the tax half to labor and half to capital.[47] As figure 2–5 shows, differing corporate-tax incidence assumptions are significant in assessing the distribution of tax burdens and tax changes.

Concerns and ambiguities about the economic incidence of taxes and tax changes create enormous problems for staffs attempting to construct distributional tables. Obviously, making firm incidence assumptions when tax incidence is uncertain or controversial can have a major influence on policy. For example, the decision to allocate the corporate-income tax burden completely to owners of capital, rather than, say, one-half to owners of capital and one-half to labor or consumption, concentrates that tax in the higher income brackets. If those analysts who contend that consumers or workers bear at least part of the burden of the corporate income tax are correct, the current distributional tables make the existing tax system appear more progressive than it actually is. Currently, to make a distributionally neutral change to offset a reduction of corporate income taxes, higher taxes must be imposed on upper-income individuals. To the extent that the corporate tax is borne in part by consumers or workers, reductions in corporate taxes would, in fact, be spread more generally across income classes. Finally, if corporate-income taxes are, as many economists believe, particularly inefficient and inhibitive of economic growth, trade-offs between efficiency and equity look quite different depending on how the incidence of the corporate tax is assigned in distribution tables.

The problem of allocating corporate income and corporate taxes by income class is further complicated by the desire that equivalent policies be treated consistently in distributional tables to maintain a

---

46.Congressional Budget Office, *The Changing Distribution of Federal Taxes, 1975–1990* (Washington, D.C.: GPO, 1987), pp. 22–23. Contrast Jane G. Gravelle, "Corporate Tax Incidence in an Open Economy," vol. 1993, *Proceedings of the National Tax Association* (1994), p. 173 (contending that corporate income taxes are borne by capital owners even in an open economy with global capital markets)

47. Kasten, "CBO's Method for Simulating," p. 8.

FIGURE 2–5

EFFECTIVE TAX RATES WITH VARYING CORPORATE TAX ALLOCATION FOR
INCOMES UP TO $452,000 AND OVER

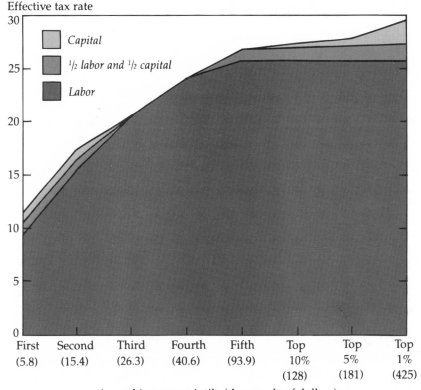

Effective tax rate

NOTES: All numbers are at 1988 income levels. The numbers in parentheses are
the average incomes for each income class.
SOURCES: CBO, *Changing Distribution*, tables 6, 7, 8; U.S. House, Committee on
Ways and Means, *1991 Greenbook: Background Material and Data on Programs
within the Jurisdiction of the Committee on Ways and Means* (Washington, D.C.:
GPO, 1991), table 14.

semblance of policy coherence and to limit gamesmanship. The pre-
1992 practice of the JCT of distributing changes in individual taxation
of corporate source income but not distributing changes at the corporate level, as suggested earlier, created a bias in favor of a dividend-
deduction method of integration over shareholder level methods, such
as a dividend exclusion or shareholder credit. This was true despite
the fact that this choice would have substantial effects on other issues,

49

such as the impact of integration on tax-exempt entities and foreign shareholders.[48] The JCT's current methodology eliminates this kind of problem by allocating the corporate tax entirely to owners of capital that would treat a dividend-deduction method of integration as generally equivalent to a shareholder credit or dividend exclusion. This parity would not exist, however, if part of the corporate tax were allocated to consumers or labor, given that the distributional tables for shareholder-level integration would be constructed using the standard assumption that the individual income tax is not shifted.[49]

A proper desire for consistency in demonstrating distributional burdens of policy equivalents creates additional conundrums for the staffs who construct distributional tables. To take an important example, JCT now distributes a value-added tax, or any other broad-based consumption tax, to wage earners and existing owners of capital rather than distributing the burden entirely to consumers, the more traditional method. JCT thus allows the distribution of consumption taxes when the income is earned, and parallels the treatment of income or wage taxes.[50] As figure 2–6 below (reproduced from the 1993 JCT distribution pamphlet) shows, however, this allocation of consumption taxes to earners rather than consumers produces a different burden of consumption taxes from that imposed by the typical allocation to consumption—particularly at the higher end of the income distribution. Again, this staff decision may have important policy implications; the new JCT method of allocating consumption taxes means that replacing income taxes with consumption taxes would require a much smaller offsetting tax increase on high-income taxpayers in order to produce neutrality in a JCT distribution table.

Consumption taxes may take a variety of forms. States in this country routinely impose retail sales taxes; the European Community uses credit-method value-added taxes; Canada uses a subtraction-method value-added tax. A subtraction-method value-added tax (or business-transfer tax) has similar incidence and should be distributed in a similar manner to a credit-method value-added tax. Some advocates of such a tax, however, much prefer the label "cash-flow corporate-income tax," "uniform-business tax," or some such appellation,

---

48. Department of the Treasury, *Corporate Tax Integration: Taxing Business Income Once* (Washington, D.C.: Superintendent of Documents, 1992).

49. For a suggestion that individual level taxes on businesses conducted in the partnership or proprietorship form might be partially shifted, see Boris I. Bittker, "Effective Tax Rates, Fact or Fancy," *University of Pennsylvania Law Review*, vol. 122 (1974): 799.

50. Joint Committee on Taxation, *Methodology and Issues*, pp. 51–60.

FIGURE 2–6

BURDEN OF A 5 PERCENT BROAD-BASED CONSUMPTION TAX AS A PERCENTAGE OF PRETAX INCOME FOR ANNUAL INCOME CLASSES FROM NO INCOME TO INCOME OF MORE THAN $200,000

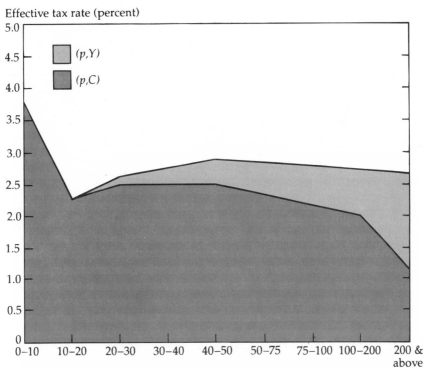

NOTES: (p,C) = traditional method of distributing a consumption tax to consumption. (p,Y) = method adopted by the JCT in 1993, distribution to wages and old capital.

SOURCE: JCT, *Methodology and Issues*, table 3.

to the value-added tax label. Needless to say, one cannot change one's judgment about tax burdens as labels change, a point that emphasizes the need to examine the details of a tax in order to know how to distribute it.

As stated earlier, capital-recovery allowances in the direction of expensing of capital purchases move the corporate–income tax burden away from capital and on to labor. This point may raise doubts about the decision made by both OTA and JCT that corporate taxes should be allocated entirely to capital in distribution tables. An allocation of the corporate tax entirely to capital, however, might be defended as the most conservative course if JCT and OTA distributional estimates are intended to protect against changes that might inadvertently make the distribution of aftertax income less equal.

The problem of assessing tax incidence is pervasive. To take one additional example, economists agree that an excise tax imposed on final consumers of a particular product is a tax on consumption, and each of the three staffs generally distributes selected excise taxes consistent with that premise, although their methodologies vary. In the short term, however, producers and workers in the industry affected may bear the burden of the tax. Recently this phenomenon was widely believed to have occurred in connection with the 10 percent excise tax on luxury boats adopted in the 1990 Budget Act. Advocates for the boating industry, some independent economists, and virtually all politicians came to believe that instead of burdening the very wealthy, high-income purchasers of luxury yachts as had been intended, the excise-tax burden in the period immediately following enactment was borne predominately by laborers engaged in the construction of such boats.[51] Putting aside the truth of this judgment,[52] the standard decision to ignore short-term distributional effects of the tax was proved wrong in this case, since the perceived short-term effects induced Congress to repeal the tax and thus turned out to be the only effects.

Political decision makers would probably like to know both near-term and long-term distributional consequences of legislative decisions, particularly when a serious impact on labor in concentrated areas or industries might reasonably be predicted. Short- and long-term differences are much more easily captured through a narrative report of the distributional consequences of proposed legislation than through distributional tables.

When the affected workers are abroad, political consequences may be the opposite. Congress, for example, might be little concerned, or even pleased, if the excise tax on so-called gas guzzling automobiles was borne by the workers who produce these automobiles, not, as the distributional tables suggest, by purchasers of these automobiles—since much of the production of these cars occurs abroad. Distribu-

---

51. The discussion in the text is a shorthand description to make the point that short-term and long-term effects may differ in significant ways that are not taken into account in the distributional tables. How the change itself is accounted for would depend importantly, for example, on whether the burden or the taxes are distributed and on a number of other factors.

52. For a contrasting view, see Dennis Zimmerman, "The Effect of the Luxury Excise Tax on the Sale of Luxury Boats," Congressional Research Service, February 10, 1992.

tional tables simply do not alert decision makers to the potential consequences of their actions in circumstances like these. Nor do they alert decision makers to regional variations in tax burden. The luxury excise tax on boats also demonstrates that regional variations in tax distribution may be significant. Regional differences, however, are generally treated as a horizontal, not a vertical equity issue, and they are not reflected at all in distributional tables.

Excise taxes enacted for the specific purpose of correcting externalities or reducing consumption of specific goods are taken up below.

Summary—Areas of Disagreement. The foregoing discussion describes important staff disagreements and differences in practice among the staffs over the incidence of certain taxes, the taxpaying unit evaluated, the appropriate measurement of income, and even the meaning of distributing a change in taxes. In principle there is nothing wrong with such disagreements. They generally reflect reasonable— but different—judgments by the various staffs about controversial questions of theory, as well as about the best compromises among theoretical purity, limitations of data, and public and politicians' understanding. Even within the same staff, however, these compromises do not seem to be made consistently. JCT emphasizes understanding and practicality over theory in its income measure and in its family classifier, while attempting to achieve greater theoretical purity in distributing burdens rather than actual taxes. OTA has reached the opposite judgment on all three of these issues, although with regard to the question of distributing tax changes or burden changes there seems to be a disagreement over the best answer, even in theory. When more than one staff is involved in the process of estimating distributional aspects of tax changes, or even when only one staff is involved but experiences personnel changes at frequent intervals, as now seems to be the case at both JCT and OTA, judgments on these issues and staff practice will vary from staff to staff and even within the same staff over time.

Controversial Areas of Staff Agreement

Tax Capitalization and Implicit Taxes. As the preceding discussion of tax incidence suggests, a fundamental issue in constructing distribution tables is how to treat market reactions to various taxes and tax changes. Obviously, by distributing taxes in accordance with their economic rather than statutory incidence, each of the staffs takes certain kinds of market responses into account in constructing distribution tables. No one could reasonably suggest that it would be more appropriate to distribute the burden of tax legislation by its legal rather than economic incidence, notwithstanding the uncertainties involved in the latter exercise. The question when to stop attempting to take market reactions into account is not an easy one, though. This problem is well illustrated by the distributional treatment of the 1986 Tax Reform Act's limitations on tax-shelter investments.

In 1986, Congress enacted a major tax reform that was said to be distributionally neutral, as well as revenue-neutral. Apparently, this was taken to mean that the legislation should be revenue-neutral in each income class.[53] During the 1970s and early 1980s, however, many high-income taxpayers had invested in a wide variety of so-called tax shelters. Investments in real estate, exploration and development of oil, gas and other natural resources, motion picture production, and certain farming activities were all eligible for tax benefits and were favored tax-shelter investments. Eliminating the widespread availability of such tax shelters was an important substantive goal of the 1986 act. In making these kinds of tax-advantaged investments under the pre-1986 law, taxpayers had reduced their income taxes, but typically at the cost of a lower pretax return from the tax-shelter investment than would have been available in an investment of similar risk that did not enjoy tax advantages. No good measurement of the adjustments to pretax returns in the tax-favored areas, however, was available for use by the relevant tax staffs.

In contrast to these tax-sheltered investments that enjoyed particular favor in the 1980s, the magnitude of the effects of tax benefits on pretax returns is generally well known in the case of tax-exempt state and local bonds, where the relationship between returns on tax-exempt and taxable bonds of similar maturity and risk is readily available. Historically, returns on state and local bonds have ranged between about 70 and 90 percent of returns on comparable taxable bonds. There is a large literature discussing the reductions in pretax rates of return for holders of tax-exempt bonds—reductions that have come to be called "implicit taxes"—and evaluating the efficiency and equity implications of the trade-off between lower interest rates and tax savings.[54] Even when data are available, however, distributional tables typically reflect these kinds of reductions in pretax rate of return only in measuring taxpayers' incomes and do not take implicit taxes into account.

---

53. Steuerle, *The Tax Decade*, pp. 106–8. If "burdens" rather than taxes were distributed, the legislation would have had to be "burden" neutral in each income class.

54. For example, Boris I. Bittker, "Equity, Efficiency and Income Tax Theory: Do Misallocations Drive Out Inequities?" in Henry J. Aaron and Michael J. Boskin, eds., *The Economics of Taxation* (Washington, D.C.: Brookings Institution, 1980), p. 19.

The best treatment of implicit taxes is far from clear, but the staffs' uniform decision to ignore the widespread tax shelter phenomenon in its distributional tables in 1986 had important effects. In determining in 1986 the level of tax rates that would be necessary to achieve distributional neutrality, distributional tables told congressional decision makers that they needed to set tax rates at a level necessary only to compensate for actual taxes paid at each income level, ignoring the implicit taxes—reductions in the pretax returns—on tax-favored assets. In combination with the direct restrictions on tax shelters in the 1986 act, this rate schedule prompted a shift away from tax-shelter investments into taxable investments, a shift that necessarily would produce higher pretax income for these upper-bracket taxpayers, and which, given substantially lowered rates on upper-income individuals of the new rate schedule, would result in a foreseeable reduction in progressivity from purportedly "distributionally neutral" tax legislation. In 1986, this effect on progressivity was exacerbated by the fact that much of the tax increase for upper-income taxpayers was in the form of retroactive tax increases on pre-1986 tax-shelter investments, tax increases that would have only a temporary impact in increasing taxes of upper-income people, even though the provisions themselves and the accompanying rate reductions were permanent changes in the law.

This standard practice of ignoring changes in pretax returns on tax-favored assets also dramatically distorts distributional tables that are produced annually by the JCT to show the distributional effects of particular tax expenditures. Using quite different methodologies, David Bradford and I (at an interval of about a decade) attempted to "correct" the official estimates of the distribution of the benefits of the exclusion of interest on tax-exempt bonds. I proposed correcting this distribution by reflecting the interest-cost savings of state and local governments—reflected in the investor's lower pretax return—on the assumption that the additional interest costs that would result from repealing the tax exemption would be made up through increased taxes by the state and local governments.[55] The difference in results of this methodology and the official estimate are depicted in figure 2–7.

David Bradford took quite a different approach and attempted to measure the implicit tax impact more directly by constructing effective tax rates, taking into account the reductions in pretax returns that result from the exclusion.[56] His results, alongside the official estimates, are depicted in figure 2–8.

---

55. Graetz, "Assessing the Distributional Effects," pp. 351–68.

56. David Bradford, *Untangling the Income Tax* (Cambridge: Harvard University Press, 1986).

FIGURE 2–7

DISTRIBUTION OF BENEFITS FROM TAX-EXEMPT STATE AND LOCAL BONDS FOR
ANNUAL INCOME CLASSES FROM NO INCOME TO MORE THAN $100,000

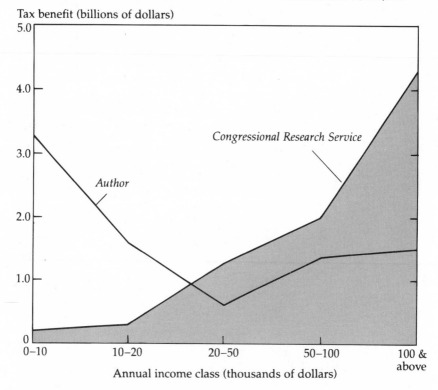

Tax benefit (billions of dollars)

Annual income class (thousands of dollars)

NOTE: The numbers for Graetz were scaled to 1990 by multiplying the percentage of total benefits for each class in Graetz, 1975, by the total amount of interest excluded in CRS, 1990.
SOURCE: Michael J. Graetz, "Assessing the Distributional Effects of Income Tax Revision," *Journal of Legal Studies* 4 (1975): 351–68.

The major revisions to the standard distributions depicted by Bradford and myself in figures 2–7 and 2–8 both reflect efforts to take into account the price effects of the exclusion of state and local bond interest, which lower the interest rate received by the upper-income purchasers of these bonds. Changes in tax rates typically will have price effects. To continue with the case of municipal bonds, prices of such bonds increased in anticipation and response to the tax-rate increases of the 1993 legislation. Martin Feldstein has argued that assessments of the equity of any tax reform should take such price effects into account and that changes in such prices attributable to a change

FIGURE 2–8
Bradford-corrected Distribution of Tax-exempt State and Local Bonds for Annual Income Classes from No Income to More than $100,000
(millions of dollars)

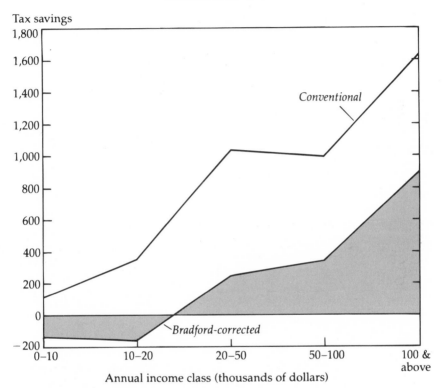

NOTE: Numbers are for 1985.
SOURCE: Bradford, *Untangling the Income Tax.*

in legislation should be treated as a departure from standard notions of horizontal equity.[57] I have disagreed with this view.[58]

Many difficult issues are involved in evaluating how and when to take market responses, such as estimated effects on pretax returns, into account. Unlike actual taxes, Congress is unable to spend the changes in investors' pretax returns, because of the repeal of tax advantages—

57. Martin Feldstein, "On the Theory of Tax Reform," *Journal of Public Economics* 6 (1976): 77.

58. Graetz, "Legal Transitions: The Case of Retroactivity in Income Tax Revision," *University of Pennsylvania Law Review* 126 (1977): 79–81.

the "implicit taxes." In fact, Congress may even have difficulties understanding the concept. It may therefore be futile for the staff to attempt to construct distribution tables that reflect reductions in pretax returns, even when the data are available. Yet distributional tables that are as misleading as the official tables distributing the benefits of the tax-exempt bond exclusion can be quite harmful when used in the tax-legislative process. In this case, for example, they disguise a change that almost certainly will reduce the after-tax income of low- and middle-income taxpayers as affecting only higher-income people.

Most economists would suggest that the way out of this dilemma, in theory at least, is to perform a general-equilibrium analysis and to examine changes in the distribution of aftertax income within a general-equilibrium framework, assuming the enactment of the proposed legislation. This approach would take into account effects of the tax rules on pretax returns both before and after the legislation. But the data demands of such general-equilibrium analyses are large, the required assumptions are many, and the answers that result are sensitive not only to the limitations of data and the assumptions made but also to the structure of the general-equilibrium model. Moreover, general-equilibrium models are typically not capable of estimating the effects of relatively small changes in policy. The mathematical elegance of general-equilibrium analyses seems likely to produce a false sense of precision, even in circumstances of consensus about the general direction of change. (Some of the false sense of precision would be eliminated if a range of estimates—a so-called confidence interval—were provided.) Nevertheless, the "black-box" quality of general-equilibrium analysis is probably no more inscrutable to a legislator than the current distributional methodology. Where the nature of the change and time permit, something may be learned from engaging in such analysis. OTA, for example, has recently published results of three differing general equilibrium analyses of corporate tax integration.[59]

Lifetime versus Annual Income. Recently public-finance economists have embraced the view that distributional burdens of taxes (and perhaps other government actions, including expenditures) should be estimated with respect to a lifetime rather than an annual measure of income.[60] Indeed, a lifetime perspective has begun to creep into the tax

---

59. Department of the Treasury, *Corporate Tax Integration*, pp. 111–52; see also Fullerton and Rogers, *Lifetime Tax Burden*.

60. See, for example, Fullerton and Rogers, *Lifetime Tax Burden*, pp. 17–21; and Alan J. Auerbach, J. Gokhale, and L. Kotlikoff, "Generational Accounts: A Meaningful Alternative to Deficit Accounting," in *Tax Policy and the Economy*, edited by David Bradford (Cambridge: MIT Press, 1991).

staffs' analysis of tax distribution. CBO recently assessed the distributional burdens of excise taxes on alcohol and tobacco with reference to a lifetime-income measure,[61] and the JCT contends that its method of distributing consumption taxes approximates a lifetime perspective.[62] But these are exceptions; generally all three staffs distribute tax changes with reference to annual rather than lifetime income.

Classifying people and measuring tax burdens with respect to their annual income has some obvious distorting characteristics, such as classifying students and elderly people as poorer than they may be. It also emphasizes equal annual earnings rather than equal annual consumption, and as a result makes early consumers seem poorer than early earners. Economists have long used a life-cycle framework in explaining much of people's saving behavior, and this view of saving as a temporary postponement of consumption has been used to argue in favor of using lifetime income as an index of people's relative well-being. There is considerable dispute in the literature as to how much of the disparity of wealth holdings is explained by life-cycle saving.[63] A full discussion of this issue is well beyond the scope of this essay, but, as figure 2–9 demonstrates for the distribution of a broad-based consumption tax, the choice between an annual and a lifetime perspective may have substantial effects on the distributions shown. Therefore, I offer here a few preliminary observations on this issue.

First, a philosophical grounding for a lifetime basis for measuring relative well-being has yet to be fully developed, even though a lifetime perspective finds substantial support in certain fundamental philosophical concepts, including the idea that people should be responsible for their actions and prudent in preparing for both old age and emergencies. A lifetime view might also be defended as a better approach in advancing equality of opportunity over equality of outcome.

The contrary view, though, also enjoys philosophical support. Derek Parfit, for example, contends that our future selves might better be thought of as persons different from who we now are and that people may rationally care far more about their present than future selves, in a manner analogous to the greater care they devote to themselves than to others.[64] This suggests philosophical difficulties that cannot be

61. Congressional Budget Office, *Federal Taxation of Tobacco, Alcoholic Beverages, and Motor Fuels* (Washington, D.C.: Superintendent of Documents, 1990).

62. Joint Committee on Taxation, *Methodology and Issues*, pp. 57–58.

63. See, for example, Atkinson, *Economics of Inequality*, pp. 76–77.

64. P. Parfit, *Reasons and Persons* (New York: Oxford University Press, 1984).

FIGURE 2–9

DISTRIBUTION OF A 5 PERCENT BROAD-BASED CONSUMPTION TAX FOR ANNUAL
INCOME CLASSES FROM NO INCOME TO MORE THAN $200,000

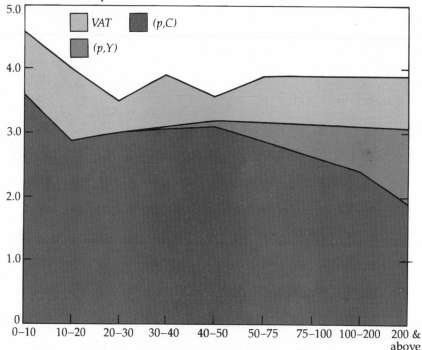

Effective tax rate (percent)

Annual income class (thousands of dollars)

NOTES: (p,C) and (p,Y) = same distributions as those of figure 2–5. The VAT is
distributed over lifetime income. The VAT plot is an approximate mapping of
Metcalf's decile distribution into JCT's income classes.
SOURCES: JCT, *Methodology and Issues*; Erik Casperson and G. Metcalf, "Is a
Value-Added Tax Progressive?" NBER working paper 4387, 1993.

solved by discounting future income to present values as a basis for
comparing people's well-being.[65]

Norman Daniels grounds an argument for the equity of a lifetime
perspective in public policy regarding health care in the claim that
"*consistent* differential treatment by age will equalize over time"—that
is, the young and the old may be treated differently at any moment in

---

65. Elmer Elhauge, "Allocating Health Care Morally," *California Law Review*
82 (1994): 1449, 1516–17, 1528–30.

time, but *over time* people will be treated both ways.[66] The validity of this argument, of course, is dependent on consistent treatment over a long period of time—something that no Congress can assure.

Most economists who have embraced a lifetime accounting of ability to pay for tax policy making have done so without either serious argument or defense—often because they prefer consumption to income taxation. Perhaps this is because of lesser deadweight costs. In the absence of perfect capital markets, high lifetime income may not reflect high current ability to pay taxes, particularly when liquidity constraints are serious. Short-term precautionary savings may operate to smooth consumption over several years rather than over a lifetime.

Moreover, major difficulties arise in assessing lifetime income. First, given pervasive uncertainty about the future, discounting future estimated income to the present is fraught with difficulties. As a consequence, some analysts simply use annual consumption as a proxy for permanent or lifetime income,[67] but it is clear that, in principle, bequests and inheritances must also be taken into account.[68] But none of the methods as yet developed for taking bequests or inheritances into account is fully satisfactory.[69]

Particularly for lower- and middle-income persons, however, annual consumption may well be a better measure of a person's ability to pay taxes than is annual income. But at the very top of the wealth distribution this is not the case.

Even if one regards a lifetime, as opposed to an annual or several years' measure of income, as having significant philosophical or economic advantages, the implications of such an advantage are far from clear in the political context in which the distributional questions are being asked. As Tom Barthold, JCT, has pointed out, politicians do not regard an individual who is making $200,000 in a current year as having the same current ability to pay taxes as an elderly individual earning $35,000, even if the present value of their lifetime incomes is

---

66. Norman Daniels, *Am I My Parents' Keeper?* (New York: Oxford University Press, 1988).

67. James Poterba, "Lifetime Incidence and the Distributional Burden of Excise Taxes," *American Economic Review* 79 (1989); and Congressional Budget Office, *Federal Taxation of Tobacco*.

68. Henry J. Aaron and Alicia H. Munnell, "Reassessing the Role for Federal Wealth Taxes," *National Tax Journal* 45 (1992): 119–43.

69. See, for example, Fullerton and Rogers, *Lifetime Tax Burden*, p. 74, who simply assume that any inheritances received must correspond to bequests transferred, an assumption that affects only the lifetime income classification of people who receive bequests.

the same.[70] A person's current ability to pay is certainly relevant, since taxes must be paid currently to finance government currently.

More significantly, our system of government does not give one Congress the power to bind the legislation of a subsequent Congress. Therefore, it is impossible for any group of legislators to make a viable, binding political commitment to fair taxation over a person's lifetime. The fact that the current Congress cannot commit the policies of future Congresses encourages self-interested people who lobby legislators to try always to maximize their *present* interests. This phenomenon alone might well make it of special concern to legislators to know who wins and who loses in their present status. In addition, it may well be appropriate that an age cohort that experiences its peak income-producing years during wartime, when higher taxes have historically been required to pay for the nation's defense, pay more in lifetime taxes than an age cohort whose peak earnings occur during peacetime, even though a lifetime perspective would regard this as unfair.

Fullerton and Rogers have suggested a strong equity criterion that would require *both* that current taxes reflect current ability to pay and that lifetime taxes reflect lifetime ability to pay.[71] Even if one embraces this criterion in principle, however, it is difficult to imagine how it would be enforced in practice. Consider figure 2–9 above, which shows the difference in distribution of a broad-based consumption tax using annual- and lifetime-income classifiers. Even if one rejects a lifetime-income measure as generally inappropriate as a basis for politicians to assess distributional fairness—on the ground that the lifetime horizon is too long relative to people's perceptions of fairness, or their behavior, or, alternatively, in light of Congress's limited ability to commit to public policies—a lifetime perspective nevertheless often offers useful and important information in assessing the fairness of tax-legislative changes. First, it suggests the importance of looking at how proposed tax changes affect different age cohorts, both as a way of alerting decision makers that measures of current income for the young and old may understate their abilities to pay and also to raise to the level of explicit decision making issues of intergenerational equity.[72] Indeed, important policy initiatives that are troublesome from an annual perspective may well be far more justified from a lifetime perspective. A

---

70. Barthold, "Measure Distribution," pp. 291–92.

71. See, for example, Fullerton and Rogers, *Lifetime Tax Burden*, p. 93, n. 2.

72. Laurence J. Kotlikoff, *Generational Accounting: Knowing Who Pays, and When, for What We Spend* (New York: Free Press, 1992); and Auerbach, Gokhale, and Kotlikoff, "Generational Accounts."

wide range of tax-legislative provisions governing retirement savings and income, for example, fall in this category.[73]

In addition, where taxes are being imposed to induce taxpayers to shift consumption away from specific harmful items of consumption, such as alcohol or tobacco, toward a less harmful consumption mix, the fact that a tax that looks regressive on an annual basis may be proportional or even progressive on a lifetime basis should give legislators greater confidence in enacting such legislation. Distributional tables, however, do not in any way distinguish the effects of taxes such as these where taxes are deliberately being used to penalize or indeed to change undesirable behavior from situations where taxes are simply being used to raise revenue. Figure 2–10 compares the effects of a cigarette-tax increase to both annual income and annual expenditures, which are often used as a proxy for lifetime income.

Congress in this context may want to examine the distributional burden over a longer time horizon than solely by reference to annual income. Tobacco taxes have been claimed to be proportional to lifetime income and alcohol taxes to be slightly progressive.[74] To the extent that legislators are preoccupied with making a JCT or other staff distributional table look "right," however, such legislation will be inhibited. In this case, distribution tables based on annual income may well poorly serve the legislative process. This effect will be exacerbated by tables that distribute burdens rather than taxes, as was shown above.

Despite the staffs' virtually universal use of annual income measures, the impact of tax legislation on various age cohorts and on intergenerational equity is important and deserves to be highlighted. More generally, the appropriate role of lifetime or multiyear income perspectives for assessing ability to pay in the political process deserves continuing attention and debate.

Distributing Transfers as Well as Taxes. All three of the staffs recognize that in distributing tax changes or existing taxes they are presenting only a partial picture of the distributional effects of government actions. The JCT, for example, remarks:

> The full effect of government policies on the economic well-being of different groups of individuals can only be determined by examining the burdens and benefits imposed by changes in expenditure policy as well as tax policy. . . . The

---

73. Michael J. Graetz, "The Troubled Marriage of Retirement Security and Tax Policies," *University of Pennsylvania Law Review* 135 (1987): 851, 852–55.

74. Congressional Budget Office, *Federal Taxation of Tobacco*, p. 80.

FIGURE 2–10

NET INCREASE IN CIGARETTE TAX AS A PERCENTAGE OF AFTER-TAX INCOME
AND EXPENDITURES, FOR ANNUAL INCOME QUINTILES, 1990

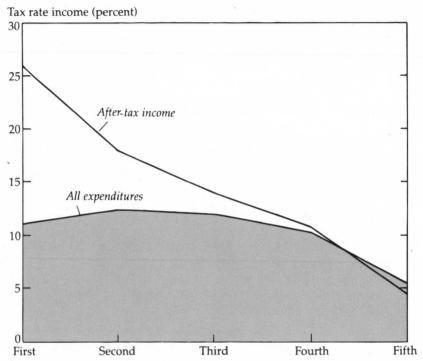

Tax rate income (percent)

SOURCE: CBO, *Changing Distribution*.

effects of . . . expenditure program[s] will be ignored in the
JCT distributional analysis, which looks only at tax changes.[75]

Yet JCT defends this practice on four grounds: (1) its staff has no particular expertise in distributing expenditures, and to do so would increase considerably the work of that staff; (2) it is impossible to
consider state and local governments' burdens and benefits—an objection that applies with equal force in distributing taxes alone; (3) most
proposals for tax changes do not have specific expenditure changes
associated with them—a claim that today seems unrealistic, particularly since most tax changes in recent years have been part of omnibus-
budget legislation and, in any event, is irrelevant; and (4) the policy

75. Joint Committee on Taxation, *Methodology and Issues*, p. 2.

FIGURE 2–11

EFFECTS OF TAXES AND TRANSFERS ON INCOME, BY INCOME QUINTILE, 1990
(average net dollars received)

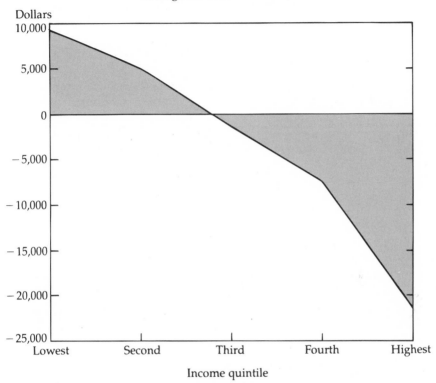

SOURCE: CEA, *Economic Report to the President.*

makers who make greatest use of JCT distributional analyses are interested in isolating the distributional effects of tax changes—in other words, the staff claims to be answering only the question that has been asked. But given the well-known alternatives to taxes as a tool for implementing governmental policies, ignoring distributional effects of nontax governmental action often gives a misleading picture.

The important difference between a distribution of taxes alone and one that combines taxes and transfers is depicted in figure 2–11, which shows an estimate of the distribution of both taxes and transfers from the 1992 *Economic Report of the President.*

The omission of transfers from the distributional tables is especially misleading in the case of payroll taxes used to finance old age, survivors', and disability insurance benefits, and health insurance ben-

65

efits under Part A of Medicare. Both programs were designed (and embraced by the American public) as programs of social insurance under which wage earners and their employers would make contributions through a payroll tax equal to a fixed percentage of wages (or some portion thereof) and, in exchange, would receive wage-replacement retirement benefits, survivors' and disability insurance, and hospital insurance during retirement. The growth of these payroll taxes as a percentage of federal revenues is the single most striking fact in the development of the nation's tax policy in recent decades. Indeed, recent expressions of concern regarding increased tax burdens on middle-class families over the past decade are largely attributable to the rise in payroll taxes.

As tax-policy analysts know, when viewed in isolation the social security payroll tax is regressive, but when benefits are taken into account, the social security system is quite progressive. Nevertheless, estimates of the existing tax burden and of changes in tax burdens since 1977 (frequently used as a baseline by CBO) or since 1980 (which marks the beginning of the Reagan administration) routinely include payroll taxes without indicating the benefits that they finance. Figure 2–12 shows the distribution of social security taxes alone, and figure 2–13 shows the distribution of social security taxes and benefits. The distributional implications of these two pictures are quite different.

Methods of distributing the benefits of government expenditures are no less disputable or demanding of questionable judgments than are distributions of taxes or tax burdens. Many of the same questions discussed here regarding the units of analysis, income classifiers, economic incidence, and the like are present in the realm of expenditure distribution and are perhaps even more controversial. Even in answering a question limited to the distribution of social security benefits, there are serious issues about how best to show the combination of taxes and benefits. For example, the picture in figure 2–13 above, which shows a current year's distribution of taxes and benefits, looks quite different from an analysis that examines payroll-tax contributions with reference to rates of return experienced by various income cohorts.[76]

The one important exception to the omission of government expenditures from tax distributional tables is the inclusion of outlays under the refundable earned-income tax credit (EITC). The most likely explanation for this practice is that EITC outlays are governed by a provision of the Internal Revenue code, rather than other titles of the

---

76. Michael Boskin et al., "Social Security: A Financial Appraisal across and within Generations," *National Tax Journal* 40 (1987): 19.

FIGURE 2–12

EFFECTIVE SOCIAL INSURANCE TAX RATE BY FAMILY QUINTILE, 1990

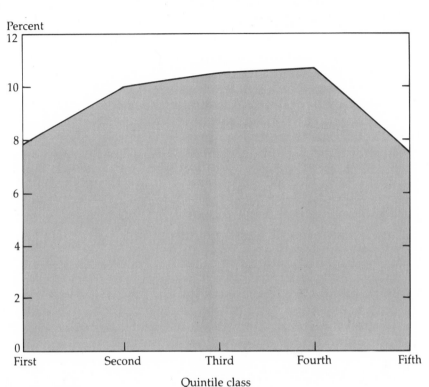

Percent

SOURCE: CBO.

Quintile class

U.S. code. But this explanation cannot be fully satisfying, even if one has come not to expect purity.

Despite the theoretical and data difficulties, ignoring government transfers in a political context is a major disservice, particularly to a nation experiencing fiscal stress caused by a long-standing federal-deficit problem. For example, ignoring government benefits makes it easier for politicians to promise and support middle-class tax cuts in apparent sympathy for the recent increase in middle-class burdens, despite the well-known fact that an enormous share of federal government entitlement expenditures benefits the middle class. The share of government expenditures targeted at people at or near the poverty level is important, but far from a full accounting. Distributional tables limited to taxes alone—particularly when social security and health payroll taxes are included—present a very misleading picture, either

FIGURE 2–13
SOCIAL SECURITY TAXES AND NET BENEFITS BY ANNUAL INCOME QUINTILE,
1987

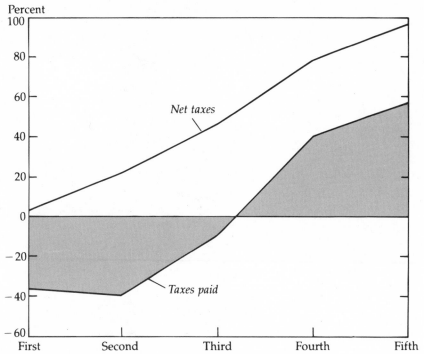

NOTES: The annual income quintiles are based on Census money income for 1987. Net taxes are equal to social security taxes paid minus social security benefits received.
SOURCE: OTA tabulations.

in the context of tax increases to fund additional spending or, vice versa, spending reductions to fund tax reductions.

Benefit Taxes and User Charges. As the discussion of tobacco and alcohol taxes earlier in this chapter suggests, the reason for enacting a tax change may influence the most appropriate method of showing the distributional effects. It is difficult and, in some cases naive, simply to ignore adverse distributions in such cases. The preceding section, which emphasizes the significance of government transfers, raises particular questions for the distribution of taxes levied on the "benefit" principle. These include both explicit user charges, such as entrance fees at the national parks or fees for animal-grazing rights on federal lands, and other benefit-based taxes, of which federal and state gasoline taxes to fund federal highway construction and repair are probably the most important.[77] The proper treatment of these taxes is not clear. Showing the burdens without the benefits is clearly misleading, as suggested above. But leaving these taxes out of the "distribution of current taxes" column or ignoring the distribution of changes in such taxes entirely is not an attractive alternative either. Providing Congress with a "distributional table" is clearly an unfortunate oversimplification.

Mandates and Regulations. Closely related to the question of distributing government expenditures or benefits along with taxes is the issue of the distributional impact of nontax regulations and government mandates. During consideration of what was to become the Clean Air Act of 1990, Congressman Pete Stark (D., Calif.) of the House Ways and Means Committee introduced a proposal for taxes based on levels of sulfur-dioxide and nitrogen-oxide emissions of electric utilities, in lieu of a regulatory emission–permit trading mechanism that was ultimately adopted by the Congress. Under standard staff practices, no distributional tables were (or would be) constructed with regard to a regulatory system controlling emissions. To the extent that a regulatory system imposes pollution-control costs on electric utilities, however, there should be little disagreement that those costs will generally be passed on to consumers in the form of higher electricity prices. If such an increase in electricity prices were distributed to income classes in a manner similar to that of an excise tax on electricity, the changes would be shown to have quite a regressive distribution.

Using the tax system rather than regulation to control harmful externalities such as pollution would induce the JCT to construct a distributional table that would depict the regressive burden of the tax change. (Recall that the JCT uses the static revenue estimate in estimating "burden," as was discussed above. If, however, the excise tax serves to induce electricity users to internalize costs they are imposing on others, there is at least a question about whether the excise tax should be counted as a burden at all.) Along with the public's general antitax sentiment and some institutional resistance to using the tax system as a regulatory device, this dramatic difference in distributional practices will inhibit the use of the tax system to control externalities, even in circumstances where a tax might prove to be a better instrument of government policy. The chlorofluorocarbon (CFCs) tax imposed by the 1989 legislation offers a good example of an effective tax enacted primarily for environmental reasons. Proposals for enacting

---

77. Congressional Budget Office, *User Charges and Benefit Taxes*, pp. 56–58.

carbon taxes (or other energy taxes) as a measure to address problems of global warming offer additional potential examples.

The issue of evaluating distributional consequences of government requirements or mandates also occurs in connection with legislation such as the Family Leave Act of 1993, where employers are mandated to provide certain benefits to employees. A far more significant example was President Clinton's health-reform proposal. Generally such mandated payments on behalf of employers are shifted to employees through reductions of wages.

In testimony in February 1994, Robert Reichauer, director of the CBO, concluded that the mandate in the Clinton health plan that would require employers to make payments for a substantial portion of the costs for their employees' health insurance coverage should be treated similarly to a tax for federal budgetary purposes. The Clinton administration had hoped to reach a different result by requiring that employers' and employees' mandatory payments be made directly to state health alliances, instead of deposited with the Internal Revenue Service, which would then pass them on to the health alliances.

Regardless of the niceties of administration of such mandates or their budgetary labels, federal requirements that employers pay a specific amount for the health insurance coverage of each employee is unmistakably an economic burden on employee wages, with distributional consequences somewhat similar to a payroll tax. If the amount required to be paid on behalf of each employee is a per capita amount rather than a percentage of payroll, the distributional burden on employees would be considerably more regressive than a flat-rate payroll tax.

Putting aside the metaphysical but politically important question of whether these mandates are taxes, constructing any distributional table for the proposed Clinton health financing proposals would have been a daunting task. First, the amounts of payments required by employers and their employees were proposed to vary across regions depending on local health care costs, and the relationship of these regional variations to regional variations in wages is difficult to know. For this and other reasons, it is impossible to tell when the proposed caps on employer contributions as a percentage of payroll (never greater than 7.9 percent) would be binding under the Clinton plan. The caps would bind for some employers but not for others, and they are more likely to be binding in some regions than in others. One can hazard a guess that if the JCT or OTA were asked to prepare a distributional table of the Clinton health plan, they would decline to do so on the grounds that the data simply do not permit fulfillment of such a task—a position similar to that the JCT took before 1992 (but has since reversed) about luxury excise taxes and corporate tax changes.

Notwithstanding the difficulties of constructing a distributional table, however, the general distributional burden of President Clinton's employer-mandate financing mechanism is clear. The burdens will be borne by employees in a manner not dissimilar to the burden of payroll taxes generally, but in some instances in a more regressive manner. Likewise, the distribution of specific tax increases on tobacco and the payroll-based assessment for corporations (which do not join regional alliances) is clear. If distributional tables were to be constructed for the Clinton health-care financing system in the manner traditional for tax proposals generally, they would prove an enormous embarrassment for the president. Such tables would suggest a major middle-class tax increase, which would not only contradict the president's campaign promises of tax cuts for the middle class but would also contrast sharply with his oft-repeated insistence that at least 70 percent of the tax increases of the 1993 budget act be borne by people with incomes above $100,000.

A full accounting of the distributional consequences of the Clinton health proposals, however, would ease this embarrassment substantially, because, as I have discussed above, government expenditures as well as taxes should be distributed in these kinds of distributional tables. This seems particularly true in a context such as health reform, where new taxes would be imposed to fund specific enumerated benefits. As with social security, combining the distributional burden of the Clinton health proposal's mandates (or taxes) and its benefits would almost certainly convert a regressive financing burden into a progressive system, although almost certainly there would be some possibly substantial net tax increase on families with incomes below $100,000.

Commentators have emphasized that the Clinton health-care financing scheme has been designed largely in response to widespread public antitax sentiment and the attendant political difficulties of enacting any broad-based tax-financing mechanism. The analysis here suggests that, in addition, relying predominantly on a complex system of mandates also avoids the considerable embarrassment to the president that would result from the normal staff distribution tables that would be prepared by OTA, CBO, or the JCT if taxes were substituted for mandates. Even without a distributional table, of course, any of these expert staffs could describe generally the likely distributional patterns of the Clinton health care proposal.

Federalism. None of the staffs distribute taxes imposed at the state rather than the federal level. Many state and local governments, however, have tied their tax systems directly to the federal system. Thus when federal income–tax law is changed, some state and local tax burdens will automatically change as a result, unless the state government enacts specific legislation to avoid the changes. Federal tax legislation may also have less direct effects on state and local tax burdens. As suggested above (see figure 2–7), repeal of the federal-tax exemption for interest on state and local bonds, for example, would necessarily involve a state and local government tax response—a response that is typically ignored in distributional tables prepared by the federal-tax staffs. Other impacts of federal tax legislation on state fiscal systems may be even less direct; for example, the repeal of the federal income-tax deduction for state sales taxes in 1986 was a major factor in Connecticut's substitution of state-income taxes for a portion of its state-sales taxes. In this case, the federal change ultimately made the state-tax system more progressive.

The decision of all the staffs to omit state-tax effects seems reasonable, given the difficulties of doing the relevant calculations and the great variations from state to state and, in some cases, even within states. However, the picture presented in the distributional tables will be incomplete. State- and local-tax effects may, in some instances, be sizable and should then be identified for policy makers.

International Aspects. Our nation's economy has become inextricably linked with worldwide markets and investments. But none of the staffs' distributional tables allocates any portion of proposed or enacted tax changes to foreigners. Nor do distributional tables typically take into account changes in Americans' behavior made possible by integrated capital markets and the global economy.

Many tax proposals now advanced are intended to change the taxation of international income, sometimes focusing on the taxation of U.S.-source income of foreign persons, sometimes on foreign-source income of U.S. persons. Moreover, many proposals primarily designed to change U.S. tax policy may substantially change the U.S. taxation of foreigners or U.S. taxation of foreign-source income of U.S. persons. Proposals for integration of the corporate-income tax and substitution of some form of broad-based consumption tax for all or a portion of either corporate income taxes or payroll taxes offer two prominent examples. Finally, international capital mobility may require different analyses of the incidence of U.S. taxes or tax incentives. The CBO, for example, grounds its decision not to allocate the entire corporate income–tax burden to owners of capital on the difference between an open and closed economy.[78]

The JCT pamphlet on distribution methodology defends its practice of ignoring the effects of U.S. tax changes on foreign persons.[79] JCT's judgment not to attempt generally to estimate such effects seems

78. CBO, "Changing Distribution"; Gravelle, "Corporate Tax Incidence."
79. Joint Committee on Taxation, *Methodology and Issues*, pp. 78–81.

reasonable, given uncertainties about how foreign governments might respond to U.S. changes and the limited current technical capacity of the staff to make such analyses. JCT also defends the omission of analysis of any impact on foreign persons on the ground that "domestic individuals or family units" are "the group with whose well-being members of Congress and others are most likely to be concerned"—a claim that is indisputable as stated but that ignores Congress's interest in shifting tax burdens to foreigners. That JCT's approach may be reasonable does not, however, make the omission of international aspects from distributional analyses any less important.

Far more questionable is JCT's decision to ignore foreign-income taxes, but not foreign-source income, of U.S. persons in its distributional tables.[80] To the extent that foreign taxes have been imposed on such income and U.S. taxes have been eliminated through the foreign-tax credit, this practice has the effect of greatly understating the tax burden on U.S. persons who earn foreign-source income relative to people who earn only domestic-source income. JCT's treatment of foreign-source income and foreign-income taxes also has the general effect of decreasing the effective tax burden that is shown for high-income people, since more foreign-source income is earned by people in the upper-income brackets. The inconsistency of the JCT decision to ignore foreign taxes while claiming to reflect welfare losses or changes in burdens in its tables is particularly striking. As more and more people expand their investment portfolios to include foreign-source income, the incompleteness of distributional tables as a result of ignoring international aspects will grow in significance.

Summary—Areas of Staff Agreement. Areas of staff agreement seem to be no less important or controversial in the construction of distributional tables than the areas of disagreement discussed in the preceding section. These include the decision to use an annual rather than lifetime or some intermediate period for measuring income, the omission of government expenditures and government regulations and mandates from distributional analyses, the omission of state and local taxes, and the failure to take into account foreign taxes. Whether the staffs agree or disagree on particular issues, the precision reflected in tables of the distributional effects of changes in the tax law is false and potentially misleading.

Conclusion

It seems impossibly difficult to communicate even the simplest facts about tax and fiscal policy to the American public. One cannot be en-

---

80. Ibid., pp. 109–110.

tirely certain whether this is because politicians are engaged in willful distortions—that is, the politicians themselves do not know the facts or are misinformed—or because, as I have demonstrated, the truth is at best elusive, and often unknowable. The most important recent illustration of public confusion about fiscal "facts" was the dispute over the proportion of tax increases and spending cuts in the 1993 act. A wide variety of estimates was offered as truth by opposing politicians. Even the experts had difficulty in sorting through the data. Much of the difficulty stemmed from routine staff practices. CBO's normal budgetary treatment of user changes as "negative outlays" rather than as taxes no doubt encouraged the Clinton administration to extend this notion by counting as spending reductions income-tax increases on social security benefits. As the analysis above makes clear, distributional facts are subject to similar debate and misunderstanding.

Moreover, the precision of distribution tables is illusory, even if they could be readily understood. Even the least disputable distributional estimates are—as Boris Bittker would put it—somewhat fanciful.[81] It is natural to read table 2–1 above to imply that the provisions of the 1993 budget act will change the average tax rate on people with $40,000–$50,000 of income from 20.9 percent to 21.19 percent. But as this chapter has demonstrated, this is an erroneous reading of the table itself and, in any event, suggests far more precision than is plausible. The footnotes to the table make clear that the interpretation of the foregoing sentence is wrong, despite the appearance of the table. The discussion above makes it clear that one should not attempt to connect these two numbers, since the first is an estimate of the relationship of taxes to income, while the second is derived from mistakenly adding an estimate of changes in burden to an estimate of taxes.

The problems of distributional tables detailed above make clear that they are often misleading and should be abandoned as a basis for legislative decision making. Their current capacity to constrain policy decisions disadvantages the tax-legislative process. The economists' typical response to empirical uncertainties—producing a range of estimates or indicating confidence intervals—is an inadequate response to the fundamental inadequacies of these tables. Politicians, journalists, and the public are incapable of reaching informed and consistent judgments about the compromises that should be made among the relevant variables; even if they were capable of such judgments, there is no reason to expect any more agreement or better results from those groups than from the professional staffs. The distributional tables that the staffs produce, however, create the illusion of precision. They endeavor

---

81. Bittker, "Effective Tax Rates, Fact or Fancy."

to tell policy makers precisely how much change in taxes (or tax burden) is anticipated for people at various income levels. They appear to predict within one-tenth of 1 percent changes in effective tax rates that are expected to result.

Ironically, the answers to distributional questions provided by these kinds of tables are probably most accurate (or, more precisely, least inaccurate) when they are of least interest: that is, when the change is narrowly targeted or very small. To know the distributional effects of significant changes in tax policy on aftertax incomes, for example, we would have to know the effect of both the tax increase (or decrease) and any accompanying spending increases (decreases), or borrowing, or other tax decreases (increases) on relative prices, as well as on the employment, consumption, savings, wages, interest, rents, and profits of the people whose change in distributional burdens is being assessed. When the changes in these relevant variables are likely to be small, their distributional effects may well be negligible and any errors reasonably, if not safely, disregarded. Likewise, the choice between distributing only the static-revenue effects (JCT's proxy for burden) and the total-revenue effects is not important when the effect of the tax change on peoples' behavior is small. But when the tax changes and their likely consequences on behavior are large, confidence in the "truth" of quantitative estimates of distributional consequences diminishes. As I have demonstrated, necessary simplifying assumptions are commonplace, but they are controversial.

In practice, if a particular distributional result is desired by powerful politicians, or if a particular distributional outcome is regarded as unacceptable by these politicians, two consequences seem likely. First, one staff's methodology must dominate the legislative process. In recent years, that staff has been the JCT. Second, important policy decisions and tax-law changes will turn on the dominant staff's distributional analysis. Clearly, the JCT's decision to provide policy makers with tables that distribute tax burdens rather than estimated tax changes inhibited, perhaps even defeated, a capital-gains reduction during the period 1989–1992. I do not wish to rehearse here whether capital-gains tax cuts are good or bad policy, but only to insist that distributional tables grounded in staff judgments, which at a minimum are controversial, should not play such a substantial role in the tax-legislative process.

To take but one other example, in 1990 rumors were rampant that the earned income tax (EITC) provisions of the 1990 act were changed at the last moment to reduce the adjustments in the amount of credits for family size in order to change a distributional result in the JCT tables that turned largely on that staff's use of tax-return filing units

75

rather than families as the distributional classifier. (The 1990 expansion of the EITC had been considered as a part of child-care legislation by the House in 1990, and both the House child-care legislation and the Senate version of the 1990 budget act included larger family-size adjustments in the EITC than were adopted.) I do not wish here to dispute the JCT's choice of that income classifier; it does not really matter whether the EITC policy was in fact changed in the way described. It was certainly plausible to those involved in the 1990 act that EITC policy might have been revised solely to reach (or avoid) a particular distributional result in the tables. If this happened, it undermined basic policy agreements made over a year's debate about the use of earned-income tax credits to offset costs of child care. Regardless of one's view about the merits of particular tax changes, this is no way to make policy decisions. The false precision of distributional tables, however, has had and in the future seems likely to have precisely that influence.

The concerns I have expressed here should not be taken to imply that I believe distributional or revenue information to be unimportant, or that policy makers should not be informed of the distributional consequences of their proposed actions. It is crucial, however, to distinguish between, first, the beneficial effects of academic, private, and staff analyses of such information, made in an effort to illuminate the existing state of affairs or proposals for change; and second, the dangers of such information presented to policy makers in the form of supposedly definitive distributional tables at the time legislative decisions are being made. My principal thesis here is that distributional information is far too important to be left to distributional tables.

The information transmitted to policy makers through the current practice of producing distributional tables is simply bad information. Typically, it is both too much information and too little. Distributional tables are not only overly precise; they also leave out important distributional matters. They do not show, for example, how different age cohorts, types of families, or regions of the country will be benefited or burdened by tax changes. In my view, Congress would be far better served by coupling a verbal description of the distributional consequences of legislation under consideration (with doubts, controversial assumptions, and uncertainties explicitly identified and discussed) with staff-produced examples of how the legislation would affect the taxes of specific types of families. If a legislator were interested in particular circumstances, examples could be readily produced with added facts—distinguishing, for example, between taxpayers above age sixty-five and younger families, or between couples where both spouses work and those where only one spouse is employed.

People seriously concerned with the tax policy–making process have reason to worry that the current use of distributional tables (and of revenue estimates) in tax policy making may prove extremely costly to sensible tax policy. For example, the substantial increases in the marriage penalties under the 1993 legislation occurred as a consequence of an effort to make both revenue estimates and distributional tables come out in a certain manner. The current emphasis on distributional tables and revenue estimates both reifies staff decisions about controversial matters and ties legislators' hands in making considered policy judgments. Many thoughtful observers of the tax-legislative process, including the JCT chief of staff, have vigorously lamented the dominant role now being played in the tax-legislative process by revenue estimates. There is serious danger that distributional tables play an equally negative role. Some thoughtful observers believe this was the case in 1990. If current practices in constructing and using distributional tables had been in vogue then, they might well have stymied the 1986 tax-reform process, although the overwhelming commitment of the relevant staffs to the substance of that legislation more likely would have induced them to put aside their standard practices for more creative uses of data to make sure that this did not happen.

Even though the distributional tables now presented to members of Congress and other tax-policy makers should be abandoned, qualitative distributional information should be given to decision makers. The bulk of this information would be noncontroversial among the staffs, and any significant disagreements among the staffs could be discussed in the presence of the decision makers. When offsetting tax increases or decreases are considered necessary for distributional reasons, staffs might also indicate their rough magnitudes. Staffs might wish to refer for their own discussion to analyses of the sort they now make available to decision makers, but with greater consideration of ambiguities, disputes, and uncertainties. As examples of the kinds of qualitative distributional information I envision, staff should inform members of Congress that substitution of a value-added tax for the income tax would reduce taxes for high-income families, but that this effect would be smaller if a longer time perspective—perhaps even a lifetime perspective—were taken; that integration of the corporate tax would be a tax reduction for higher-income people to the extent that the incidence of the tax is now on owners of capital, but less so to the extent the corporate tax is borne by labor or consumers. Likewise, staff should inform decision makers that a tobacco-tax increase would be borne largely by younger low- and middle-income people and is regressive when viewed vis-à-vis annual income but may be proportional if viewed on a lifetime basis. Calculations of the effects of proposals or a combination of proposals on the tax returns of typical families also should be made available. The continuing production of distributional tables for policy alternatives should come to a halt.

No doubt, the views I am expressing here will be regarded by those who produce such data and perhaps by the economics profession at large as an effort to deprive legislators of the best data that economic science can now produce, given the limitations that the legislative timetable demands. So be it. Ronald Coase, the Nobel laureate in economics, once remarked, "In my youth it was said that what was too silly to be said may be sung. In modern economics it may be put into mathematics."[82] In an even less charitable moment, he observed: "If you torture the data enough, nature will always confess."[83]

On March 23, 1995, the *Wall Street Journal* reported that the Treasury Department and the Joint Committee on Taxation substantially changed their methodologies for distributing benefits of tax reductions proposed by the new Republican congressional majority. *Both* Treasury and JCT *reversed* their positions on distributing changes in taxes versus changes in burdens of proposals for capital gains rate reductions. The Treasury distributed the static-revenue cost of the change as an estimate of the change in tax burdens (JCT's prior practice), and JCT distributed the actual anticipated change in taxes (Treasury's prior practice). JCT abandoned its practice of allocating changes in corporate taxes to owners of capital and instead did not include any of the benefits of corporate tax reductions in its distribution tables. JCT distributed tax reductions for the year 2000; Treasury distributed fully phased-in tax changes. As the *Wall Street Journal* correctly reported: "The Treasury's changes make the Republican tax-cut bill look extremely generous to the rich. Changes by the congressional Joint Committee on Taxation make the same tax cuts look less generous to the wealthy."[84]

These methodological changes should shake anyone's remaining confidence that the various staffs' resolutions of the difficult distributional issues discussed in this chapter are—or even can be— determined by economic science rather than politics. The mystery deepens as to why these distributional tables should be used to determine tax legislative outcomes. I rest my case.

---

82. Ronald W. Coase, *The Firm, the Market and the Law* (Chicago: University of Chicago Press, 1988), p. 185.

83. Coase, *How Should Economists Choose?* (Washington, D.C.: American Enterprise Institute, 1982), p. 16. See also Michael A. Fitts, "Can Ignorance Be Bliss? Imperfect Information as a Positive Influence in Political Institutions," *Michigan Law Review*, vol. 88 (1990): 917–82.

84. Lucinda Harper, "Treasury, Congress Disagree How Much GOP's Gains-Tax Cut Benefits the Rich," *Wall Street Journal*, March 23, 1995, A3.

PART TWO

The Current
State of the Art

3
Distributional Tables and Tax Policy

R. Glenn Hubbard

The distribution of tax burdens and government expenditures is a fundamental question in both public economics and public policy. Positive and normative analyses in public economics have focused on *incidence*, effects of tax and expenditure policies on the distribution of economic well-being. Tax policy debates among policy makers are grounded in no small part in their perceptions of the effects of policy changes on the distribution of economic well-being. The study of incidence is an active area of research among economists, though the contributions of recent research are not always integrated in the distributional assessments presented to policy makers.

Since 1990, the preparation of "distribution tables" has been an area of increasing activity for staff economists in the administration and Congress and for economists in private organizations advising taxpayers—as well as for academic economists serving in the government. While there are many reasons for this recent growth, two seem particularly prominent: first, the heightened concern over income inequality in the 1980s, with the attendant concerns that the federal tax system may have been partially responsible and, in any event, should be used to redress changes; and second, the increasing ability of staff economists to prepare detailed tables quickly, using modern computer technology and microsimulation models. Whatever the reason, the higher profile of distribution tables has aroused worries by economists

I am grateful to Anne Alstott, Alan Auerbach, David Bradford, Martin Feldstein, Bill Gale, Michael Graetz, Jim Nunns, Jim Poterba, Jon Skinner, and Joel Slemrod for helpful comments and suggestions. This chapter draws on some of the many lessons I learned, especially from Jim Nunns, while serving as deputy assistant secretary for tax analysis in the Treasury Department. While in no way implicating my former colleagues in the Office of Tax Analysis for this chapter, I acknowledge that debt.

in and out of government that the tables do not necessarily convey the appropriate information (or, in some cases, lack of information) to decision makers. In this chapter, I argue that economic analysis has much to offer decision makers in forming their judgments about tax fairness.

On one level, economic analysis has made significant contributions to the study of distributional effects of government policies. It is well understood, for example, that the burden (or benefit) of a tax change is not necessarily borne by (does not necessarily accrue to) the groups that bear the legal liability to remit the tax. That is, changing the structure of taxes alters the economy's equilibrium by altering prices of goods, labor, and capital.[1] The concept of shifting the burden of the tax *is* incorporated in the distributional analysis presented by policy makers in the executive branch and Congress. There is much controversy, however, over *how* the economy's equilibrium changes in response to many taxes, for example, the corporate income tax or a broad-based consumption tax. Such controversy notwithstanding, I argue that economic analysis contributes a framework for deciding the appropriate questions and for gathering information.

In the following section, I present some questions posed by economic analysis for the presentation of distribution tables and then review "answers" in practice. The next section illustrates some methodological issues in measuring the distribution of the tax burden in the context of proposals for a broad-based federal consumption tax. The final section suggests a strategy for bringing theory and practice closer together.

Applying Economic Analysis

A basic methodological issue in distributional analysis is how to measure incidence. Economists' reflexive answer is to calculate the compensating variation, a monetary measure—in absolute terms or relative to lifetime resources—of the effect of a particular policy change on economic well-being. This "answer" is by no means a simple one in practice, since it requires the calculation of the extra resources needed to restore the individual to his or her initial level of well-being given a

---

1. For a survey of the academic literature, see Laurence J. Kotlikoff and Lawrence H. Summers, "Tax Incidence," in Alan J. Auerbach and Martin Feldstein, eds., *Handbook of Public Economics*, vol. 2 (Amsterdam: North-Holland, 1985). An excellent review of practical problems is presented in U.S. Congress, Joint Committee on Taxation, "Methodology and Issues in Measuring Changes in the Distribution of Tax Burdens," Washington, D.C., June 14, 1993.

change in prices.[2] Most applied analyses do not attempt to calculate this measure, generally emphasizing effects of taxes on after-tax current incomes of individuals or households with different pretax incomes.[3]

Economists' analytical approaches to studying incidence have generally used static computable general equilibrium (CGE) models[4] or life-cycle overlapping-generations models.[5] These models permit the calculation of compensating variations for different groups in the population at a point in time, in the case of the CGE model, and in some cases across different lifetime-income groups or generations, in the case of the life-cycle simulation models. As analytical devices, such models have been used to assess actual and potential tax reforms. They have not, however, been the principal guiding force in shaping distributional analysis presented to policy makers.[6]

---

2. Another measure is the equivalent variation, which uses the after-tax-change level of economic well-being as the point of reference.

3. Another issue relates to the disposition of tax revenue. The distributional effect of a tax policy change depends in general on whether the revenue is used to finance changes in other (current or future) taxes or government spending. Some analyses of alternative tax reforms therefore focus on differential incidence, a comparison of the distributional consequences of alternative equal-revenue tax instruments.

4. See, for example, Charles L. Ballard, Don Fullerton, John B. Shoven, and John Whalley, *A General Equilibrium Model for Tax Policy Evaluation* (Chicago: University of Chicago Press, 1985); and John B. Shoven and John Whalley, "Applied General Equilibrium Models of Taxation and International Trade: An Introduction and Survey," *Journal of Economic Literature* 22 (September 1984), pp. 1007–51.

5. See, for example, Alan J. Auerbach and Laurence J. Kotlikoff, *Dynamic Fiscal Policy* (Cambridge: Cambridge University Press, 1987); R. Glenn Hubbard and Kenneth L. Judd, "Social Security and Individual Welfare: Precautionary Saving, Borrowing Constraints, and the Payroll Tax," *American Economic Review* 77 (September 1987), 630–46; R. Glenn Hubbard, Jonathan Skinner, and Stephen P. Zeldes, "Precautionary Saving and Social Insurance," *Journal of Political Economy* 103 (April 1995), pp. 360–99; and R. Glenn Hubbard, Jonathan Skinner, and Stephen P. Zeldes, "The Importance of Precautionary Motives in Explaining Individual and Aggregate Saving," *Carnegie-Rochester Conference Series on Public Policy* (1994).

6. In another line of inquiry, research by Jorgenson and his collaborators has focused on money-metric individual welfare (incorporating compensating and equivalent variations in total expenditure by defining the concept as money measures of individual welfare corresponding to each policy, expressed in terms of a common price system); see Dale W. Jorgenson, Laurence J. Lau, and Thomas M. Stoker, "Welfare Comparison under Exact Aggregation," *American Economic Review* 70 (May 1980), pp. 268–72; and Dale W. Jorgenson,

Applied analyses of the distribution of the tax burden have been more heavily influenced by empirical studies that have proceeded in two steps: first, hypothesizing the incidence of each principal tax; then, using cross-sectional or panel data on households to estimate the distribution of the composite tax burden by income class.[7] Among academic economists, the results of such empirical studies have generated controversy both because they rely on ad hoc assumptions about the incidence of particular taxes[8] and, relatedly, because *tax collections* may bear a poor relation to tax burdens.[9]

Rather than examining in more detail the controversy among alternative approaches to distributional analysis, I focus on some questions suggested by economic analysis and on "answers" implemented in practice. The number of alternative answers, in principle, to central questions suggests the desirability of more sensitivity analysis in distribution tables than is the case under current practice.

The Construction of Distribution Tables in Principle. It is instructive to begin by describing the essential elements of the typical distribution tables of tax burdens used by policy makers, to wit: Which taxes are included? What is the definition of income? What are the underlying assumptions about incidence? What measure of the tax burden is used? How are temporary tax provisions treated?

"Correct" answers to these questions depend, of course, both on the professional judgment of staff economists and economic policy makers and on the purpose for which the table is used. While senior

---

"Aggregate Consumer Behavior and the Measurement of Social Welfare," *Econometrica* 58 (September 1990), pp. 1007–40; and money-metric social welfare (providing a complete ordering of economic policies by defining the concept as the difference between money measures of social welfare corresponding to each policy, expressed in terms of a common price system); see Dale W. Jorgenson and Daniel T. Slesnick, "Aggregate Consumer Behavior and the Measurement of Inequality," *Review of Economic Studies* 51 (July 1984), pp. 369–92. While day-to-day application to distributional analysis is probably not around the corner, these approaches offer valuable developments for decomposing impacts of proposed policy into "efficiency" and "equity" effects.

7. See Joseph A. Pechman and Benjamin A. Okner, *Who Bears the Tax Burden?* (Washington, D.C.: Brookings Institution, 1974); Edgar K. Browning and William R. Johnson, *The Distribution of the Tax Burden* (Washington, D.C.: American Enterprise Institute, 1979); and Joseph A. Pechman, *Who Paid the Taxes, 1966–1985* (Washington, D.C.: Brookings Institution, 1985).

8. The incidence of the corporate income tax is particularly controversial.

9. For example, a high rate of tax on realized capital gains may raise little revenue, but generate a significant tax burden for holders of assets.

policy makers often use distribution tables to guide them in implementing "equity" goals, comparatively little review of these five questions takes place by officials, though the technical staffs of the Treasury Department's Office of Tax Analysis (OTA), the Joint Committee on Taxation (JCT), and the Congressional Budget Office (CBO) are keenly aware of their importance.

Which taxes are included? A tax-burden table may include all taxes (federal, state, and local), all federal taxes, or only a specific set of federal taxes. Criteria for inclusion depend on the purpose of the table, but in practice judgments over how certain taxes are—or how well they can be—distributed are important.

What is the definition of income? The way in which incomes are classified is in principle chosen to distinguish taxpaying units by their economic well-being. At one level, members of Congress and administration policy makers are interested in narrowly defined concepts such as money income; at another level, economists have generally stressed broader definitions matching more closely conceptual notions of income. The common economists' measure of a household's economic income, the Haig-Simons measure of annual income, equals the annual change in the household's wealth plus the market value of consumption over the year.[10]

A second issue in defining income relates to the specification of an economic unit: income may be defined on a family basis (as a proxy for an economic unit) or on a tax-return basis (which corresponds to current income-tax reporting).[11] Differences in distributional estimates from different sources sometimes reflect this distinction.

A third issue relates to the time period under consideration. Generally, distribution tables produced for policy makers are based on current annual income, while many analysts have argued for greater

---

10. As discussed later, this concept of economic income is difficult to measure. Staff economists for policy makers have used different sets of approximations of economic income.

11. For a discussion of the distinctions among these concepts, see Susan C. Nelson, "Family Economic Income and Other Income Concepts Used in Analyzing Tax Reform," in *Compendium of Tax Research, 1987*, Washington, D.C.: U.S. Department of the Treasury, Office of Tax Analysis, 1987; and U.S. Department of the Treasury, Office of Tax Analysis, "Household Income Mobility during the 1980s: A Statistical Assessment Based on Tax Return Data," *Tax Notes* (June 1, 1992); and U.S. Department of the Treasury, Office of Tax Analysis, "Household Income Changes over Time: Some Basic Questions and Facts," *Tax Notes* (August 24, 1992).

emphasis on permanent income.[12] The length of the period over which one analyzes the distributional consequences of a policy change is important for two reasons. First, the progressivity or regressivity of a tax change can be overstated in the short run to the extent that annual variations in income overestimate long-run or lifetime differences.[13] Abstracting from lifetime income differences, the consumption-smoothing feature of the familiar life-cycle model predicts that differences in annual income over the life cycle are larger than differences in annual consumption (which corresponds more closely to permanent income). Second, significant reforms entail periods of transition.[14] A switch from a wage tax to a consumption tax, for example, burdens the current elderly in the short run, who paid wage taxes and now in retirement must pay consumption taxes; the introduction of investment incentives reduces the value of old capital in the short run; and the introduction of an actuarially fair pay-as-you-go social security scheme benefits the first generation to participate relative to future generations.

What are the underlying assumptions about incidence? Staff economists rely on theoretical arguments and empirical evidence about the

---

12. Advocates of a permanent income measure argue that it removes transitory fluctuations in annual income and better reflects long-run well-being; advocates of a current annual income measure argue that it is better (or, at least, less controversially measured) and corresponds to man-in-the-street notions of income.

A still broader question is whether to consider intergenerational redistribution of the tax system. See, for example, Alan J. Auerbach, Jagadeesh Gokhale, and Laurence J. Kotlikoff, "Generational Accounting: A Meaningful Way to Evaluate Fiscal Policy," *Journal of Economic Perspectives* 7 (Summer 1993); and Alan J. Auerbach, "Public Finance in Theory and Practice," *National Tax Journal* 4 (December 1993), pp. 527–538.

13. Don Fullerton and Diane Lim Rogers conclude in their study, however, that, in practice, lifetime and annual-income incidence of the U.S. tax system are not markedly different. See Don Fullerton and Diane Lim Rogers, *Who Bears the Lifetime Tax Burden?* (Washington, D.C.: Brookings Institution, 1993). See also the discussion in James M. Poterba, "Lifetime Incidence and the Distributional Burden of Excise Taxes," *American Economic Review* 79 (May 1989), pp. 325–30; OTA, "Household Income Changes over Time"; and OTA, "Household Income Mobility during the 1980s."

14. Transition effects are discussed in Douglas B. Bernheim, "A Note on Dynamic Tax Incidence," *Quarterly Journal of Economics* (1981), pp. 705–23; Christophe Chamley, "The Welfare Cost of Capital Income Taxation in a Growing Economy," *Journal of Political Economy* (June 1981), pp. 468–91; and Hubbard and Judd, "Social Security and Individual Welfare."

incidence of particular taxes. For many taxes, such as the individual income tax, there is broad professional agreement on incidence; for other taxes, notably the corporation income tax, there is considerably less professional agreement. Though not often scrutinized by consumers of the tables, alternative incidence assumptions can have a significant effect on distribution tables of tax burdens.

What measure of tax burden is used? Tax burdens are measured in practice as the amount of taxes paid, or reduction in taxes paid; they do not incorporate notions of excess burden. The distribution tables attempt to convert "taxes paid" into indicators of the economic burden of taxes, including the effective tax rate—that is, taxes divided by income—the percentage change in taxes, the percentage change in after-tax income, or the share of taxes paid. The choice of indicator is not innocuous: the indicators do not necessarily present the same "answer" regarding the progressivity or regressivity of current taxes or a change in taxes, nor do they relate in the same way to theoretical measures of economic well-being.

How are temporary tax provisions treated? Both current federal tax law and proposed policy changes often incorporate temporary measures; such provisions may be included in a distribution table or given special treatment in an ancillary table. An additional complication arises on account of provisions with a timing element. Individual retirement account or Keogh contributions from pretax income, for example, reduce current tax payments while increasing tax payments in future years when withdrawals are subject to tax.[15] Analysts must make decisions about how to treat such timing changes.

In addition to the questions raised above, a serious question arises over which proposals merit the detailed distributional analysis found in distribution tables. At the risk of sounding simplistic, such analysis should be submitted only when it informs the debate. I would argue that such situations arise relatively rarely—for example, the submission of the president's budget or a proposal to change the structure of the tax system significantly.

The Construction of Distribution Tables in Practice. In part because of the flurry of interest created by the fashioning of the Omnibus Budget Reconciliation Act of 1990, in the early 1990s the Office of Tax Analysis prepared numerous distribution tables to explain current-law tax

---

15. The net tax benefit of such tax-favored savings schemes is, of course, the sheltering of accumulated earnings from taxation (plus a gain upon disbursement of funds if the tax rate is lower at that time).

burdens and effects of tax policy changes on those burdens. As a rule, distribution tables are prepared for the use of administration officials and are not released publicly. The Joint Committee on Taxation and the Congressional Budget Office do release distributional tables to congressional decision makers.

The Office of Tax Analysis, the Joint Committee on Taxation, and the Congressional Budget Office have offered "answers" to the five questions raised earlier:

Which taxes are included? Following the work of the late Joseph Pechman,[16] the CBO, OTA, and JCT staffs decided to count only federal taxes, including individual income and corporate income taxes, payroll (social security and unemployment insurance) taxes, and excise taxes.[17] Customs duties are not incorporated. The JCT staff has not previously distributed the corporate income tax, although its 1993 pamphlet on distributional analysis suggests that it will do so in the future, at least for changes in elements of the tax; the CBO and OTA do distribute the burden of the corporate income tax.

What is the definition of income? The OTA, JCT, and CBO use "current annual income" to define income. Each staff tries to approximate economic income. The JCT uses a very narrow definition, relying almost exclusively on items reported on tax returns. Specifically, the JCT adds back to adjusted gross income tax-exempt interest, workers' compensation, nontaxable social security benefits, deductible contributions to individual retirement accounts (IRAs), employer contributions for health and life insurance, tax preferences under the alternative tax, and net losses in excess of minimum tax preferences from passive business activities. In addition to the categories in the JCT definition, the CBO includes all government cash transfers, all cash pension benefits, the employer share of payroll taxes, and a portion of the corporate income tax.

The OTA uses the broadest annual income concept, called family economic income (FEI), which adds to adjusted gross income a proxy for unreported and underreported income; deductible contributions to IRA and Keogh plans; nontaxable transfer payments (such as excludable income from social security and Aid to Families with Dependent

---

16. See Pechman and Okner, *Who Bears the Tax Burden?* and Pechman, *Who Paid the Taxes, 1966–1985.*

17. For a description of taxes included by the three groups, see U.S. Congressional Budget Office, *The Changing Distribution of Federal Taxes: 1975–1990* (Washington, D.C.: CBO, 1987); Nelson, "Family Economic Income"; and JCT, "Methodology and Issues."

Children benefits); employer-provided fringe benefits; inside buildup on private pensions, IRAs, Keoghs, and life insurance; tax-exempt interest; and imputed rent on owner-occupied housing.[18] In contrast to the JCT and CBO, the OTA computes capital gains on an accrual basis, adjusted for inflation, to the extent permitted by reliable data. In addition, inflationary losses of lenders are subtracted, and gains of borrowers are added. Finally, FEI includes the value of food stamps received but excludes other in-kind transfers, such as the value of public housing and Medicaid payments.[19]

To represent income units, the JCT uses tax returns. The CBO uses families but for some distributions also adjusts for family size by dividing each family's income by the poverty level for a family of that size. The OTA's FEI is calculated on a family, rather than on a tax-return, basis. The economic incomes of all members of a family unit are added to arrive at the family's income used as a classifier in the distributions.

I noted earlier that an additional question in deciding the appropriate income concept relates to the time horizon for analysis. One option is to shift from annual measures of economic income to lifetime measures. Indeed, Don Fullerton and Diane Lim Rogers have produced an ambitious examination of lifetime tax burdens borne by groups in the population,[20] and staff economists at the OTA and JCT are analyzing various measures of permanent income. Lifetime incidence calculations, while informative, are not likely to become the principal summary measures for policy makers for two reasons. First, on a conceptual level, lifetime income and incidence calculations assume perfect insurance and lending markets; recent research shows that for

---

18. See Nelson, "Family Economic Income." In earlier work, Pechman and Okner, *Who Bears the Tax Burden?* and Pechman, *Who Paid the Taxes, 1966–1985,* also incorporated in "income" imputed rent on owner-occupied housing, measures of accrued rather than realized capital gains, and noncash transfer payments. William G. Gale reviews issues in deciding on the appropriate income concepts in "Comment on 'Trends in Federal Tax Progressivity, 1980–93,'" mimeo, Brookings Institution, October 1992.

19. The difference between the OTA and JCT approaches to defining economic income essentially represents differences in judgments about whether existing data permit the development of information about some components of Haig-Simons income relative to the OTA's family economic income. Some of the data sets used by the JCT staff for other purposes described in the pamphlet could have been applied to the construction of a more comprehensive measure of economic income. Whether imperfections in such data make more comprehensive measures less meaningful is, of course, an open question with reasonable positions on either side.

20. Fullerton and Rogers, *Who Bears the Lifetime Tax Burden?*

most groups in the population, consumption moves more closely with income than perfect-markets models suggest.[21] Thus current income provides information about economic well-being not captured by permanent income. Second, since revenue estimates are presented for relatively short time horizons (generally a five-year budget period), policy makers are likely to request distributional analysis for a comparable period.[22] A related point is raised by the concern over "transition issues": to the extent that policy makers are concerned with the near-term effects of policies, the incidence of the tax change may be different from that suggested by "long-run" calculations.

What are the underlying assumptions about incidence? The basic incidence assumptions used by the OTA are as follows. The individual income tax is assumed to be borne by payers, the corporate income tax by capital income generally,[23] payroll taxes (employer and employee shares) by labor (that is, wages and self-employment income), excise taxes on purchases by individuals by the purchaser, and excise taxes on purchases by business in proportion to total consumption expenditures. The same incidence assumptions are used in distributing current-law burdens and proposed changes. With the exception of the corporate income tax, the OTA, JCT, and CBO follow very similar incidence assumptions. The CBO generally assumes that half the corporate tax burden is borne by all capital income and that half is borne by labor income. As of this writing, the JCT distributes neither the corporate income tax nor the proposed changes in the corporate income tax. The JCT suggests, however, that it will in the future distribute *changes* in the corporate tax burdens.[24]

What measure of the tax burden is used? Distribution tables prepared by the Office of Tax Analysis have traditionally measured tax burdens by the amount of taxes paid (or the reduction in taxes paid, for a tax reduction), in absolute terms or in terms of an effective tax rate. While such measures provide a consistent means of distributing current-law

---

21. See, for example, Christopher D. Carroll, "The Buffer Stock Theory of Saving: Some Macroeconomic Evidence," *Brookings Papers on Economic Activity* no. 1 (1992): 61–135; and Hubbard, Skinner, and Zeldes, "The Importance of Precautionary Motives."

22. A compromise approach taken by the JCT staff is outlined in JCT, "Methodology and Issues."

23. For a review of the issues surrounding the incidence of the corporate income tax, see U.S. Department of the Treasury, *Integration of the Individual and Corporate Tax Systems* (Washington, D.C.: U.S. Government Printing Office, January 1992).

24. See JCT, "Methodology and Issues."

taxes and proposed changes, they do not incorporate excess burden. The JCT and CBO economists have also traditionally measured direct tax burdens by tax payments or decreases in tax payments.[25] According to its 1993 pamphlet, the JCT staff has now adopted as measures of the tax burden effective tax rates and the percentage change in taxes paid. CBO staff and, if developments during my experience are continuing, OTA staff are emphasizing the percentage change in after-tax income as a straightforwardly computable measure of the tax burden and proxy for the change in economic well-being.

How are temporary tax provisions treated? OTA staff economists define as "permanent" the law at the end of the five-year budget period. The burdens of permanent tax changes are then distributed assuming *long-run* (end-of-budget-period) behavioral responses and *current* levels of income. Temporary tax changes are indicated in "short-run" distribution tables, which incorporate the effect of the first full year of the temporary provisions. Proposed policy changes involving "timing" effects (IRAs, for example) are evaluated by the Office of Tax Analysis at long-run levels.[26] Provisions with irregular effects on tax liabilities (such as changes in the timing of depreciation allowances) are assessed using the present value of taxes over the budget period. When I was at the Office of Tax Analysis, I was not always certain of the CBO and JCT procedures for distributing burdens or benefits of temporary tax changes or timing tax provisions. Prospective JCT procedures are outlined in the 1993 pamphlet.

Distributing the Burden of a Consumption Tax

A number of proposals over the past two decades have suggested fundamental restructuring of the federal income tax, both individual and corporate, to be financed by a broad-based consumption tax. The 1992 proposal of Nicholas Brady, former secretary of the Treasury, for example, recommended a broad-based business transfer tax—namely, a tax on business gross receipts with expensing of purchases from other

---

25. A notable exception is the JCT staff's measurement of the burden of the capital gains tax as the "static" revenue loss (the change in revenue by income class, assuming no behavioral response to changes in the tax).

26. For the case of tax-favored savings vehicles such as IRAs, the long-run effect could be characterized by the tax savings from the earnings from one year's deposits in a steady-state year. I believe that the Office of Tax Analysis follows this procedure.

firms, including new investment[27]—to finance reductions in individual and corporate taxes. Claims that such a restructuring would improve economic efficiency are often countered with arguments that it would be regressive. The design of the Brady proposal was influenced by distributional considerations to ensure that the package did not reduce the progressivity of federal tax burdens; similar considerations have figured in the deliberations over a proposal for a broad-based consumption tax by Senators David Boren and John Danforth.[28]

Economists generally argue that, over the lifetime of a given individual, a flat-rate, broad-based consumption tax is equivalent to a flat-rate tax on wages plus a flat-rate tax on existing capital at the time the tax is introduced.[29] This equivalence arises because a consumption tax is likely to lead to price increases in the long run, reducing the purchasing power of wage income and income from existing capital. The returns to new investment are untaxed under a broad-based consumption tax.

This lifetime equivalence for a given individual does not imply that commonly produced distribution tables would generate identical answers under the two approaches. Since annual consumption exceeds

---

27. The business transfer tax is a variant of a subtraction-method value-added tax. There is no reason to believe that the incidence of a subtraction-method value-added tax and the more familiar (in practice) credit-invoice value-added tax are different. For discussions of this point, see David F. Bradford, *Untangling the Income Tax* (Cambridge, Mass.: Harvard University Press); U.S. Congressional Budget Office, *Effects of Adopting a Value-added Tax* (Washington, D.C.: GPO, 1992); JCT, "Methodology and Issues"; Charles E. McLure, Jr., "The Mechanics of Three Consumption Taxes," in *The Value Added Tax: Coming to America?* (Arlington, Va.: Tax Analysts, 1993); and Nicholas F. Brady, "Remarks Presented at the Graduate School of Business of Columbia University," December 10, 1992.

28. In estimating the distributional impact of the plan, the Office of Tax Analysis used the most conservative assumptions (to satisfy the Secretary's request that the proposal not reduce overall progressivity of the federal tax system): The consumption tax was assumed to raise prices, so that its burden was distributed across households according to their consumption. Taxes on corporate capital income (which were reduced in the plan through corporate tax integration) were assumed to be borne by owners of capital. Distributional analysis for the Boren-Danforth plan is (as of this writing in September 1993) being provided by JCT staff economists. As discussed later, the JCT assumes that the burden of the tax is borne by wages and old capital as the income is earned.

29. This equivalence is true in a benchmark case in which credit and insurance markets are perfect.

measured annual income for very low-income individuals on account of transfers and unmeasured income, distributing the burden of a consumption tax proportionally to consumption will make the tax appear regressive at low-income levels.[30] In contrast, distributing the burden of the tax to wage income and old capital income increases the progressivity of taxes at low- and high-income levels relative to the previous case.[31]

To the extent that tables showing the distribution of the tax burden by economic income class are to represent the short-run or medium-run incidence of tax changes, the JCT staff's decision to distribute the burden of a broad-based consumption tax to factor incomes (wages and returns to existing capital) is appropriate. During the period of transition from an income tax to a consumption tax, the burden borne by owners of existing capital enhances the current-annual-income progressivity of a flat-rate broad-based consumption tax.[32]

The decision regarding the distribution of a broad-based consumption tax is not the only incidence assumption required in analyzing the distributional consequences of a policy change involving such a tax. If a business transfer tax were used to reduce federal corporate income taxes and individual income taxes, for example, incidence assumptions for those taxes are also needed. If, on the one hand, the corporate income tax were borne by owners of capital, replacing corporate tax revenue with consumption tax revenue would be regressive on an annual-income basis. If, on the other hand, part of the burden of the

---

30. This assumes that prices rise because of the tax, and that not all transfer payments are indexed. John Sabelhaus, "What is the Distributional Burden of Taxing Consumption?" Mimeo., Congressional Budget Office, December 1992, suggests that consumption taxes are likely to be less regressive than previously believed when distributed this way. This is because the traditionally used Consumer Expenditure Surveys overstate dissaving by very low-income households and saving by very high-income households. Sabelhaus and the JCT staff have used the Federal Reserve's Survey of Consumer Finances data on saving rates to impute consumption. These data suggest that income is higher relative to consumption for very low-income households and lower relative to consumption for very high-income households. The Brady proposal provided a refundable tax credit for low-income households rather than specifically indexing individual transfer programs.

31. See, for example, JCT, "Methodology and Issues," p. 55.

32. This distributional approach does suggest different burdens for holders of nominal and real claims on existing capital. Nominal bondholders will not be affected by the reduction in returns to existing capital. Owners of real physical capital bear this burden.

corporate tax were borne by workers or by consumers of corporate goods, the distributional consequences would be less regressive.[33]

An additional complication is raised by the distributional assumptions that accompany incremental reforms in the direction of a consumption tax. Suppose that a series of business income tax reforms was introduced gradually: expensing of investment, phasing out of interest deductions, and phasing out of deductions for compensation. At each step, the distributional analysis should be consistent with the distributional analysis of a broad-based consumption tax, the final result of the three steps. It would be inconsistent, for example, to distribute incremental reforms on the basis of factor incomes (wage and capital income) and to distribute the final result (a consumption tax) on the basis of consumption. The approach suggested by the JCT staff in its 1993 pamphlet—to distribute the burden of a broad-based consumption tax on wages and returns to existing capital—ensures greater consistency between distributional analysis of incremental and large-scale tax reforms.

To summarize, examining the distributional analysis of a broad-based consumption tax illustrates many of the issues surrounding the design of distributional information for policy makers, including assumptions about incidence and appropriate concepts of income and time horizon.

Conclusions

As with many areas in public economics, the gap between the theory and the practice of distributional analysis is noticeable to economists and policy makers. Moreover, economic researchers and staff economists often want to present guarded and qualified answers to questions about the distribution of the federal tax burden to policy makers desiring much more specific answers. The temptation to satisfy policy makers' growing appetite for distribution tables should, in my view, be resisted in favor of the following three-part strategy:

• Staff economists should continue their efforts to instruct decision makers on what one can and cannot learn from "distribution tables." The 1993 Joint Committee pamphlet and the 1987 Office of Tax Analysis *Compendium* are excellent examples of this educational proc-

33. See, for example, the discussions in JCT, "Methodology and Issues," and Fullerton and Rogers, *Who Bears the Lifetime Tax Burden?* While I understand the spirit of the exercise, the JCT staff's decision that the incidence of the existing corporate tax is not well understood but that the distribution of straightforward changes is easily accomplished puzzled me on a technical level.

ess. Seminars for new legislators (particularly for those on tax-writing committees) or administration officials could also devote time to the examination of assumptions and judgments lying behind the distributional analysis of specific proposals.

• Staff economists should stress that distributional analysis is most useful for examining the distribution of fiscal policies generally[34] and much less useful in considering small changes in policy. Reporting of tax-burden tables for the existing federal tax system, presidential budget packages, or significant reforms—accompanied by the caveats to which I referred earlier—informs the policy process. Producing such tables for a large number of individual proposals gives decision makers the misleading appearance of exactitude and can cause confusion by drawing attention away from interactions of the effects of individual policies.[35] Specific statements qualifying such distribution tables should become a part of staff economists' response to specific requests for distributional tables for individual policy changes.

• Economists engaged in research on incidence can help improve the quality of applied distributional analyses by working with staff economists in the administration and Congress. Recent research on lifetime incidence, generational differences in tax burden, and burdens and benefits of public policies under imperfect insurance and capital markets can make potentially significant contributions to applied distributional analysis.[36]

In short, economic analysis can best contribute to distributional analysis in much the same way as it can to other areas of public policy decision making—by posing central questions for study, designing a framework for gathering information, and imposing basic tests for consistency of analyses communicated to policy makers. These contributions, sometimes ignored by decision makers, will serve those decision makers better than merely producing information of the type they demand.

---

34. I use the term *fiscal policies* to underscore the need for more effort to report to policy makers the distributional consequences of federal expenditures.

35. My former Treasury colleague Michael Graetz told me on more than one occasion that the flurry of distribution tables produced for "1990 budget summit" conferees at Andrews Air Force Base crossed the border between sublime and ridiculous early in the game.

36. One example is the discussion of intergenerational differences in federal tax burdens in President Bush's Fiscal Year 1993 Budget. That informative description built on research in Auerbach, Gokhale, and Kotlikoff, "Generational Accounting," *Journal of Economic Perspectives*, vol. 8 (Winter 1994), pp. 73–94, with assistance from those authors.

4

A Comparison of Distribution Methodologies

Thomas A. Barthold, James R. Nunns, and Eric Toder

The Congressional Budget Office (CBO), the Department of the Treasury's Office of Tax Analysis (OTA), and the staff of the Joint Committee on Taxation (JCT) all routinely supply policy makers with distributional analyses of proposals to change the nation's tax laws. The CBO has also presented analyses showing how the distribution of the tax burden has changed over time.[1]

Any distributional analysis of tax legislation is an attempt to represent changes in the economic burden of taxation. Tables 4–1, 4–2, and 4–3 reproduce the distributional analyses prepared by the CBO, the OTA and the JCT staff, for the Omnibus Budget Reconciliation Act of 1993 (OBRA). Because economics is not an exact science and the three agencies perform these analyses independently, it is not surprising that their estimates do not coincide exactly. Because the three agencies base their estimates on the same economic principles, however, it is also not surprising that their qualitative findings about how OBRA altered the distribution of tax burdens are broadly similar.

All three entities base their estimates primarily on large microsimulation models of the U.S. tax system. In practice, such modeling

The authors originally prepared this chapter as a paper for the American Enterprise Institute's conference "Distributional Analysis for Making Tax Policy," in Washington, D.C., December 16–17, 1993. We thank Tom Bowne, Billy Jack, and Rick Kasten for helpful comments. While descriptive of the methodologies of the Joint Committee on Taxation, the Congressional Budget Office, and the Office of Tax Analysis, this chapter represents the views of the authors alone. It should not be construed as representing the views or policies of the U.S. Department of the Treasury, the Joint Committee on Taxation, the Congressional Budget Office, or any member of Congress.

1. See, for example, *The Changing Distribution of Federal Taxes: 1975–1990*, Congressional Budget Office, October 1987; and Committee on Ways and Means, U.S. House of Representatives, *1993 Green Book*, appendix K.

TABLE 4-1
TAX BURDENS BEFORE AND AFTER THE 1993 OBRA, BY ADJUSTED FAMILY INCOME AND BY FAMILY DOLLAR INCOME
(1994 income levels and 1998 law)

	All Federal Taxes			Income after Taxes		Effective Tax Rates		Share of Total Change
	Average	Change	Percent change	Average	Percent change	Current law	With option	
Families by Adjusted Family Income								
All families								
First	589	−166	−28.1	7,878	2.1	7.0	5.0	−8.3
Second	3,119	−35	−1.1	17,623	0.2	15.0	14.9	−1.8
Third	6,498	64	1.0	27,156	−0.2	19.3	19.5	3.2
Fourth	10,800	110	1.0	38,172	−0.3	22.1	22.3	5.7
Fifth	29,203	1,884	6.5	82,111	−2.3	26.2	27.9	100.9
All quintiles	10,107	382	3.8	34,129	−1.1	22.8	23.7	100.0
Top 10	41,225	3,473	8.4	111,727	−3.1	27.0	29.2	94.6
Top 5	59,374	6,521	11.0	157,427	−4.1	27.4	30.4	89.4
Top 1	158,719	29,417	18.5	408,157	−7.2	28.0	33.2	76.3
81–90%	16,757	239	1.4	51,452	−0.5	24.6	24.9	6.3
91–95%	22,859	388	1.7	65,483	−0.6	25.9	26.3	5.3
96–99%	36,188	1,177	3.3	98,908	−1.2	26.8	27.7	13.1
Families with children								
First	559	−380	−68.0	10,493	3.6	5.1	1.6	−25.8
Second	4,811	−134	−2.8	23,585	0.6	16.9	16.5	−8.8

(Table continues)

TABLE 4-1 (continued)

	All Federal Taxes			Income after Taxes		Effective Tax Rates		Share of Total Change
	Average	Change	Percent change	Average	Percent change	Current law	With option	
Families by Adjusted Family Income								
Third	9,665	73	0.8	35,240	-0.2	21.5	21.7	4.7
Fourth	15,305	144	0.9	49,663	-0.3	23.6	23.8	8.1
81–90%	22,402	223	1.0	66,243	-0.3	25.3	25.5	5.0
Top 10	54,694	6,450	11.8	147,793	-4.4	27.0	30.2	116.5
All quintiles	11,178	336	3.0	37,610	-0.9	22.9	23.6	100.0
Families with head age 65 +								
First	200	9	4.6	7,336	-0.1	2.6	2.8	0.5
Second	718	27	3.8	15,412	-0.2	4.4	4.6	1.6
Third	2,169	60	2.8	25,121	-0.2	7.9	8.2	2.9
Fourth	5,037	115	2.3	36,149	-0.3	12.2	12.5	4.5
81–90%	10,178	651	6.4	50,892	-1.3	16.7	17.7	10.4
Top 10	38,198	3,753	9.8	119,182	-3.1	24.3	26.7	80.0
All quintiles	5,615	421	7.5	30,663	-1.4	15.5	16.6	100.0
Other families								
First	876	-37	-4.3	5,276	0.7	14.2	13.6	-1.4
Second	3,060	25	0.8	13,066	-0.2	19.0	19.1	1.0
Third	5,842	58	1.0	20,787	-0.3	21.9	22.2	2.5
Fourth	9,843	86	0.9	31,412	-0.3	23.9	24.1	4.7

81–90%	15,848	153	1.0	45,329	−0.3	25.9	26.2	5.1
Top 10	37,798	2,450	6.5	98,197	−2.5	27.8	29.6	87.7
All quintiles	11,308	399	3.5	33,074	−1.2	25.5	26.4	100.0

Families by Dollar Income

Less than $10,000	455	−68	−14.9	5,577	1.2	7.5	6.4	−2.5
10,000–20,000	1,718	−86	−5.0	13,258	0.6	11.5	10.9	−3.9
20,000–30,000	4,240	−41	−1.0	20,775	0.2	16.9	16.8	−1.7
30,000–40,000	6,891	50	0.7	27,970	−0.2	19.8	19.9	1.6
40,000–50,000	9,667	105	1.1	35,062	−0.3	21.6	21.8	2.7
50,000–75,000	14,295	192	1.3	46,719	−0.4	23.4	23.7	7.8
75,000–100,000	21,604	312	1.4	64,185	−0.5	25.2	25.5	5.6
100,000–200,000	33,910	649	1.9	95,854	−0.7	26.1	26.6	8.8
200,000 or more	135,359	23,521	17.4	350,578	−6.7	27.9	32.7	81.3
All incomes	10,107	382	3.8	34,129	−1.1	22.8	23.7	100.0

NOTES: Figures are based on January 1993 economic assumptions. Pretax family income is the sum of wages, salaries, self-employment income, rents, taxable and nontaxable interest, dividends, realized capital gains, and all cash transfer payments. Income also includes the employer share of social security and federal unemployment insurance payroll taxes, and the corporate income tax. For purposes of ranking by adjusted family income, income for each family is divided by the projected 1994 poverty threshold for a family of that size. Quintiles contain equal numbers of people. Families with zero or negative income are excluded from the lowest income category but included in the total.

Changes in individual income taxes, premiums, and entitlements are distributed directly to families paying those taxes and premiums, or receiving those benefits. Changes in payroll taxes are distributed to families paying those taxes directly, or indirectly through their employers. Changes in federal excise taxes are distributed to families according to their consumption of the taxed good or service. Changes in corporate income taxes are distributed to families according to their income from capital.

SOURCE: Congressional Budget Office.

TABLE 4–2

DISTRIBUTION OF THE ESTIMATED CHANGE IN TAX LIABILITIES DUE TO PROVISIONS IN OBRA, INCLUDING TAXATION OF SOCIAL SECURITY BENEFITS AND EXPANSION OF EITC AND FOOD STAMPS

(1994 income levels)

Family Economic Income Class[a] (thousands of dollars)	Federal Taxes under Current Law[b]			Change in Federal Taxes[c]			Total Federal Taxes after Change		
	Amount (billions of $)	As a percent of pretax income	As a percent of after-tax income (%)	Amount (billions of $)	As a percent of pretax income (%)	As a percent of after-tax income (%)	Amount (billions of $)	As a percent of pretax income (%)	As a percent of after-tax income (%)
0– 10	6.7	7.8	8.5	−0.5	−0.6	−0.6	6.2	7.2	7.9
10– 20	26.9	9.8	10.9	−1.4	−0.5	−0.6	25.5	9.3	10.3
20– 30	55.7	14.0	16.3	−0.7	−0.2	−0.2	54.9	13.8	16.1
30– 50	152.1	17.3	20.9	1.6	0.2	0.2	153.7	17.4	21.1
50– 75	203.1	19.0	23.5	3.2	0.3	0.4	206.3	19.3	23.8
75–100	174.3	20.4	25.6	3.0	0.4	0.4	177.3	20.7	26.0
100–200	242.6	21.2	26.8	5.3	0.5	0.6	247.9	21.6	27.4

| 200 and over | 247.5 | 20.9 | 26.5 | 32.4 | 2.7 | 3.5 | 279.9 | 23.7 | 30.0 |
| Total[d] | 1,110.5 | 19.0 | 23.4 | 42.9 | 0.7 | 0.9 | 1,153.3 | 19.7 | 24.3 |

NOTE: This table distributes the estimated change in tax liabilities due to the revenue provisions in OBRA including taxation of social security benefits. Included is a total of $6.4 billion of expansions in the EITC and a $.6 billion expansion of food stamps. Tables 4–2 and 5–1 are the same.

a. Family economic income (FEI) is a broad-based income concept. FEI is constructed by adding to adjusted gross income unreported and underreported income; IRA and Keogh deductions; nontaxable transfer payments such as social security and AFDC; employer-provided fringe benefits; inside build-up on pensions, IRAs, Keoghs, and life insurance; tax-exempt interest; and imputed rent on owner-occupied housing. Capital gains are computed on an accrual basis, adjusted for inflation to the extent reliable data allow. Inflationary losses of lenders are subtracted and of borrowers are added. There is also an adjustment for accelerated depreciation of noncorporate businesses. FEI is shown on a family rather than on a tax return basis. The economic incomes of all members of a family unit are added to arrive at the family's economic income used in the distributions.

b. The taxes included are individual and corporate income, payroll (social security and unemployment), and excises. Estate and gift taxes and customs duties are excluded. The individual income tax is assumed to be borne by payers, the corporate income tax by capital income generally, payroll taxes (employer and employee shares) by labor (wages and self-employment income), excises on purchases by individuals by the purchaser, and excises on purchases by business in proportion to total consumption expenditures. Taxes due to provisions that expire before the end of the budget period (that is, before 1999) are excluded.

c. The change in federal taxes is estimated at 1994 levels but assuming fully phased-in (1998) law and long-run (1998) behavior. All excise and payroll tax effects on indexed transfers and tax brackets are accounted for. All income, payroll, and excise tax changes are included, with the exception that provisions that affect only the timing of tax collections are excluded. The incidence assumptions for tax changes are the same as for current law taxes (see footnote b).

d. Families with negative incomes are included in the total line but not shown separately.

SOURCE: Department of the Treasury, Office of Tax Analysis.

TABLE 4–3

DISTRIBUTIONAL EFFECTS OF THE REVENUE PROVISIONS CONTAINED IN THE
1993 OBRA AS AGREED TO BY THE CONFEREES
(1993 income levels)

Expanded Income Class[a]	Present-Law Federal Taxes[b] (billions of $)	Present-Law Average Tax Rate[c] (%)	Proposed Change in Tax Burden[d] (millions of $)	Burden Change as Share of Income (%)
Less than $10,000	9	10.4	−1,152	−1.28
10,000– 20,000	39	11.9	−993	−0.30
20,000– 30,000	72	17.0	94	0.02
30,000– 40,000	86	19.1	949	0.21
40,000– 50,000	93	20.9	1,271	0.29
50,000– 75,000	201	22.3	3,517	0.39
75,000–100,000	120	24.6	2,653	0.54
100,000–200,000	142	26.6	4,598	0.86
200,000 and over	168	30.2	29,863	5.39
Total, all taxpayers	930	22.1	40,800	0.97

a. The income concept used to place tax returns into income categories is adjusted gross income plus: (1) tax-exempt interest; (2) employer contributions for health plans and life insurance; (3) employer share of FICA tax; (4) workers' compensation; (5) nontaxable social security benefits; (6) insurance value of Medicare benefits; (7) corporate income tax liability attributed to stockholders; (8) alternative minimum tax preference items; and (9) excluded income of U.S. citizens living abroad.
b. Includes individual income tax, FICA and Self Employment Contributions Act taxes, excise taxes, estate and gift taxes, and corporate income tax.
c. Present-law federal taxes as a share of expanded income.
d. Includes all revenue provisions except: Individual and corporate estimated tax changes, information reporting for discharge of indebtedness, targeted jobs credit, capital gains incentives, provisions affecting qualified pension plans, mortgage revenue bonds, low-income housing credit, luxury tax provisions, excise tax on diesel fuel used in noncommercial motorboats, empowerment zones and enterprise communities, vaccine excise tax, Generalized System of Preferences (a tariff item) and Federal Unemployment Tax Act extensions, transfer of Federal Reserve funds, deduction disallowance for certain health plans, orphan drug credit, and diesel fuel compliance.
SOURCE: Joint Committee on Taxation, August 3, 1993.

requires a number of decisions that can lead to differences in reported estimates of changes in economic burden. These decisions fall into three main categories: measuring the pretax distribution of income, selecting a time frame of analysis, and measuring and reporting tax burdens.

Measuring the Pretax Income Distribution

Deriving a measure of the distribution of income involves four main steps: constructing a database, choosing a unit of analysis, deciding what to include in the measure of income, and deciding how to classify and rank people. The construction of a database often requires merging separate data sources because no data source includes all the information the modeler needs. Although all three agencies use the same basic data sources as a starting point, they differ in the way they construct the database, group people into units of analysis, measure pretax income, and classify and rank people.

The Database. The main data sources the three agencies use are a large sample of individual income tax returns produced by the Statistics of Income Division of the Internal Revenue Service, the Current Population Survey produced by the U.S. Bureau of the Census, and the Consumer Expenditure Survey produced by the U.S. Bureau of Labor Statistics. The agencies also use other data sources for imputations such as those for employer contributions toward employer-provided health insurance and the value of home equity loans.

The OTA and the JCT staff use the Statistics of Income as the base for their microsimulation models. The OTA and the JCT staff use data from the Current Population Survey to represent families (tax-filing units in the case of the JCT) that are not required to file tax returns and to augment tax return data. The OTA also uses Current Population Survey data to reconfigure tax return units into family units. The CBO uses the Current Population Survey as its base population for its microsimulation model. The CBO then adjusts those data to match income totals and distributions from the Statistics of Income, and imputes itemized deductions and other tax return data to families. All three agencies use the Consumer Expenditure Survey and other data sources to impute consumption and wealth data to their models.

Although the agencies use different methods of matching databases, the distribution of income that all three use primarily reflects tax return data. Consequently, there is probably little difference in estimates prepared by the three agencies because of how they develop the database for their microsimulation models.

Unit of Analysis. The CBO and the OTA both make the family the unit of analysis. The CBO uses the same family concept as the Bureau of the Census but also counts one-person households as families. The OTA creates families statistically by matching tax returns (for example, matching returns of dependent children and their parents), based on Current Population Survey data.

The JCT staff uses "tax-filing units" as the unit of analysis, a notion that corresponds roughly to tax returns. Thus, in the case of joint returns, head-of-household returns, and many single returns, the tax return represents a family. In the case of returns of married couples filing separately, obviously the tax-filing unit is smaller than a family. The JCT staff generally deletes separately filed returns of dependents from its distributional analysis. Because its unit of analysis is smaller than a family, the JCT shows more total units, with less income per unit, than the CBO or the OTA analyses.

Measurement of Income. All three agencies measure income in a current year; none attempts to measure permanent or lifetime income. The agencies represent their measures as pretax income. To do so, all three agencies add to reported income of their individual tax units or families the taxes that businesses pay on behalf of their employees or shareholders. Thus, for example, all three agencies include a unit's allocated share of corporate income taxes.

The agencies differ in their degree of inclusion of government transfers in their respective income measures. The OTA and the CBO include most nontaxable cash transfer payments such as social security benefits and payments for Aid to Families with Dependent Children. The OTA also includes the value of food stamps but excludes other transfers in-kind, such as Medicaid. The CBO excludes in-kind transfers. The JCT staff includes a narrower set of government transfer payments in income, limiting inclusion to social security benefits, workers' compensation, and the insurance value of Medicare.

The agencies differ most in how they include income from capital in their measure of income. The OTA uses the broadest measure of income (family economic income). Family economic income attempts to approximate the Haig-Simons comprehensive income concept. Thus, OTA includes in its income measure accrued capital gains (whether or not realized), net rental income from owner-occupied housing, accruing pension benefits, and other fringe benefits. The OTA also includes income that is unreported or underreported on tax returns and in survey data. The OTA adjusts capital income, interest expense, and depreciation for inflation. Because these items do not

TABLE 4–4

PERCENTAGE OF FAMILIES (CBO AND OTA) AND TAX-FILING UNITS (JCT)
WITH INCOMES ABOVE A GIVEN THRESHOLD, 1993 AND 1994

Income Threshold	CBO	OTA	JCT
$20,000	68.6	69.1	64.0
$50,000	28.8	35.2	25.1
$100,000	6.5	10.1	5.1
$200,000	1.3	2.2	1.1

NOTE: The CBO and OTA figures are at 1994 income levels; the JCT figures are at 1993 income levels.
SOURCE: Joint Committee on Taxation, *Methodology and Issues in Measuring Changes in the Distribution of Tax Burdens*, June 14, 1993, p. 106; unpublished tabulations of the OTA microsimulation model and the CBO tax simulation model.

appear on individual tax returns or in census data, the OTA has developed imputation methods to distribute them among families.

The CBO and the JCT staff use narrower income concepts. (The CBO calls its measure realized cash income; the JCT, expanded income.) Both agencies include capital gains and pension benefits in income when they are realized instead of as they accrue. Neither agency includes imputed rental income from owner-occupied housing. The JCT staff imputes the value of employer-provided health insurance and some other fringe benefits; the CBO currently does not.

With a broader income measure, tax return or family units will appear to be higher in an income distribution measured by fixed-dollar cutoffs. Hence, the OTA model will generally show a higher percentage of taxpayers in the higher income classes than will the CBO or JCT staff estimates. Table 4–4 shows the percentage of tax-filing units (JCT) or families (CBO and OTA) above various income thresholds.

Classifying and Ranking Units of Analysis. The OTA and the JCT staff classify families (tax units, for the JCT) into income groupings based on family economic income (OTA) and expanded income (JCT). They rank families according to their measure of income.

In many of its distributional tables, the CBO classifies families into groupings and ranks them by adjusted family income. To compute adjusted family income, the CBO divides a family's realized cash income by the official census poverty threshold for a family of that size. Ranking families by adjusted family income instead of by family income places larger families lower in the income distribution than smaller families with the same income.

Timing Issues

The second important modeling decision is the time period of analysis. Tax burdens can be measured in the current year, over a taxpayer's lifetime, or over some intermediate time period. Changes in tax policy highlight a number of timing issues. Some tax provisions, for example, are phased in. One could model the burden of a proposal that changes over time in different ways. The CBO, the JCT staff, and the OTA each model these timing questions differently.

The OTA and CBO generally analyze the tax burden of a proposal based on the law as it will be in the long run or in a steady state.[2] That is, the burden is measured as an annual burden for each provision of proposed legislation when that provision is permanent or in a steady state. For these purposes, provisions are taken to be "permanent" legislatively as they will apply in the last year of the five-year budget window. Long-run economic incidence is assumed to be appropriate for the end of the budget period.

The JCT staff, as explained in the chapter by Barthold and Jack, measures the change in the tax burden over the five-year period of the federal government's budget planning horizon. The JCT staff calculates an annual burden for each of the five years and then computes the annuity equivalent of the five-year stream of burdens as its measure of the annual value of the burden. The importance of the choice of time period of analysis is that the JCT staff analysis is much more an analysis of the short- to medium-run burden of taxation, while the OTA and CBO analyses are long-run estimates of the burden of the tax change.

Choosing a time period of analysis may only partially answer how the analyst models the burden of tax provisions that change through time. For proposed legislation containing significant temporary provisions, the OTA and the CBO often produce separate short-run distribution tables, which include the effect of the first full year of the temporary provision. For provisions with irregular effects on tax liability over the budget period (such as some depreciation proposals), the OTA may calculate the average present value over the budget period.

The JCT staff, as noted above, combines these separate calculations into one estimate of the five-year distributional burden. The annuitization means that a provision that is to take effect in year five is measured as less burdensome than an identical provision effective only in year one. Provisions that phase in or phase out within the five-year period are measured as less burdensome than permanent provi-

---

2. In its studies of how tax burdens have changed over time, CBO compares current-year tax burdens in different years.

sions. But all provisions that vary over time are presented as equivalent to provisions in effect in all five years.

Measuring and Reporting Tax Burdens

The final group of decisions includes choices of which tax changes to include, how to estimate tax burdens, and how to report tax burdens. These include decisions about what taxes are to be covered in the analysis, how to measure tax burdens, and how to display them. For some tax proposals, the most difficult problem is determining the incidence of the tax—that is, its effects on prices of goods and returns to factors of production. As with the other groups of decisions, the three staffs approach these issues differently.

Taxes Included in the Analysis. The CBO, the JCT staff, and the OTA each restrict its analysis to federal taxes. The CBO and the OTA generally include the individual and corporate income taxes, payroll taxes, and excise taxes. To this list, the JCT staff adds estate taxes (but not gift taxes). None of the agencies includes customs duties in its distributional analyses. The JCT staff, however, will not always distribute changes in burden arising from changes in specific features of any of these taxes. This situation might arise where the JCT staff believes there are insufficient data from which to calculate a distribution of the change in burden.[3] On similar grounds, the CBO and the OTA also will not necessarily supply a distributional estimate for all tax proposals.

Because the differences in coverage are slight, differences in reported estimates of the distribution of the tax burden of major tax legislation cannot generally be attributed to differences in taxes covered.

How the Burden Is Measured. The OTA measures the burden of present law taxes by tax liabilities and measures changes in burden by changes in the amount of tax liability.[4] The JCT staff and the CBO measure the change in burden by the change in tax rate multiplied by the prechange level of economic activity. Some refer to this as the "static" loss or gain.

---

3. For example, the JCT staff estimate in table 4–3 does not include a distribution of the change in tax burden resulting from the repeal of the luxury excise tax on certain goods.

4. The OTA measure of change in burden is not equal to a revenue estimate because the burden estimates are generally made on a calendar rather than on a fiscal year basis and generally reflect long-run, fully phased in changes at the current (or next) year's income level. In contrast, revenue estimates embody year-by-year provisions, behavior, and levels of economic activity.

Measuring the tax burden by the static instead of by the actual revenue changes usually raises the measured burden of tax increases and also raises the measured decline in burden from tax reductions. When behavioral responses are small, however, estimating tax receipts will not be substantially different from estimating burdens by a measure of static loss or gain. Therefore, in many cases this difference in methodology does not substantially alter the relative magnitudes of burdens estimated by the CBO, the JCT staff, and the OTA.

How the Burden Is Reported. The OTA presents the distribution of current-law total federal taxes, the proposed tax change, and total federal taxes after the change both in nominal amounts and expressed as a percentage of pretax and after-tax family economic income (see table 4–2). The OTA presents this information for families classified into fixed family economic income groups.

The JCT staff generally presents only the estimated change in tax burden and the change in burden as a percentage of pretax income. Like the OTA, the JCT staff presents this information stratified by groups of tax-filing units classified by income ranges (see table 4–3).

The CBO reports the distribution of effective federal tax rates under both current law and proposed law, the change in the tax burden per family, and the change in taxes paid as percentages of total taxes paid and after-tax income. The CBO usually presents this information for families grouped by quintiles, with additional detail within the top quintile, but also displays the effects on families grouped by nominal income (see table 4–1).

The CBO burden estimates can differ from those of the JCT staff and the OTA because the CBO groups families by quintile and, by using the adjusted family income measure, places larger families at a lower position in the income distribution. Thus, tax changes that are relatively more favorable to larger families would appear to be more progressive in the CBO measure than in the JCT staff or the OTA measure.

Incidence Assumptions. The incidence assumptions of the OTA, the CBO, and the JCT staff are broadly similar. Each agency assumes that taxes on labor income are borne by labor, including both the employee and the employer share of payroll taxes. All three agencies assume that taxes on individual-level capital income are borne by recipients of that income.

The CBO, the OTA and the JCT staff differ modestly regarding the assumed incidence of the corporate income tax. In some of its historical studies, the CBO assumes the corporate income tax is borne half by all owners of capital and half by labor. (The CBO also displays tables in which the corporate tax is borne either by all labor or by all capital.) The OTA assumes the corporate income tax is borne by all owners of capital. In a more short-run view, the JCT staff assumes the corporate income tax is borne by the owners of corporate capital. The JCT also distinguishes saving and the formation of "new" capital from old capital by assuming that taxes on saving or the creation of broad-based investment incentives are borne (or received) by savers, rather than by all owners of capital. (That is, the JCT staff treats incentives for new saving and investment as a partial conversion of the income tax to a consumption tax.)

The CBO, the OTA, and the JCT staff also make different incidence assumptions regarding excise taxes and consumption taxes. The OTA and the CBO assume that the burden of excise taxes and consumption taxes is borne by the purchaser of taxed goods in the year he or she consumes the goods. In the case of the excise taxes on business purchases, the burden is assumed to fall on consumers in proportion to total consumption expenditures. The JCT staff takes a different approach with regard to the timing of the tax burden, as described in more detail in the chapter by Barthold and Jack. In brief, the JCT converts the consumption (or excise) tax to an equivalent income-based tax and attributes the burden to individuals based on their wages and income from old capital (weighted by the expenditure shares of the taxed good or goods). That is, the JCT assumes that income earners accrue consumption tax liabilities as they earn income. The effect of this assumption is to make consumption and excise taxes appear less regressive relative to the measures used by the CBO and the OTA.

The JCT staff does not generally distribute a measured burden to the extent that such burden (for corporate taxes, for example) is believed to fall on nonprofit organizations or non-U.S. citizens in their capacity as owners of capital. The OTA and the CBO distribute 100 percent of such burdens. This difference would make the aggregate burden reported by the JCT staff somewhat smaller than that of the OTA and the CBO.

In summary, the CBO, the JCT staff, and the OTA make identical assumptions regarding the incidence of taxes on labor income. The agencies display modest differences in their treatment of the taxation of capital income. The JCT staff differs from the CBO and the OTA in its analysis of consumption taxation.

Summary

Although we have detailed many areas of difference among the CBO, the JCT staff, and the OTA in the modeling of changes in tax burden, there are many broad areas of similarity. The three agencies are likely to produce similar estimates of proposals that affect individual income tax burdens directly, such as changes in marginal tax rates, personal exemptions and the standard deduction, itemized deductions, and exclusions from adjusted gross income (such as the partial exclusion for social security benefits). The agencies are also likely to produce similar estimates for proposals that change payroll taxes.

In contrast, the agencies may produce quite different distributional estimates of changes in consumption taxes, saving and investment incentives, and proposals that primarily affect corporate taxes. They may also differ in their treatment of certain narrowly targeted tax changes.

While particular legislative initiatives may highlight differences among the agencies' estimates, a package of proposals such as OBRA that raises a large share of its revenue from direct increases in individual income taxes and payroll taxes produces broadly similar estimates of changes in the tax burden.

5
Distributional Analysis
at the Office of Tax Analysis

James R. Nunns

The Treasury Department's Office of Tax Analysis (OTA) prepares analyses of how proposed changes in the tax law would affect the distribution of tax burdens across income classes. This chapter describes the methodology followed by OTA in preparing these analyses. The first section summarizes OTA's methodology for distributing tax burdens under current law, which provides the base line for evaluating changes in tax burdens. OTA's general methodology for distributing proposed changes in the tax law is covered in the second section. The third and final section describes the application of OTA's methodology to the provisions of the 1993 deficit reduction bill, the Omnibus Budget Reconciliation Act of 1993 (OBRA).

Distribution of Current-Law Taxes

In its distribution of current-law taxes, OTA includes federal individual and corporate income taxes, payroll taxes (social security and unemployment), and excises.[1] The burden of these taxes is measured by tax liabilities in the succeeding calendar year, as estimated by OTA in the preparation of forecasts of tax receipts for the budget.[2] To ensure consistency between the distribution of current-law taxes and the distribu-

---

While descriptive of the methodology of the Office of Tax Analysis, this chapter represents the views of the author alone and should not be construed as representing the views or policies of the U.S. Department of the Treasury.

1. Estate and gift taxes and customs duties, which are relatively minor sources of tax revenue and rarely changed in significant amounts, are excluded.

2. These tax liability estimates assume the current level of taxpayer compliance, so that the distinction between liabilities and receipts is the timing of actual tax payments.

tion of proposed changes, estimated liabilities exclude amounts due to provisions of current law that are scheduled to expire before the end of the five-year budget period.[3]

The incidence assumptions OTA follows are that individual income taxes are borne by payers, corporate income taxes by capital income generally, payroll taxes (employer and employee shares) by labor (wages and self-employment income included in the payroll tax base), excises on purchases by individuals by the purchaser, and excises on purchases by business in proportion to total consumption expenditures. All of the tax burden is distributed to individuals according to these incidence assumptions.

OTA groups individuals into families, which generally operate as an economic unit. Families are then ranked by their "family economic income," which is a broad measure of annual pretax income based on the Haig-Simons definition. Family economic income adds to adjusted gross income as reported on tax returns the AGI of nonfilers; income unreported and underreported on tax returns and in survey data; IRA, Keogh, and 401(k) deductions; nontaxable cash transfer payments such as AFDC and excluded social security benefits; food stamps (but no other noncash transfers); employer-provided fringe benefits; inside buildup on pensions, IRAs, Keoghs, and life insurance; tax-exempt interest; and the net imputed rent on owner-occupied housing. Capital gains are computed on an accrual basis, adjusted for inflation. Inflationary losses of lenders are subtracted and the inflationary gains of borrowers added. There is also an adjustment for accelerated depreciation of noncorporate businesses.

The distribution of current-law taxes to families by family economic income class is based on tabulations from OTA's individual tax model. The model is based on the statistics of income (SOI) sample of individual income tax returns.[4] Data on nonfilers, nontaxable sources of income, and family structure are taken from the Current Population Survey (CPS) conducted annually by the Bureau of the Census. Tax-filing rules are applied to each adult in each CPS household, and potential filing units are constructed from the CPS file. The SOI and CPS files are then statistically merged, and families formed based on relationships from the CPS records. A similar matching procedure is used

---

3. Consistent with federal budget conventions, excise tax receipts that are dedicated to trust funds are treated as permanent, even if they have a legislated expiration date.

4. The SOI sample available to OTA and the Joint Committee on Taxation staff is considerably larger, and contains many more data items, than the public use SOI file.

to add information on consumption expenditures by category from the Consumer Expenditure Survey conducted by the Bureau of Labor Statistics. Extensive imputations are then added to the merged records. Transfer payments reported on the CPS, for example, are corrected for underreporting using aggregate payments data and other information from administrative records. Underreported income on tax returns is corrected using information from the Taxpayer Compliance Measurement Program of the Internal Revenue Service. Wealth data are imputed from the Federal Reserve Board's Survey of Consumer Finances and other sources.[5]

In addition to its detailed data base, the individual tax model consists of an extensive set of computer programs used to simulate individual income tax law. These programs simulate individual income tax liabilities under current law, which are then tabulated by family economic income class. Tabulations from the model by family economic income class are also made of the data items necessary to distribute other current-law federal taxes according to the incidence assumptions given above—capital income (for distributing the corporate income tax), wages and self-employment income subject to tax (for distributing payroll taxes), and various items of consumption and total consumption expenditures (for distributing the excises).

OTA's final distribution of current-law taxes is prepared in a spreadsheet. Estimated liabilities for each tax are distributed by family economic income class using the individual tax model tabulation of the appropriate item(s).[6] These distributions are then summed to provide the total distribution of current-law taxes, and the taxes are expressed as a percentage of pretax and after-tax family economic income. The figures for 1994 (*before* taking into account the effects of OBRA) are shown in the first three columns of table 5–1. Of the $1.1 trillion of federal taxes in 1994, the table shows, for example, that $152 billion is estimated to be paid by families with economic incomes between $30,000 and $50,000, and these taxes would represent 17.3 per-

---

5. The accuracy of the matching and imputation procedures cannot be independently verified, because no single data source contains all the income, consumption, and wealth data necessary for such a verification. For distributional purposes, however, the methods need only provide a reasonably accurate distribution of certain variables by broad family economic income classes.

6. Because of such factors as collections from IRS enforcement activities and the difference in timing between tax payments and tax liabilities, individual income tax liabilities simulated on the individual tax model do not exactly match the liabilities forecast for budget purposes. Therefore, the individual tax model distribution of individual income tax liabilities is adjusted to the budget forecast amount.

TABLE 5-1

Distribution of the Estimated Change in Tax Liabilities Due to Provisions in OBRA, Including Taxation of Social Security Benefits and Expansion of EITC and Food Stamps

(1994 income levels)

Family Economic Income Class[a] (thousands of dollars)	Federal Taxes under Current Law[b]			Change in Federal Taxes[c]			Total Federal Taxes after Change		
	Amount (billions of $)	As a percent of pretax income	As a percent of after-tax income (%)	Amount (billions of $)	As a percent of pretax income (%)	As a percent of after-tax income (%)	Amount (billions of $)	As a percent of pretax income (%)	As a percent of after-tax income (%)
0– 10	6.7	7.8	8.5	−0.5	−0.6	−0.6	6.2	7.2	7.9
10– 20	26.9	9.8	10.9	−1.4	−0.5	−0.6	25.5	9.3	10.3
20– 30	55.7	14.0	16.3	−0.7	−0.2	−0.2	54.9	13.8	16.1
30– 50	152.1	17.3	20.9	1.6	0.2	0.2	153.7	17.4	21.1
50– 75	203.1	19.0	23.5	3.2	0.3	0.4	206.3	19.3	23.8
75–100	174.3	20.4	25.6	3.0	0.4	0.4	177.3	20.7	26.0
100–200	242.6	21.2	26.8	5.3	0.5	0.6	247.9	21.6	27.4

| 200 and over | 247.5 | 20.9 | 26.5 | 32.4 | 2.7 | 3.5 | 279.9 | 23.7 | 30.0 |
| Total[d] | 1,110.5 | 19.0 | 23.4 | 42.9 | 0.7 | 0.9 | 1,153.3 | 19.7 | 24.3 |

NOTE: This table distributes the estimated change in tax liabilities due to the revenue provisions in OBRA including taxation of social security benefits. Included is a total of $6.4 billion of expansions in the EITC and a $.6 billion expansion of food stamps. Tables 4–2 and 5–1 are the same.

a. Family economic income (FEI) is a broad-based income concept. FEI is constructed by adding to adjusted gross income unreported and underreported income; IRA and Keogh deductions; nontaxable transfer payments such as social security and AFDC; employer-provided fringe benefits; inside build-up on pensions, IRAs, Keoghs, and life insurance; tax-exempt interest; and imputed rent on owner-occupied housing. Capital gains are computed on an accrual basis, adjusted for inflation to the extent reliable data allow. Inflationary losses of lenders are subtracted and of borrowers are added. There is also an adjustment for accelerated depreciation of noncorporate businesses. FEI is shown on a family rather than on a tax return basis. The economic incomes of all members of a family unit are added to arrive at the family's economic income used in the distributions.

b. The taxes included are individual and corporate income, payroll (social security and unemployment), and excises. Estate and gift taxes and customs duties are excluded. The individual income tax is assumed to be borne by payers, the corporate income tax by capital income generally, payroll taxes (employer and employee shares) by labor (wages and self-employment income), excises on purchases by individuals by the purchaser, and excises on purchases by business in proportion to total consumption expenditures. Taxes due to provisions that expire before the end of the budget period (that is, before 1999) are excluded.

c. The change in federal taxes is estimated at 1994 levels but assuming fully phased-in (1998) law and long-run (1998) behavior. All income, payroll, and excise tax effects on indexed transfers and tax brackets are accounted for. All income, payroll, and excise tax changes are included, with the exception that provisions that affect only the timing of tax collections are excluded. The incidence assumptions for tax changes are the same as for current law taxes (see footnote b).

d. Families with negative incomes are included in the total line but not shown separately.

SOURCE: Department of the Treasury, Office of Tax Analysis.

cent of these families' pretax incomes and 20.9 percent of their after-tax incomes. According to OTA's distributional analysis, the federal tax system before OBRA was progressive, except at the highest income levels.

Distribution of Proposed Changes in Tax Law

When a proposed tax change is enacted, it becomes part of "current law" in subsequent years, and its effect would then be distributed as part of the distribution of current-law taxes in the manner described in the preceding section. OTA's general methodological approach to distributing proposed changes in tax law is to estimate how the current-law distribution would be changed at the end of the five-year budget period if the proposal were adopted (holding income and its distribution at its current level).

The burden of proposed changes to federal income, payroll, and excise taxes is measured by the effect of the changes on annual tax liabilities at current income levels, but assuming fully phased-in law and long-run behavioral responses of taxpayers. For these purposes, the law is taken to be fully phased in as it applies in the last year of the five-year budget period, and long-run behavior is assumed to apply in the last year of the budget period. These burden measures differ from revenue estimates in several respects: revenue estimates are made on a fiscal-year-by-fiscal-year basis rather than on a single-calendar-year basis, reflect the level of income and economic activity in each year, and incorporate anticipated taxpayer behavioral responses in each year. There is also a difference in the way the income offset is incorporated for excises. For revenue-estimating purposes, the budget-estimating convention of fixed gross domestic product and a fixed price level are followed. Indirect business taxes therefore reduce factor payments and consequently reduce revenues from income and payroll taxes. For distributional analyses, preoffset liabilities (measured at current income levels and assuming long-run law and behavior) are distributed, and in the case of payroll taxes, so is the income offset.[7] In the case of excises, however, it is assumed that the price level rises by the amount of the excise, and the effect of this inflation on indexed transfer payments and income tax parameters is distributed in place of the offset.[8]

---

7. The assumption is that payroll taxes reduce factor incomes (wages and self-employment income) even if the budget-estimating conventions are relaxed.

8. The offset generally exceeds the effect of inflation on transfers and income tax revenues, creating a further difference between the revenue estimate and the net amount distributed.

Following OTA's methodology, provisions that affect the timing of tax receipts across fiscal years but not tax liabilities in any year are not distributed. Provisions that expire before the end of the budget period are also excluded from the analysis. For proposals that include major temporary provisions, however, OTA prepares a separate distributional analysis that includes the temporary provision at its first full-year level.

The incidence assumptions followed in distributing current-law taxes are also followed in distributing proposed changes in tax law. The use of the individual tax model for tabulations by family economic income classes is also the same. These tabulations, together with the burden measures, are then combined in the spreadsheet in the same manner to produce the final distribution of the proposal.

Distributional Analysis of OBRA

The Omnibus Budget Reconciliation Act contains many tax provisions, but nearly all the revenue effect, and the change in tax burdens, is due to a few provisions. These provisions were distributed across family economic income classes as follows:

• *Individual income taxes.* OBRA added two new rates of 36 percent and 39.6 percent, increased the alternative minimum tax rate to 28 percent, and made permanent the phaseout of personal exemptions and the limitation on itemized deductions for higher-income taxpayers.[9] These provisions were modeled as a unit on the individual tax model and tabulated by family economic income class. The modeled amount was then adjusted to the long-run, fully phased-in revenue estimate at 1994 income levels, which takes into account off-model behavioral adjustments.

• *Taxation of social security benefits.* The percentage of social security benefits subject to tax for higher-income taxpayers was increased to 85 percent. Like the rate changes, this provision was modeled on the individual tax model and tabulated by family economic income class and then adjusted to the measure of tax burden.

• *Medicare (HI) tax wage cap.* The $135,000 limit on wages (and self-employment income) subject to the Medicare tax (1.45 percent on both employers and employees) was repealed. The distribution of the base above the cap was tabulated on the individual tax model by family economic income class. The calendar 1994 revenue estimate (which is

9. The distribution of current law (pre-OBRA) taxes excluded these last two items because they were scheduled to expire before the end of the five-year budget period.

net of the income offset) was then distributed according to this tabulation.

• *Deduction for business meals and entertainment.* The percentage of meal and entertainment expenses deductible by businesses was reduced from 80 percent to 50 percent. The corporate portion was distributed like other corporate income tax changes to all capital income. The noncorporate portion was distributed according to noncorporate business deductions for these expenses, as tabulated by family economic income classes from the individual tax model.

• *Corporate income tax rate.* The top corporate rate was increased from 34 percent to 35 percent. This was distributed by family economic income class according to all capital income.

• *Transportation fuels.* A new 4.3 cent per gallon transportation fuels tax was added, and the 2.5 cent per gallon motor fuels rate for deficit reduction passed in 1990 was made permanent.[10] Preoffset revenues (calculated at 1994 income levels and 1998 behavior) from both taxes were distributed by family economic income class on the basis of direct consumption of taxed goods and total consumption expenditures (for the tax on fuels purchased by businesses), as tabulated from the individual tax model. The price-level effect of the taxes was computed by the ratio of preoffset revenues to total consumption expenditures. This price-level effect was converted to an inflation adjustment for indexed transfer payments and for indexed income tax parameters. Tabulations of indexed transfer payments and simulations of the income tax effect of indexation, both by family economic income classes, were then taken from the individual tax model and used to distribute the indexation amounts.

• *Earned income tax credit.* The basic earned income tax credit was substantially increased and expanded over several years, and the supplemental credits for young children and for children's health insurance were repealed. The fully phased-in changes were simulated on the individual tax model and tabulated by family economic income class. The simulated amount was then adjusted to the fully phased-in revenue estimate at 1994 income levels.

The results of distributing these and all other permanent provisions of OBRA are shown in the fourth through sixth columns of table 5–1. As is clear from the nature of its major provisions, the table shows that the distributional effect of OBRA is quite progressive. The final three

---

10. The current (pre-OBRA) law distribution excluded the 2.5 cent per gallon motor fuels tax because it was scheduled to expire before the end of the budget period and receipts from the rate are not dedicated to a trust fund.

columns of the table show the estimated distribution of post-OBRA law as it would appear at the end of the budget period, but at the 1994 level and distribution of income. The effect of OBRA, by estimates of the Office of Tax Analysis, was to make the federal tax system more progressive, and progressive even at the highest income levels.

6

Distributional Analysis at the Congressional Budget Office

Richard A. Kasten and Eric J. Toder

The Congressional Budget Office has developed a model for analyzing the federal tax system. We use it both in studies of changes in the distribution of tax payments over time and in estimates of proposed changes in tax law. CBO's distributional analyses include federal individual and corporate income taxes, payroll taxes, and federal excise taxes but not customs duties or estate and gift taxes. The unit of analysis is the family—all related individuals living at the same address. (Single individuals are considered to be families of one.)

CBO measures family income on a cash receipts basis, consistent with, but more comprehensive than, the way income is counted by the federal individual income tax. The individual income tax system generally treats income as cash received. It excludes certain types of cash income, such as welfare benefits and, for the majority of taxpayers, social security benefits. Nonmonetary payments such as food stamps, Medicare, Medicaid, and employer-provided health insurance are not included in income. Appreciation of financial and physical assets is taxed only when these gains are realized, and the gains, like other income from capital, are not adjusted for inflation. Pension benefits are taxed when they are received rather than as they accrue.

The major differences between family income and adjusted gross income (AGI) are that family income includes all cash transfer payments and is measured before all federal taxes. Family income equals the sum of wages, salaries, self-employment income, personal rents, interest, dividends, government cash transfer payments, cash pension benefits, and realized capital gains. To lessen the distortion in measured incomes that results from incentives to realize capital losses but to defer capital gains, following the tax code, capital losses in excess of capital gains are limited to $3,000 per return. (If gains were measured on an accrual basis, it would be appropriate to net total accrued gains against total accrued losses.)

In order to measure income before reductions for any federal taxes, employer contributions for federal social insurance and federal corporate income taxes are added to family income. Most economists agree that payroll taxes are borne by wage earners, and CBO uses this assumption. Although the corporate income tax is collected from corporations, families are assumed ultimately to bear the economic burden of the tax. Economists disagree, however, whether families bear the tax as shareholders in corporations, owners of all capital assets, employees, or consumers. In some recent studies, CBO assumed that half the corporate income tax falls on all income from capital and half falls on labor income. (In the analysis of changes in corporate taxation in Omnibus Budget Reconciliation Act of 1993 (OBRA-93), however, CBO allocated the burden of most of those changes to families in proportion to their realized income from capital.)

Although income in our data differs both from comparable national income aggregates and from a comprehensive measure of real accrued income, we have not made any attempt to adjust incomes to these aggregates. Using a nominal cash income measure avoids the difficult problems of valuing noncash and in-kind income, measuring accrued and unreported income, adjusting incomes for inflationary gains and losses, and assigning these constructed values to the appropriate families in the income distribution. While some of these adjustments are conceptually feasible, in practice each would introduce new problems and would shift the measured distribution of income into uncharted regions away from the anchor of reported incomes in the microdata files. Unless federal taxes were recomputed on the basis of adjusted incomes, there would be a mismatch between the bases on which taxes and incomes are measured. If taxes were recomputed, however, reported taxes would bear little relation to actual tax payments for many families.

In its historical analyses, CBO uses adjusted family income— family income as a fraction of the poverty line—to rank families. In its analyses of proposals, CBO uses both adjusted family income (AFI) and the more common dollar-income categories. While AFI may not perfectly assess differential needs of families of different sizes, it falls between the extremes of unadjusted and per capita family incomes. We use a simplified set of poverty thresholds, based on the official Bureau of the Census thresholds, that vary only with family size and not with the age of the head of the family or the number of children in the family.

CBO divides the population into equal fifths (quintiles) ranked according to incomes. Because there is continuing interest about the taxes paid by the most affluent families, CBO provides additional detail on family income groups within the highest income quintile. CBO defines percentiles of the income distribution based on people, not families.

CBO's estimates are based on data from three sources. The source of family income and demographic information is the March Current Population Survey (CPS). The CPS is a monthly survey of approximately 60,000 families conducted by the Bureau of the Census. The March survey contains detailed information about current family characteristics and family income in the previous calendar year. Income tax data are an alternative and, for estimation of tax burdens, a superior source of income information. These data are available from the annual Statistics of Income (SOI) individual income tax return model, provided by the Internal Revenue Service. The SOI is an extensive annual sample of approximately 100,000 actual individual income tax returns. The Consumer Expenditure Survey (CEX) provides data on consumer expenditures. The CEX Interview Survey is a quarterly panel survey conducted by the Bureau of Labor Statistics. The survey collects detailed data on household expenditures over a twelve-month period.

Because it combines individuals into families and provides good data on transfer benefits and health insurance, CBO uses the CPS as its base data set. The SOI, however, is used to make extensive modifications to the CPS. We add tax information not included in the survey and modify the income information to make it consistent with tax data. The CEX provides information about consumption necessary to allocate excise taxes and other proposed consumption taxes. The analysis of OBRA-93 was based on the March 1991 CPS, the SOI for 1990, and CEX data for 1989.

Analysis of OBRA-93

Early in 1993, CBO analyzed the tax provisions in the president's budget proposals, in the House and Senate bills, and in OBRA-93. Table 6-1 shows CBO's estimates of the effects of the tax changes in OBRA-93. (OBRA-93 also included changes in outlays—especially Medicare—but no distributional analysis was done for those changes.)

In analyzing the effects of legislation, CBO's usual procedure is to look at a bill as if it were "fully implemented" in the next calendar year. We ignore the effects of temporary provisions and treat phased-in changes as if they were implemented immediately. We also treat temporary provisions of prior law as if they had already expired; thus, permanent extension of temporary provisions counts as a change in

TABLE 6–1

Tax Burdens before and after OBRA-1993
(1994 income levels and 1998 tax law)

| | All Federal Taxes | | | Income after Taxes | | | Effective Tax Rates | | Share of Total change % |
	Average $	Change $	Percent change	Average $	Percent change		Current law %	With option %	

Families by Adjusted Family Income

All families									
First	589	−166	−28.1	7,878	2.1		7.0	5.0	−8.3
Second	3,119	−35	−1.1	17,623	0.2		15.0	14.9	−1.8
Third	6,498	64	1.0	27,156	−0.2		19.3	19.5	3.2
Fourth	10,800	110	1.0	38,172	−0.3		22.1	22.3	5.7
Fifth	29,203	1,884	6.5	82,111	−2.3		26.2	27.9	100.9
All quintiles	10,107	382	3.8	34,129	−1.1		22.8	23.7	100.0
Top 10	41,225	3,473	8.4	111,727	−3.1		27.0	29.2	94.6
Top 5	59,374	6,521	11.0	157,427	−4.1		27.4	30.4	89.4
Top 1	158,719	29,417	18.5	408,157	−7.2		28.0	33.2	76.3
81–90%	16,757	239	1.4	51,452	−0.5		24.6	24.9	6.3
91–95%	22,859	388	1.7	65,483	−0.6		25.9	26.3	5.3
96–99%	36,188	1,177	3.3	98,908	−1.2		26.8	27.7	13.1
Families with children									
First	559	−380	−68.0	10,493	3.6		5.1	1.6	−25.8
Second	4,811	−134	−2.8	23,585	0.6		16.9	16.5	−8.8

(Table continues)

123

TABLE 6–1 (continued)

	All Federal Taxes			Income after Taxes		Effective Tax Rates		Share of Total change %
	Average $	Change $	Percent change	Average $	Percent change	Current law %	With option %	
Families by Adjusted Family Income								
Third	9,665	73	0.8	35,240	−0.2	21.5	21.7	4.7
Fourth	15,305	144	0.9	49,663	−0.3	23.6	23.8	8.1
81–90%	22,402	223	1.0	66,243	−0.3	25.3	25.5	5.0
Top 10	54,694	6,450	11.8	147,793	−4.4	27.0	30.2	116.5
All quintiles	11,178	336	3.0	37,610	−0.9	22.9	23.6	100.0
Families with head age 65 +								
First	200	9	4.6	7,336	−0.1	2.6	2.8	0.5
Second	718	27	3.8	15,412	−0.2	4.4	4.6	1.6
Third	2,169	60	2.8	25,121	−0.2	7.9	8.2	2.9
Fourth	5,037	115	2.3	36,149	−0.3	12.2	12.5	4.5
81–90%	10,178	651	6.4	50,892	−1.3	16.7	17.7	10.4
Top 10	38,198	3,753	9.8	119,182	−3.1	24.3	26.7	80.0
All quintiles	5,615	421	7.5	30,663	−1.4	15.5	16.6	100.0
Other families								
First	876	−37	−4.3	5,276	0.7	14.2	13.6	−1.4
Second	3,060	25	0.8	13,066	−0.2	19.0	19.1	1.0
Third	5,842	58	1.0	20,787	−0.3	21.9	22.2	2.5
Fourth	9,843	86	0.9	31,412	−0.3	23.9	24.1	4.7
81–90%	15,848	153	1.0	45,329	−0.3	25.9	26.2	5.1

Top 10	37,798	2,450	6.5	98,197	−2.5	27.8	29.6	87.7
All quintiles	11,308	399	3.5	33,074	−1.2	25.5	26.4	100.0

Families by Dollar Income

Less than $10,000	455	−68	−14.9	5,577	1.2	7.5	6.4	−2.5
$10,000–$20,000	1,718	−86	−5.0	13,258	0.6	11.5	10.9	−3.9
$20,000–$30,000	4,240	−41	−1.0	20,775	0.2	16.9	16.8	−1.7
$30,000–$40,000	6,891	50	0.7	27,970	−0.2	19.8	19.9	1.6
$40,000–$50,000	9,667	105	1.1	35,062	−0.3	21.6	21.8	2.7
$50,000–$75,000	14,295	192	1.3	46,719	−0.4	23.4	23.7	7.8
$75,000–$100,000	21,604	312	1.4	64,185	−0.5	25.2	25.5	5.6
$100,000–$200,000	33,910	649	1.9	95,854	−0.7	26.1	26.6	8.8
$200,000 or more	135,359	23,521	17.4	350,578	−6.7	27.9	32.7	81.3
All incomes	10,107	382	3.8	34,129	−1.1	22.8	23.7	100.0

NOTES: Pretax family income is the sum of wages, salaries, self-employment income, rents, taxable and nontaxable interest, dividends, realized capital gains, and all cash transfer payments. Income also includes the employer share of social security and federal unemployment insurance payroll taxes and the corporate income tax. For purposes of ranking by adjusted family income (AFI), income for each family is divided by the projected 1994 poverty threshold for a family of that size. Quintiles contain equal numbers of people. Families with zero or negative income are excluded from the lowest income category but included in the total.

Changes in individual income taxes are distributed directly to families paying those taxes. Changes in payroll taxes are distributed to families paying those taxes directly or indirectly, through their employers. Changes in federal excise taxes are distributed to families according to their consumption of the taxed good or service. Changes in corporate income taxes are distributed to families according to their income from capital.

Based on 1993 economic assumptions.

SOURCE: Simulations by Congressional Budget Office.

taxes. In the case of OBRA-93, we displayed the effect of the tax changes at 1994 income levels, but we used 1998 tax parameters and revenue estimates, adjusted for differences between 1994 and 1998 incomes. By 1998, the changes in the earned income tax credit (EITC) will be fully implemented, and the major expiring provisions of pre-OBRA-93 law—the phaseout of personal exemptions (PEP), the limitation on itemized deductions for high-income taxpayers (Pease), and 2.5 cents of the gasoline tax—would have expired. CBO's distributional analysis omits provisions that change only the timing of liabilities, such as estimated payment rules, and provisions that improve compliance.

Most changes in OBRA-93 that affected individual income taxes and payroll taxes were simulated using CBO's tax simulation model. For changes in corporate taxes and excise taxes, we used the Joint Committee on Taxation (JCT)'s estimate of the revenue of a provision and allocated the effect to families according to the assumptions of tax incidence discussed below.

CBO's tax simulation models were used to simulate the effect of the rate increases for high-income individuals, the extensions of Pease and PEP, the modifications to the AMT, the elimination of the cap on earnings subject to the Medicare (HI) tax, and the expansion of the EITC. The effect of these provisions was simulated at 1994 income levels. Since the effects were simulated under the assumption that there would be no changes in taxpayer behavior because of OBRA-93, the effects of the rate increases on tax burdens are larger than the expected revenue from them. Wage earners are assumed to bear the effect of both the employee and the employer share of the HI tax increase, with an adjustment to their individual income taxes to reflect the assumption that their wages would be lower.

Gross revenue from excise tax changes was allocated by consumption—the same method used to assign the tax in our historical analyses. Part of the tax was allocated to the direct consumption of the taxed good. The part of the tax that affects intermediate inputs to consumer goods was allocated to general consumption. We assumed that the price level would rise because of the excise tax. Payments from indexed transfer payments such as social security, federal pensions, and Supplemental Security Income (SSI) were raised and individual income tax payments were lowered to reflect more indexing of personal exemptions, EITC brackets, and other tax parameters. These changes in transfers and individual income tax payments offset some of the burden of the higher excise tax.

Although the corporate income tax under current law is assumed to be borne half by capital and half by labor, we made a different assumption about the effect of changes in the tax. We assumed that most changes were borne by families in proportion to their capital income, but there were a few exceptions. The limitation on the deductibility of compensation over $1 million was assumed to affect only those in the highest income category, under the assumption that the incomes of highly paid executives will be affected. The higher corporate tax payments from the further limitation of the deductibility of meals and entertainment expenses were allocated to employees, with the proportional effect rising with income; the higher tax payments of noncorporate firms were assigned to families in proportion to their taxes on business income. For all business taxes, the amount of the tax assigned was the JCT revenue estimate for 1998, reduced to account for the growth in income between 1994 and 1998.

7
Distributional Analysis at the Joint Committee on Taxation

Thomas A. Barthold

In August 1993, President Clinton signed the Omnibus Budget Reconciliation Act of 1993 (OBRA). It contained a large revenue component, estimated to raise $240.4 billion during fiscal years 1994 through 1998. In addition to raising substantial revenue, the bill attempted to fulfill President Clinton's campaign promise to increase the progressivity of the federal tax system. Analysis of the distribution of the burden of the new taxes became an important policy consideration in meeting that goal.

Table 4–3 presents the analysis of the distributional effects of the 1993 act as estimated by the staff of the Joint Committee on Taxation (JCT). As calculated by the JCT, the act produced a more progressive federal revenue system by decreasing the tax burden by more than 1 percent of income for tax filers with annual incomes less than $10,000, while increasing the tax burden by more than 5 percent of income for tax filers with annual incomes in excess of $200,000. The following chapter by Thomas Barthold and William Jack in this volume presents the details of the JCT distribution methodology, and this chapter discusses, at an intuitive level, how that methodology produced the results reported in the table.

Column 1 of the table displays the JCT's income categories. The JCT reports the distribution of the tax burden by the annual income of the tax-filing unit. Tax-filing units correspond approximately to tax returns with adjustments for returns filed by dependents and for individuals (generally low-income individuals) who are not required to

---

While descriptive of the distribution methodology of the staff of the Joint Committee on Taxation, this chapter represents the views of the author alone. It should not be construed as representing the views or policies of the staff of the Joint Committee on Taxation or of any member of Congress.

file tax returns. Readers of table 4–3 should recognize that single and joint returns are reported together on the same table.[1]

The JCT's annual income concept, called "expanded income," is a broader measure of income than cash income. It includes, for example, the value of employer-provided health insurance, the employer's share of payroll taxes, and corporate income taxes paid on behalf of shareholders. Recognizing the breadth of this measure is important to understanding the estimate of the burden of the 1993 act. A key component of the act was the creation of a 36 percent marginal tax rate on joint returns with taxable incomes in excess of $140,000. When the $140,000 in taxable income is adjusted for personal exemptions and deductions, one arrives at an adjusted gross income of approximately $180,000. Adding in the noncash components of income implies that most returns affected by this new income tax rate fall in the JCT's highest income category. From column 1, the importance of knowing that the break points between the income classes were not chosen to have equal numbers of tax-filing units in each group can be inferred. At 1993 income levels, the JCT's bottom category contained approximately 17 million returns, while the top category contained 1.2 million returns.[2]

Columns 2 and 3 are the same in any JCT table for a given year. These columns serve as a reference point for the analysis. Column 2 reports a measure of total federal taxes paid under present law, attributed to tax-filing units in the different income classes. This simple accounting of current revenues attributes individual income payments to the individual who remits payment, excise tax payments to consumers of the taxed products, corporate income taxes to shareholders of corporations, and payroll taxes (both portions) to the wage earner.[3] The JCT offers this as a reference point but pointedly states that the JCT staff does not interpret this as a measure of the burden of the current tax system.[4] The third column divides column 2 by the total income of all tax-filing units within the income class. Thus, the table attributes $201 million dollars in current federal tax receipts to tax-filing units with incomes between $50,000 and $75,000. These tax payments average 22.3 percent of the income of those taxpayers.

The total burden reported in column 4 is $40.8 billion. This figure

---

1. To see how single and joint returns might fall differently across the JCT income classes, see Joint Committee on Taxation, "Methodology and Issues in Measuring Changes in the Distribution of Tax Burdens" (JCS-7-93), June 14, 1993, p. 118.

2. Ibid.

3. Estate tax payments are attributed to the income class of the deceased.

4. JCT, "Methodology and Issues," p. 18.

does not equal the JCT's revenue estimate for any year of the 1993 act, for four reasons. Most important, column 4, unlike column 2, is the JCT staff's estimate of burden, not revenue. The JCT staff estimates the burden as the change in revenue that would occur if there were no change in taxpayer behavior. That is, burden is approximated by static behavior, while revenue estimates account for a wide variety of behavior. When the behavioral response is estimated to be small, however, revenue estimates will be similar to burden estimates. An additional reason why the burden measure deviates from the revenue estimates of the act is that the burden estimate is calculated against calendar year income (1993 income levels in the table) rather than by fiscal year as are revenue estimates. The reported burden estimate also represents the average, or annuitized, value of five years' burdens, corresponding to the five years of the burden period.[5] Last, while the JCT's revenue estimates include every aspect of the revenue measures of the act, the JCT has not distributed the burden of all the changes. Burdens associated with changes in estimated tax changes, for example, are not estimated. The JCT does not estimate a burden when it believes it has insufficient data or there is insufficient knowledge of the likely burden.

While the JCT distributional analysis of the 1993 act does not include all the tax provisions of the bill, it includes the vast majority on a dollar-weighted basis. The changes in individual income tax rates (36 and 39.6 percent rates, 26 and 28 percent individual alternative minimum tax rates, the phaseout of personal exemptions, and the limitation on itemized deductions), the removal of the cap on wages subject to the payroll tax, the increase in the percentage of social security benefits subject to income taxation, the increase in the top corporate rate to 35 percent, and the 4.3 cents-per-gallon transportation fuels tax (and extension of the 2.5 cents per gallon enacted in 1990) account for $217 billion of the nearly $268 billion in gross revenue raised over the 1994 through 1998 budget period.[6] In addition, the expansion of the earned-income tax credit, estimated to cost $20.8 billion over the period, represents nearly 9 percent of the net revenue of the bill. Logically, these six components of the 1993 act should account for the majority of the change in burden estimated by the JCT staff.

---

5. See Thomas A. Barthold and William Jack, "Summary of the JCT Distribution Methodology," Paper prepared for the American Enterprise Institute conference "Distributional Analysis for Making Tax Policy," Washington, D.C., December 16 and 17, 1993, for discussion of this procedure.

6. See Joint Committee on Taxation, "Summary of the Revenue Provisions of the Omnibus Budget Reconciliation Act of 1993" (H.R. 2264) (JCS-11-93), August 23, 1993, appendix table A, pp. 32–41.

The JCT staff assumes that across-the-board changes in individual rates that apply to both income from labor and income from capital are borne by the individuals who pay the taxes. As noted above, for married couples filing joint returns the burden attributable to the increased individual income taxes will fall predominantly in the highest income class. For single filers, however, the 36 percent rate applies to taxable incomes in excess of $115,000. Such a taxable income generally translates into a JCT expanded income of less than $200,000. Thus, some of the burden of the individual income tax provisions also falls below the highest income category in the JCT analysis.

The JCT assumes that changes in payroll taxes, both employer and employee shares, are borne by the wage earner. Thus, the JCT would estimate the removal of the $135,000 cap on wages subject to the health insurance portion of the payroll tax would fall on taxpayers in the highest two income categories. Likewise, as a broadly applied income tax provision, the JCT assumes the increased inclusion of social security benefits in the income tax base would be borne by the taxpayers (the social security recipients). Thus, the JCT would estimate an increased burden on a subset of taxpayers in the income categories of $30,000 and above.

The JCT assumes that changes in the burden of the corporate income tax during the five-year period fall on the owners of corporations. While pension funds hold a growing proportion of corporate shares, most individual shareholders of corporate shares are in the upper end of the income distribution, particularly at the very top. This distinction in corporate shareholding is potentially significant in the JCT analysis because the JCT does not distribute across the income classes that portion of the burden of changes in the corporate income tax attributable to pension fund ownership of corporate shares. The JCT distributes only that portion of the burden of changes in the corporate income tax attributable to individual ownership. Consequently, the JCT estimates that changes in burden attributable to changes in the corporate income tax will affect primarily higher income taxpayers.

The JCT analysis of consumption and excise taxes makes the distribution of the burden from increases in such taxes appear less regressive than conventional wisdom holds. Conventional wisdom distributes the burden of such taxes to consumers as they purchase taxable goods. The JCT distributes the burden of such taxes to consumers as they earn the income that will ultimately be used to consume taxed goods.[7] In the JCT analysis of a fuels tax, the burden of the tax

7. For a discussion of why the JCT adopted this approach and how it applies the approach, see Barthold and Jack, "Summary of the JCT Distribution Methodology"; and JCT, "Methodology and Issues," where tables 3 and 5 display how this approach appears less regressive than the conventional approach.

change as a share of income is approximately twice as great in the under $10,000 income class as for any other income group less than $100,000 and four to five times as great as that of the income classes above $100,000.[8] The burden of the tax change is roughly proportional in the middle ranges.

The last major component of the 1993 act is the enhancement of the earned income tax credit (EITC). As an across-the-board individual income tax change, the JCT distributes the benefits of this expansion to those who claim the credit. This is predominantly the bottom two of the JCT's expanded income categories.

Intuitively, then, one should expect a large increase in the EITC to swamp a modest transportation fuels tax at the low end of the income scale. In the middle range of the income scale, the transportation fuels tax should produce near proportional results, tempered somewhat by the effects of increased inclusion of social security benefits in the income tax base. At the top end of the income scale, individual income tax rate increases, repeal of the health insurance wage cap, and corporate income tax rate increases should add an increased burden. This intuition provides a good qualitative description of the results of the JCT's estimate of the distributional effects of the revenue provisions contained in the Omnibus Budget Reconciliation Act of 1993.

---

8. See JCT, "Methodology and Issues," table 4.

PART THREE

Advances in Distributional Analysis

8
Public Finance and Tax Policy

Alan J. Auerbach

There is little dispute that distributional concerns have a valid role in the design of fiscal policy or that policy makers should be able to obtain information about the distributional effects of a fiscal policy they are considering. But what questions should distributional analysis address? And what role should economists play in determining these questions?

At first thought, the answers seem relatively simple. We care about distributional effects because of our concern about the well-being of different groups of individuals. Thus, distributional analysis should be aimed at identifying the effects of policies on well-being. The way to accomplish this goal is through tax incidence analysis. The methods of tax incidence analysis should be determined by those professionally trained to perform it, namely economists, based on a careful reading of the public finance literature.

The process of translating the academic literature into usable distribution tables, however, is not straightforward. Academic research, with its often inconclusive findings and abstract simplifications, is often ill suited to the needs of the policy process, which requires fast, clear answers. Moreover, even with translation, many of those who must explain to policy makers the findings of distributional analysis are themselves unfamiliar with even the most basic economic principles.

As a result of these difficulties, the information and advice that policy makers receive often ignore valuable lessons that academic research, and indeed basic economic reasoning, can provide. The chal-

This chapter was first presented as a paper at an AEI conference, "Distributional Analysis for Making Tax Policy," and draws heavily on one that appeared in the December 1993 issue of the *National Tax Journal* under the title, "Public Finance in Theory and Practice." I am grateful to David Bradford, Joel Slemrod, former colleagues at the U.S. Joint Committee on Taxation, and participants in the AEI conference for comments on earlier drafts.

lenge to economists involved in the policy process is to produce information that policy makers and those working with them can understand, without altering the message itself. As an important part of this process, economists should acquaint the purveyors and the ultimate "consumers" of distributional analysis with simple economic principles and the nature of economic research, to help them accept that in some instances a question they pose may have no clear answer or may in fact be the wrong question. Despite the limits to what economic theory and empirical evidence can tell us, there are often valuable lessons to be learned.

In this chapter, I illustrate the challenges facing economists involved in the tax policy process and some of the lessons we can offer. While my discussion will ultimately focus on the measurement of the distributional effects of proposed tax changes, I will begin with the important and closely related issue of revenue analysis. Considering these issues together highlights common problems. Indeed, I will argue that the questions underlying revenue and distributional analysis are more similar than many have recognized. In addition, some of the perceived problems with existing distribution tables arise from attempts to reconcile them with parallel revenue estimates. Each of these subjects is dealt with in considerably more detail in two publications of the Joint Committee on Taxation.[1]

Revenue Analysis

Revenue estimation per se is rarely covered as a separate subject in the academic public finance curriculum, and it has been the focus of relatively little academic research. Yet, a growing share of the staff time of economists at the Joint Committee on Taxation (JCT) and the Treasury's Office of Tax Analysis (OTA) is spent in the production of revenue estimates for specific legislative proposals. A typical revenue estimate presents an agency's prediction of "the" change in tax revenue (or expenditures) that will result over a period of time, typically five fiscal years, if a particular proposal is adopted.

The importance of revenue analysis in the policy process has grown over the years with the institution of specific budget control measures that impose restrictions on taxes and expenditures based on official revenue estimates. Under the Budget Enforcement Act of 1990,

---

1. U.S. Congress, Joint Committee on Taxation, *Discussion of Revenue Estimation Methodology and Process.* JCS-14-92 (Washington, D.C.: GPO, 1992), and *Methodology and Issues in Measuring Changes in the Distribution of Tax Burdens.* JCS-7-93 (Washington, D.C.: 1993).

for example, a proposal that results in the loss of tax revenue must be offset by one that raises at least as much. Despite the attention that the revenue estimates themselves receive, however, little thought has been given to what information the estimates actually convey and the role they *should* play in the policy process, along with other relevant information about proposals. Several issues deserve particular mention.

Uncertainty

No matter how high the quality of data and the skill of the econometrician, any statistical estimate carries with it a measure of error. Indeed, the conditions under which government revenue estimators labor are far more unfavorable than those faced by the academic researcher. Often, revenue analysis must be performed quickly and in the absence of any reasonable empirical research or the appropriate data. Yet existing rules and institutions leave no room for confidence intervals (which indicate the range of variation in the estimates that cannot reasonably be ruled out), the normal method of indicating the degree of statistical uncertainty.[2]

If each revenue estimate were provided with such a range of error (which itself would often be hard to gauge), legislators might realize just how limited the information was and would be warned to depend less on revenue estimates (and more on other relevant considerations) in making policy decisions and budget rules. Unfortunately, economists have not succeeded in communicating to legislators the inevitability of this uncertainty—and that those outside government who offer "rival" estimates with more precision than is technically feasible are not better economists, but simply not economists.

The Nature of the Experiment

Even if revenue estimates could be made without statistical error, arriving at meaningful estimates still requires many assumptions about the nature of the "experiment" under consideration. These questions include the government's revenue and spending policy responses in current and future years that will offset any change in revenue and the specification of the "base line"—what would happen if the proposal were not adopted.

---

2. This implied lack of uncertainty places the producers of revenue estimates in a very awkward position on those occasions when revenue estimates simply must be revised to account for compelling new information about taxpayer behavior.

Suppose, for example, an increase in the federal excise tax on tobacco were proposed. Armed with the aggregate elasticities of demand and supply for tobacco, we still do not know how the revenue to be raised will be used. Will other taxes be reduced? Will expenditures increase? When will the offsetting changes in revenues or expenditures occur? The answers to these questions should affect the revenue estimate itself, for they influence the behavioral response, even if no offsetting fiscal changes are anticipated in the current year. Finally, once we have predicted the new level of revenue to be raised under the excise tax, we must ask, Relative to what *initial* level of revenue should we measure this *new* revenue level, to determine the change in revenue?

The revenue-estimating process has developed conventions to deal with many of these ambiguities, including "offsets" to take account of changes in other taxes and expenditures, but there is no "correct" set of assumptions to make, and the conventions can produce counterintuitive results. If the existing excise tax were about to expire, for example, then the revenue estimate would measure revenue relative to a zero rate of tax, even if everyone already expected that the tax would be renewed at least at its current level. If the excise tax were replaced with an equivalent tax levied at the same rate directly on households in proportion to their tobacco consumption, the estimated revenue would change because of the convention that holds nominal gross domestic product fixed. Because indirect taxes are included in GDP and direct taxes are not (this is a convention imposed by national income accountants), the total level of household expenditures inclusive of the tobacco tax would be presumed higher under the direct tax than under the indirect one.

With such inherent ambiguities, the added pressure of budget enforcement rules has wrought havoc, leading legislators to seek ways of "raising revenue" without really doing so. Given that a five-year budget "window" is used to measure each proposal's revenue effects, a proposal can be altered in arbitrary ways to change the amount of estimated revenue for budget periods beyond the first five years. Choosing, for example, to make what is intended to be a permanent tax increase expire after five years has no effect on the initial five-year revenue estimate but allows legislators to "count" the revenue again and again as they extend the date of expiration in subsequent years, relative to the base line that does not include the tax.[3]

---

3. A revenue "increase" of this type included in the Omnibus Budget Reconciliation Act of 1993 was the extension of the high-income phaseouts of itemized deductions and personal exemptions originally introduced in 1990. In this case, though, legislators opted for permanent extension, forgoing future opportunities to "use" this revenue source.

The Meaning of the Numbers

Revenue estimates have a number of uses. Whatever their limitations, they typically help legislators determine the general scope and magnitude of a provision under consideration. They are used for much more than this, however. Given the current nature of the budget process, the revenue estimate for a proposal is used to tell us how much the proposal increases or reduces the corresponding year's budget deficit. But even if we can resolve the ambiguities just discussed, what does the change in the budget deficit actually tell us? Unfortunately, it may provide little information about the proposal's macroeconomic effects or about how the fiscal burden is being shifted among taxpayers.

While policy makers are accustomed to thinking of a deficit-reducing measure as being contractionary, alleviating pressure on interest rates and imposing more of the fiscal burden on current generations, recent history provides us with many counterexamples to these presumptions.

In 1992, for example, Congress considered several "revenue-increasing" proposals that in all likelihood would have reduced the present value of revenues collected from current taxpayers. Though the proposals differed in their specifics, each offered taxpayers a net (in present-value terms) tax reduction to induce them to accelerate payments. Whether the taxpayer was prepaying the tax on a withdrawal from an individual retirement account to put the funds into a more attractive "back-end" IRA, or accepting the government's compromise offer regarding the disputed amortization of intangible assets, he or she was paying more tax during the budget period but less total; this was how voluntary participation was guaranteed. Yet these proposals were treated as if they improved the government's fiscal position and were used to relax the constraints imposed by the budget process.

Some have reacted to this sort of gamesmanship by suggesting stricter rules, to attempt to distinguish "good" from "bad" revenue increases. Such arbitrary procedures, however, have no objective principles to guide them and are bound to discourage perfectly reasonable proposals simply because they happen to have the timing characteristics of "budget gimmicks." The problem is really too fundamental to be dealt with in this way, for it reflects serious defects in the concept of deficit accounting itself.

Simply put, the annual budget deficit does not provide answers to our questions about fiscal performance. The problem is not the lack of inflation adjustment or a capital budget. As long as we look at a one-year, or even a five-year deficit forecast, timing games are inevitable, and policy will be distorted by a bias toward adopting policies that, by chance or by design, deliver less of their revenue loss, or more of their revenue gain, during the relevant budget period.

What solution does economic research suggest? If we wish to determine the fiscal effect of a policy, we must know not only its long-run budget impact—the present value of the revenues it generates or loses—but also who bears the burden of these changes. While indicating the long-run revenue consequences of a policy represents an improvement over current practice, a policy—an increase in the pay-as-you-go social security benefits, for example—could change revenue in no year but still have "deficit-like" effects by shifting resources from the young to the elderly.

This combination of looking at long-run budget effects *and* their distribution among cohorts leads to the calculation of *generational accounts* as an alternative to deficit accounting.[4] A generational account equals the present value of taxes, net of transfers, that each generation can expect to pay in the future, based on current policy. By considering how proposals affect the accounts of different generations and the residual of government obligations being left to future generations, we can gain a better indication of the shifting of fiscal burdens that underlies any prospective policy change.

Generational accounting is a methodology still under development but already being used by the government.[5] A frequent criticism of generational accounting, and even of more modest attempts at calculating a proposal's long-run revenue consequences, is that information about the distant future is imprecise and should not be used as a basis for current decisions. There is little rationale for discarding partial information in favor of ignorance, however. The perceived advantages of restricting attention to the short run are even less convincing once one recognizes the uncertainty already inherent in the revenue-estimating process.

Should budget enforcement rules be based on generational accounting? Generational accounts have the capacity to provide information that deficit accounting cannot. But, in cynical hands, even

---

4. For a nontechnical description and illustration of the generational accounting approach, see Alan J. Auerbach, Jagadeesh Gokhale, and Laurence J. Kotlikoff, "Generational Accounting: A Meaningful Way to Evaluate Fiscal Policy," *Journal of Economic Perspective*, Spring 1994.

5. See U.S. Office of Management and Budget, *Budget of the United States Government, Fiscal Year 1993* (Washington, D.C.: GPO, 1992), *Budget Baselines, Historical Data, and Alternatives for the Future* (Washington, D.C.: GPO, 1993), and *Budget of the United States Government, Fiscal Year 1995: Analytical Perspectives* (Washington, D.C.: GPO, 1994).

generational accounting can be distorted through the use of inappropriate economic assumptions about the future. While budget enforcement rules based on generational accounting would represent an improvement over the current practice, I am unconvinced that policy makers who lack the will to make hard decisions can rely on such rules to make them do so.

The Problems of Ambiguity

An important issue in the revenue estimation process in recent years has been the extent to which behavioral effects are taken into account. The general rule followed at the Joint Committee on Taxation and other agencies is to incorporate behavioral effects at the micro level but not at the macro level. Thus, while demand and supply responses in individual markets and changes in the composition of consumption or investment may be incorporated, estimates by JCT (or the Office of Tax Analysis) take the aggregate output, employment, and prices forecast by the Congressional Budget Office (or the Office of Management and Budget) as given. The revenue loss generated by an investment tax credit, for example, will account for shifts in the mixture of investment but not the increased investment, output, employment, or prices that such investment shifts may cause.

Whether to include such macroeconomic "feedback" effects is perhaps the most controversial question in revenue estimation. But the controversy is not really about whether taxes have macroeconomic effects: essentially *all* taxes have macroeconomic effects. The question is whether revenue estimates should incorporate these effects. Because the underlying goal of revenue estimation is unclear, so is the answer to this question.

As a start toward an answer, it helps to consider the question in terms of the three issues already discussed. First, short-term macroeconomic forecasts, about, for instance, the level of output, involve an additional type of uncertainty not present when forecasting the composition of output, namely, uncertainty about the ability of fiscal policy to influence macroeconomic activity. Without making such uncertainty explicit, incorporating feedback effects places the estimator in the very uncomfortable position of having to claim confidence in an estimate in which no sensible person could have much confidence. Second, the feedback effects cannot be estimated without knowledge of the implicit macroeconomic policy response to the particular proposal—how fiscal and monetary policy will react to incipient changes in output and the price level.

Finally, it is not immediately clear that we should care to know

141

the net revenue impact of a proposal. One of the purposes of estimating revenue, admittedly served rather poorly by the current process, is to determine how the intergenerational fiscal burden is affected by a proposal. As the discussion of distributional analysis below emphasizes, an important distinction exists between tax revenues and the tax burden. A better measure of the tax burden may actually be provided by estimates that ignore all or some behavioral effects. This observation does not necessarily indicate that we should ignore feedback effects but certainly makes the decision a more complex one.

Distributional Analysis

Like revenue analysis, distributional analysis often confronts a serious lack of information, because many of the proposals that must be evaluated require a level of detail that outstrips available information. As with revenue analysis, many questions, often the same ones, must be answered and conventions adopted before "the" distributional effects of a proposal can be specified, statistical difficulties notwithstanding. Here again, perhaps the most important contribution that economics has to offer is guidance in framing the discussion, identifying which questions to ask and what information is useful.

What Should the Horizon Be?

In economics, the simplest incidence analysis takes place in a static context. We ask who bears a particular tax, without paying much attention to the element of time. Traditionally, government distribution tables have taken this static approach, considering the distributional burden of taxes in one particular year. As the previous discussion of revenue estimation suggests, though, time can be an important element in determining the revenue effects, and hence the burden, of a particular tax.

In the case of the consumption tax, for example, the horizon used to evaluate incidence affects the degree of measured progressivity or regressivity, because annual variations in income among individuals tend to overstate longer-run differences in their ability to pay. The life-cycle model of consumption predicts that individuals will smooth consumption over their lifetime, supporting consumption during their relatively low-income retirement years by saving during their relatively high-income working years. The same prediction comes from the permanent income hypothesis, which suggests that household consumption will smooth out transitory shocks to income.

As in the case of revenue analysis, an attractive solution is to shift to a lifetime perspective, to measure the burden a tax imposes over each generation's lifetime. This approach could then be extended by looking within each generation at the burden on different income classes.[6] The use of short horizons in the revenue estimation process, however, makes it difficult to adopt the lifetime approach in performing distributional analysis. The challenge, then, is to develop an approach that, like a lifetime incidence calculation, is not sensitive to the timing of an individual's tax payments but is still based on a shorter time horizon.

One method,[7] is to associate all taxes with the earning of income, regardless of when the taxes are actually paid. In the case of consumption taxes, this methodology takes advantage of the fact that, under normal market conditions, a broad-based consumption tax is economically equivalent to a broad-based income tax that provides an exclusion for income from new saving.[8] Hence, the consumption taxes attributed to any individual over a five-year period are those taxes that would be paid under the equivalent tax on income from labor and preexisting assets. The approach has the effect of treating, for purposes of timing, the deduction for saving provided under a consumption tax as if it were the equivalent exemption from tax of the capital income earned on that saving.

This same methodology can also be used for consumption taxes with narrower bases and for analyzing saving and investment incentives that take what might be called the "consumption tax" form—that is, that provide a deduction for saving and a tax on dissaving—in terms of the equivalent income tax exemptions for the income from that saving or investment. The result is a consistent distributional analysis of provisions that differ with respect to timing but not substance, such as "front-end" versus "back-end" IRAs or investment tax credits versus accelerated depreciation.

What Is the Incidence of the Corporate Tax?

As economists have struggled through the years with the question of corporate tax incidence, policy-oriented distributional analysis has

---

6. For a recent application of the lifetime incidence approach, see Don Fullerton and Diane Lim Rogers, *Who Bears the Lifetime Tax Burden?* (Washington, D.C.: Brookings Institution, 1993).

7. See, for example, U.S. Congress, *Factors Affecting the International Competitiveness of the United States*, JCS-6-91 (Washington, D.C.: GPO, 1991), and *Methodology and Issues*.

8. See, for example, the discussion in Alan J. Auerbach and Laurence J. Kotlikoff, *Dynamic Fiscal Policy* (Cambridge: Cambridge University Press, 1987).

dealt with the issue in a variety of unsatisfactory ways, ranging from ignoring it to arbitrarily assigning it to one group or another. Beyond making the obvious point that *someone* must bear this tax, we can improve on past approaches by recognizing that the corporate tax, like the individual income tax, has different components that may be more easily analyzed separately than as a whole.

Basic incidence theory instructs us that shifting the responsibility for the actual payment of a tax from an individual to a corporation does not necessarily alter the incidence of the tax. A common illustration of this point is the payroll tax, the incidence of which should generally be independent of whether the employer or the employee is assessed. Let us consider the implications of this point for the distribution of a corporate-level tax that may be part of a system of consumption taxation.

A broad-based consumption tax can be collected in a variety of ways: at the retail level as a retail sales tax; through the stages of production as a credit-and-invoice value-added tax; at the individual level as a personal consumption tax; or, as noted above, as a combination of a tax on wages plus the income from capital with a deduction for new saving. With the same base and the same tax rate, the incidence should be the same (ignoring administrative differences with respect to compliance and the like), and any distributional analysis should indicate this.

For the last variant with the tax on existing capital collected at the business level as a cash-flow tax, however, most of which would be collected from corporations, the simple rules often used for distributing the burden of the corporate income tax need not lead to this result. A corporate cash-flow tax would be treated as a corporate income tax with reduced collections rather than the combination of a corporate income tax plus a deduction for new investment. Treating these components separately, and applying the timing methodology described above, provides a desirable consistency among the different consumption tax approaches and between each and other, equivalent, forms of taxation. The important lesson is that we cannot distribute the burden of the corporate tax without considering its form.

Distinguishing Taxes Paid from Tax Burden

The two major concepts of welfare economics used in public finance are equity and efficiency; in analyzing the effects of taxation, we ask who bears the tax burden and how taxes distort behavior. When taxes worsen economic efficiency, there is a difference between the taxes individuals pay and the burdens they bear, equal to the "deadweight loss," or "excess burden" of taxation.

In computing the incidence of a tax, one computes the burden of the tax borne by different individuals, equal for each to that individual's reduction in economic well-being. The sum of these burdens equals total taxes paid plus the deadweight loss of the taxes. The difference between the total burden and the sum of tax payments is important, because it indicates how large the deadweight loss of taxation is. But this is a measure of efficiency, not equity or incidence.

The failure to distinguish between the burden of taxation and the level of taxes paid has precipitated confusion and controversy in the interpretation of distributional analyses. A reduction in the rate of capital gains taxation, for example, might have a relatively modest impact on net revenues, if by relaxing the distortion of individual realization decisions it prompted more frequent realizations. Measured properly—and there are many additional issues involved in ensuring that this is accomplished—the total revenue loss would be smaller than the total benefit resulting from the tax reduction by the associated reduction in deadweight loss. But the size of the revenue loss is irrelevant to the question of burden. Indeed, to a first approximation, the change in the taxpayer's burden is the "income effect" of the tax change—the change in taxes that would result in the absence of any taxpayer response.

Still, many individuals unfamiliar with basic economics cling to the notion that the change in taxes paid is the correct measure of total burden, with the ridiculous implication that, should a tax be so distortionary that reducing it actually increases revenue, the burden of taxation increases. Others use somewhat more sophisticated logic in defense of the "taxes paid" approach, arguing that we cannot be certain of tax incidence but we can measure quite accurately the taxes that people pay. But this argument fails just as badly, and for the same underlying reason: the classification of a payment by an individual as a tax is completely arbitrary unless it is guided by economic analysis. Logically, this approach would require us to ignore, among other items, the corporate tax, the employer portion of the payroll tax, and indirect taxes not formally paid by households. Assigning these taxes to households is impossible without incidence assumptions based on economic logic. Once we opt to assign to individuals taxes that they do not pay, we are pursuing a measure of economic burden. Why, then, should we intentionally assign to them a greater or lesser burden than they bear?

The difficulty of reconciling measures of aggregate revenues and the sum of measured tax burdens frustrates policy makers. But there is no inconsistency between the measures, simply a lack of adequate explanation. The real problem is that we offer no independent measure of changes in economic efficiency as a bridge between the tables. Lacking this, policy makers not only are confused but also have no way of making informed decisions about the trade-off between equity and efficiency.

In principle, a measure of deadweight loss might actually be obtained from the discrepancies between revenue tables and distribution tables, since the former attempt to measure taxes paid. There are many problems in doing so, however, as not all revenue effects are necessarily incorporated in the revenue calculation and the timing conventions are different. Even if there were no behavioral change or associated deadweight loss, for example, the revenue impact of a consumption tax would differ from the total burden associated with such a tax over a one-year or five-year interval unless the consumption tax burden were distributed on the same cash-flow basis as the revenue estimate, a procedure most economists would reject. But these difficulties simply point out once again the need to clarify exactly what revenue estimates are supposed to represent.

Conclusions

Revenue and distributional analysis are important tax policy tools supplied by economists and supposedly grounded in economic theory and practice. Yet, as the demands of the process increase and the stress put on these tools increases, it is important to return to the foundations of these processes, to ask what purposes they are supposed to serve and what information they are intended to convey. Without solving all the disputes raging within the economics profession, we may progress beyond the present conditions simply by highlighting, and forcing policy makers to confront, the weaknesses and inconsistencies of the current methods. Among the steps that will help us achieve this objective are:

- the education of those involved in the policy process in the most basic principles of economics
- the provision of more complete information about the long-run and distributional effects of tax proposals
- the rejection of meaningless measures of fiscal responsibility, based on specific revenue estimates
- the insistence that information on the revenue and distributional impact of proposals meet the most basic tests of economic consistency
- the refusal to provide information when such information does not exist and indication of the quality of information that is provided

At worst, we may be ignored, as economists often are when their message is inconvenient—as when pointing out, for example, that price controls causes shortages or that the current account deficit must, by identity, equal the domestic imbalance between saving and investment[9]—but we will not be guilty of the complicity of silence.

---

9. See, for example, the discussion in Auerbach and Kotlikoff, *Dynamic Fiscal Policy*.

9
Innovations in the JCT Distribution Methodology

Thomas A. Barthold and William Jack

The staff of the Joint Committee on Taxation is involved in all aspects of the tax legislative process from the initial markup of tax laws in the House of Representatives through the final voting on House-Senate conference agreements. A nonpartisan staff serving both houses of Congress, the JCT[1] is Congress's primary resource for tax policy analysis and technical assistance on legislation. In addition to providing information and analysis of tax legislation to the tax-writing committees and members of Congress, under the terms of the Budget Act of 1974 the JCT is to estimate the revenue effects of proposed tax legislation.

Efforts to control the federal budget over the past decade have,

The staff of the Joint Committee on Taxation has recently revised its methodology for reporting distributional effects of tax changes to the U.S. Congress. The results of this study may be found in Joint Committee on Taxation, "Methodology and Issues in Measuring Changes in the Distribution of Tax Burdens," Washington, D.C., June 14, 1993. For this reason, the thoughts in this chapter stem from the work of many staff economists of the committee who, over the past two years, have contributed to the staff's debate of these issues, including Alan Auerbach, Tom Bowne, Pat Driessen, Ron Jeremias, Cathy Koch, Tom Koerner, Mark Mazur, Pam Moomau, John O'Hare, Bernard Schmitt, Louise Sheiner, Martin A. Sullivan, William Sutton, Michael Udell, Alan Viard, Laura Wheeler, and Judy Xanthopoulos. The authors, while retaining responsibility for any errors, are also grateful to David Bradford and the other participants in the American Enterprise Institute conference, "Distributional Analysis for Making Tax Policy," December 16 and 17, 1993, Washington, D.C., for which this chapter was prepared. While descriptive of the distribution methodology of the staff of the Joint Committee on Taxation, this chapter represents the views of the authors alone. It should not be construed as representing the views or policies of the staff of the Joint Committee on Taxation or any member of the U.S. Congress or the International Monetary Fund.

1. Throughout this chapter, we will use JCT as shorthand for JCT staff.

on the one hand, elevated the importance of quantitative estimates of receipts and outlays. On the other hand, policy makers have long recognized that revenue or expenditure goals may conflict with goals of equity. Concomitantly, demand has grown for precise estimates of the burdens or benefits that policy changes impose on different individuals. A lack of consensus within the economics profession over how best to measure tax burdens as well as a lack of understanding among many policy makers makes this task difficult.

As a general rule, the JCT strives to produce tax burden analysis that represents "good economics" that is useful to policy makers. Not all good economic analysis, however, is useful to policy makers. Sometimes concepts familiar to academic economists are not understood by, or relevant to, policy makers. A computation of lifetime burden, for example, may not be relevant to policy makers who see policy as a dynamic, ever-changing process. Similarly, some economic concepts, such as imputed income from the ownership of consumer durables, may be difficult for the noneconomist policy maker to appreciate. Another guiding principle employed by the JCT is to present burden estimates that are consistent across economically similar proposals. Consistency, while attractive from an intellectual viewpoint, also serves the important function of building both understanding and credibility. Recognition of these kinds of constraints is important to the JCT staff's distribution methodology.

In choosing a method by which to analyze the burden or benefit of tax changes, one must make four fundamental choices: the measure by which taxpayers are grouped for comparison, the time period over which the analysis is undertaken, the measure of burden or benefit, and the incidence assumptions. In its recent revision of distributional analysis, the JCT has chosen methodologies that differ from those of most other analyses with respect to three of these four fundamental choices:

- The JCT's measure of taxpayer well-being, "expanded income," is neither a cash measure, a Haig-Simons measure, nor a lifetime measure.
- The JCT calculates changes in burden over the federal government's five-year planning horizon, rather than on a fully phased-in, steady-state basis, on a lifetime basis, or on a one-year basis.
- The JCT measures the burden or benefit of changes in consumption taxes, excise taxes, and certain investment incentives as taxpayers earn income, rather than as they consume or invest.

To understand how these three choices are important to the JCT's analysis of the burden of taxation, we first briefly summarize the general methodology and then discuss these three decisions in more detail.

The JCT Distribution Methodology in a Nutshell

The Classification of Taxpayers. The JCT groups individuals by "tax-filing unit." That is, the unit of analysis is determined by how individuals file their tax returns.[2] The JCT classifies these tax-filing units on the basis of a measure of pretax and transfer income,[3] referred to as "expanded income." JCT expanded income starts with a taxpayer's adjusted gross income (AGI) as reported on the tax return. Several sources of current cash receipts that are not included in AGI are added into expanded income. In addition, certain forms of nontaxable, non-cash compensation, for example, the value of employer-provided health insurance, are included in expanded income. Expanded income includes the full value of social security benefits received and the insurance value of Medicare. Expanded income also includes certain adjustments permitted in computing AGI, such as the excess of accelerated depreciation over the Accelerated Cost Recovery System (ACRS) depreciation. Last, corporate income tax payments are imputed as income to owners of corporations.[4]

Time Period of Analysis. The JCT methodology uses a finite horizon for its distributional analyses. Distributional analyses are based on predicted changes in policy and taxpayer behavior that occur within the five-year budget planning horizon of the federal government. The JCT method computes the change in burden for each of the five years and then computes an annuitized annual value of the five years' worth of changes.

The Measure of Burden. The JCT staff attempts to estimate the economic burden of changes in tax policy. The JCT methodology approximates the changes in individual well-being by static revenue changes. That is, the change in burden is measured as the change in tax revenue that would result if output or consumption of the taxed good or activ-

---

2. Dependent returns are disregarded in the analysis. Because only a small percentage of married couples file separately, a tax return can generally be viewed as a household. The tax filing unit concept, however, is not the same as the Bureau of the Census's concept of a household.

3. Alternative schemes could group individuals as families or as separate individuals and could classify these groups by their aftertax and transfer income, their permanent or lifetime income, or their consumption.

4. AGI already includes dividends paid by corporations and capital gains realized on corporate stock (attributable, in part, to retained earnings), so to have a consistent measure of pretax income it is necessary to attribute corporate income taxes to shareholders.

ity did not change. This measure is most accurate when consumer and producer behavioral responses to tax changes are small and tends to overestimate increases in burden and underestimate decreases in burden. The measure is also more accurate in the short run, as short-run elasticities are smaller than long-run elasticities.[5]

It is important to emphasize what the JCT's estimate is not. It is not an estimate of the burden of the existing tax structure but only of incremental changes to that structure. It is also not the same as the total amount of tax revenue collected, so the JCT's estimate of loss of taxpayer well-being should not be confused with an estimate of revenue gained by the federal government. Last, while it accounts for many interactions between markets, the JCT's estimate does not result from a general equilibrium model.

Incidence Assumptions. The JCT assumes that taxes on labor income, both the individual income tax and the payroll tax, are borne by wage and salary earners as they earn the income. The JCT assumes that individual taxes on capital income are borne by all owners of capital as that capital produces income and that the corporate income tax is borne by the owners of corporate capital as corporate income is produced. The JCT assumes that the burden of changes in broad-based saving incentives are borne by savers, not owners of existing capital, as income from the new savings is earned. The JCT analysis measures the benefit of a deductible IRA, for example, in terms of the exemption of interest earnings from tax as opposed to the value of the up-front deduction.

These assumptions are reasonably standard. Perhaps somewhat unusual is the assumption that corporate income taxes are borne by the owners of corporate capital rather than by owners of all capital. This assumption is justified on the basis of the relatively short-run nature of the JCT analysis (the five-year horizon) and on the fact that the ownership of corporate capital is sufficiently similar to the distribution of all capital that the more narrow attribution will not have a large effect on any distributional analysis. The most novel incidence analysis used by the JCT involves consumption taxes. The JCT assumes, as is common, that such taxes are borne generally by consumers but assumes that the burden is borne as taxpayers earn income rather than as taxpayers consume taxed goods. This distinction is important because, for most taxpayers, the timing of income is different from the

5. If steady-state analysis were employed, only long-run elasticities would be relevant. As discussed below, the JCT methodology employs a shorter time horizon. For this reason, the distinction between short- and long-run elasticities may be important.

timing of consumption. This timing issue is important when the analysis is restricted to the federal government's five-year budget planning horizon.

The JCT does not distribute the burdens of several types of taxes (or portions of the burden of certain taxes). It does not generally distribute burdens of tax changes that affect the taxation of pension funds or other exempt organizations, for example. Nor does the JCT report a burden of taxes borne by foreign persons. As a consequence, because foreign persons and tax-exempt organizations may own corporate equities, the burden of changes in the corporate tax reported by the JCT may underestimate the total burden of the tax change.

Highlights from the JCT's Revision of Methodology

Choice of the Income Classifier. One usually thinks of classifying taxpayers by one of two general methods: a broad, annual measure of income such as the Haig-Simons definition of all increases in net worth or some measure of permanent or lifetime income. Each of these measures is difficult to compute and somewhat counterintuitive for policy makers. The Haig-Simons income concept is difficult to compute because of the many imputations that must be made: imputed net income from owner-occupied housing and other durable goods, annual accrued capital gains, annual accrued pension benefits, imputed values for other employer-provided fringe benefits, and more. Measures of permanent income are similarly difficult to compute because of imputations that must be made about individuals' age and earnings profiles. The breadth of the Haig-Simons concept with its inclusion of all of a worker's fringe benefits and the long-run nature of a permanent income measure with its averaging of working years with nonworking years make both approaches counterintuitive to policy makers accustomed to categorizing households as a "family of four where the husband makes $35,000 at the auto plant" or "the retired couple living on social security." The reference point of policy makers is much closer to a narrow measure of annual income.

For its analysis, the JCT staff has chosen an annual measure of pretax income, but not one as broad as the Haig-Simons measure. Data limitations and uncertainty over the necessary imputations motivate most departures from Haig-Simons income. As discussed above, the JCT measure of income, "expanded income," starts with a taxpayer's adjusted gross income as reported on the tax return. Several sources of cash receipts not included in AGI are added into expanded income, among them: social security benefits, excluded income of U.S. citizens living abroad, tax-exempt interest, and workers' compensation. Each clearly represents current resources available for consumption or saving.

In addition, expanded income includes certain nontaxable, non-cash compensation such as the value of employer-provided health and life insurance and the employer's share of payroll taxes. Like cash, these each represent compensation received currently, albeit in kind. Such compensation is often bargained in lieu of cash compensation. Consistency demands that an employee who chooses a compensation package with substantial medical insurance benefits but perhaps low cash wages be measured as no less well-off than an employee who makes the opposite decision and pays for more health care out of higher received cash wages.

While the same argument could be made for the inclusion of all fringe benefits, the JCT includes only employer-provided health and life insurance. This decision is motivated primarily by data availability. While the JCT can impute the employer's share of payroll taxes or a retiree's social security benefits to taxpayers by using taxpayer identification numbers to match exactly such income to taxpayers' income tax returns, untaxed fringe benefits must be imputed to taxpayers by statistically matching other data, such as Census data, to the JCT's underlying sample of tax returns. The prevalence of health and life insurance as fringe benefits and the existence of an active market placing values on such coverage lend reliability to the statistical match and the value of income imputed. The same could not as readily be said for employer-provided exercise rooms, for example. The error from omission of employer-provided benefits other than pension benefits (see below) and health benefits is likely to be small, as these two benefits are by far the largest.

Medicare is comparable to both social security benefits and employer-provided health insurance. As an annual in-kind benefit, the insurance value of Medicare is included in expanded income. The insurance value of Medicare is calculated as the government's projected Medicare expenditures net of premiums collected, divided by the Medicare eligible population. This figure is exactly matched to the Medicare eligible population in the JCT model. In addition, certain adjustments permitted in computing AGI, such as the excess of accelerated depreciation over ACRS depreciation, are added back to AGI. This is an attempt to measure economic income accurately. Last, corporate income tax payments are imputed as income to owners of corporations.

Significant departures from Haig-Simons income include the failure to impute income to the ownership of housing and consumer durables, including income from nominal capital gains as realized rather

153

than as real accrued gains, and not including the value of all employer-provided fringe benefits. To move toward the Haig-Simons concept would require substantial imputations. Another significant departure from the Haig-Simons concept is the inclusion of pension contributions and earnings upon distribution rather than as accrued, a decision made primarily because data on pension distributions (reported on the tax return) are more reliable than imputations of accruing pension benefits. This decision moves what is otherwise an annual measure part of the way toward being a measure of permanent income. This treatment of pensions may also comport with policy makers' intuitive notion of income. In contrast, the inclusion of some nontaxable fringe benefits, the employer's share of payroll taxes, and corporate tax payments generally does not comport with policy makers' intuitive notion of income. Nevertheless, as an annual measure less broad than Haig-Simons income, the JCT's measure of income probably deviates less from intuitive notions of income than do other potential measures.

Choice of Reporting Horizon. The natural way to measure the burden of a tax change over time would be to calculate an individual's compensating variation (or a similar measure) in a model where utility is a function of consumption bundles in the current, and each future, time period. If utility is assumed to be additively separable across time, then the sum of annual utility changes can be used to measure aggregate burden or benefit. Further, when utility in year i is the discounted value of the same function of year i consumption as year 1 utility is of year 1 consumption, then the total welfare change equals the discounted sum of all future annual burdens.[6]

There are a number of problems with infinite-horizon present-value calculations. First, since the JCT's income classifier is an annual measure, infinite-horizon present-values are not meaningfully comparable. It would be necessary to use a measure of lifetime income in this case, but, as discussed above, such calculations are difficult. Second, infinite-horizon present-value calculations are sensitive to the choice of discount rate. Because the discount rate is essentially subjective, it is undesirable to present results that are too sensitive to this selection. Third, long-term economic forecasts are inherently unreliable, so projections of burdens and incomes in the distant future are not very meaningful. Finally, it is not clear how the well-being of future genera-

---

6. Although this suggests that the temporal pattern of consumption determines the allocation of burdens over time, the appropriate assignment depends on the way we classify individuals. This is discussed further below, in the context of consumption taxes in particular.

tions should be weighted relative to the future well-being of current generations. Some version of the observed market interest rate can be used for the latter, but the appropriate intergenerational discount rate depends on value judgments concerning the obligations each generation has to its descendants. Furthermore, it is unclear how future individuals should be classified, since an individual who is considered relatively rich now may, because of growth in average incomes, be considered middle class at some time in the future.

These constraints and problems led the JCT to employ a shorter time horizon. In the short run, burdens are more comparable to annual income measures, discount rate sensitivity is less problematic, projections of economic activity are more reliable, and the problem of future generations is avoided to a large extent. Until recently, the JCT distribution method was based on single-year measures of burden and income, despite the possible exclusion of important future events from the analysis, particularly for phased-in proposals. In addition, the relevant year needs to be chosen, and a natural choice is the year in which a proposal is fully phased in. This is problematic to the extent that, first, a given package may contain provisions that become fully effective at different future dates and, second, any temporary provision will be shown to have no effect (since the fully phased-in version of a temporary provision is no provision).

The JCT therefore uses a five-year window to measure the distributional effect of changes to the tax code. This time span represents a reasoned compromise between the otherwise ideal infinite horizon approach and the simple but sometimes misleading single-year method. It is also consistent with the JCT's revenue-estimating methodology, which calculates changes in federal budget receipts over a five-year period.[7] The burden measures are five-year annuitized values.

Burden of Consumption Taxes. The restriction of JCT analysis to the five-year window means that the way tax burdens are assigned over time matters.[8] The JCT measures the burden of consumption taxes as income is earned. As explained below, this method (1) allows consistent treatment with most other tax provisions; (2) is consistent with the

---

7. See Joint Committee on Taxation, "Methodology and Issues in Measuring Changes in the Distribution of Tax Burdens," June 14, 1993.

8. If an infinite horizon present value were calculated, the timing would matter relatively more the higher the discount rate was. In our analysis, the discount rate on burdens outside the window is infinite, so timing is of particular importance.

measure of well-being used to classify individuals; and (3) yields a stream of burdens over time that reduces the mismeasurement of burden relative to income caused by the restriction of the analysis to the five-year window. To distribute the burden of any tax, policy makers must determine *which* individuals bear the burden of the tax and *when* the individuals are deemed to bear the burden. This observation is used to motivate and explain the income-based method for the distribution of general consumption taxes below.

A consumption tax can lead to increases in the general price level in the economy or to reductions in nominal wages and profit rates. For wage earners, the distinction is unimportant, because they will suffer the same reduction in buying power whether their nominal wage falls or the prices they face increase. In either case, their real wage falls. The distinction, however, is important for individuals with incomes fixed in nominal dollars—those with government transfers and those receiving or paying interest. Individuals whose income consists only of non-indexed government transfers, for example, are burdened if prices rise but not if wages fall. Whether a consumption tax leads to nominal wage and profit declines or to price increases depends on the monetary policy of the Federal Reserve, which is hard to predict. The distributional effects of consumption taxes under both alternatives are explored below.

Equivalent income-based taxes. It is well known that a broad-based consumption tax is equivalent to a tax on wages plus a tax on income from existing capital (but exempting income from new investment). To see this, suppose a consumption tax is introduced that increases the general price level in the economy. The real value of an individual's present and future wages will fall immediately, as will the value of any accumulated savings. Thus, the individual would be identically affected if nominal wages were cut and some of the accumulated capital were taxed by the government. Since, in competitive markets, the value of existing capital assets is equal to their (expected) future stream of income, taxing the old capital is equivalent to taxing the income generated from that capital. This equivalence means that a consumption tax can be distributed either as a tax on income or as a tax on consumption. To be consistent with the distribution of other tax changes, the JCT staff distributes the burden of consumption taxes as the burden of equivalent taxes on certain types of income.[9]

---

9. Clearly, it is only if individuals save or borrow that allocating the burden of a consumption tax when income is earned yields different results from allocating the burden when consumption occurs.

The equivalence between a broad-based consumption tax and a tax on wages and the returns to old capital allows a meaningful income-based allocation of the burden of the consumption tax over time. It also highlights the importance of specifying which nominal prices adjust in response to the consumption tax. Since nominal price levels are determined in part by the independent actions of the Federal Reserve, they cannot generally be predicted in advance.

When prices rise, the value of all income falls, unless the income is specifically indexed to changes in the price level. An individual living entirely on an indexed social security pension, for example, will not be affected by a uniform price increase.[10] Similarly, an individual receiving Medicare services will be partially protected against the price rise, because the in-kind transfer of health care is effectively indexed.[11] A further source of indexation that partially protects individuals from price increases is the indexation of income tax brackets. To the extent that bracket limits are increased as prices rise, nominal income tax payments are reduced, offsetting the negative effect of the consumption tax. The benefits of such indexation are not uniformly distributed across individuals.

If, in contrast, nominal wages and the returns to old assets fall, only certain types of income are affected. Recipients of fixed nominal transfers are not hurt by the tax. Such transfer payments include both indexed payments mentioned above as well as nonindexed government transfers such as Aid to Families with Dependent Children (AFDC). In addition, any private contracts with fixed nominal payments are unaffected by the tax. In particular, holders of existing bonds receive the same nominal interest payments as before, since the introduction of the tax does not change any contractual agreements between issuers and holders.

Alternative distribution methods. The two major issues in the distribution of consumption taxes—timing and nominal price adjustments—yield four potential methods for distributing a consumption tax. The following labels are useful for distinguishing the four approaches:

- (p, C). Prices are assumed to rise, and the burden is assigned as

---

10. This assumes that the fraction of the pension that is taxed and the applicable tax rate are fixed.

11. Food stamps are another example, since the nominal value of food stamps available to individuals is indexed to the price of a designated basket of food.

157

TABLE 9–1

BURDEN OF A 5 PERCENT BROAD-BASED CONSUMPTION TAX AS A PERCENTAGE
OF EXPANDED INCOME

Adjusted Income Class (dollars)	Distribution Method			
	(p, C)	(p, Y)	(w, Y)	(w, C)
0–10,000	3.70	3.69	2.84	2.85
10,000–20,000	2.66	2.68	2.86	2.83
20,000–30,000	2.90	3.00	3.10	2.99
30,000–40,000	2.92	3.04	3.20	3.07
40,000–50,000	2.94	3.10	3.26	3.10
50,000–75,000	2.77	2.97	3.21	2.99
75,000–100,000	2.63	2.88	3.01	2.74
100,000–200,000	2.50	2.84	2.92	2.57
200,000 and over	1.76	2.78	2.86	1.76

SOURCE: Joint Committee on Taxation, "Methodology and Issues in Measuring Changes in the Distribution of Tax Burdens," June 14, 1993.

consumption occurs (the traditional method of distributing a consumption tax).

- (p, Y). Prices are again assumed to rise, but the burden is assigned over time as income is earned.
- (w, C). Wages (and the returns to old capital) are assumed to fall, goods prices remain fixed, and the burden is assigned as consumption occurs.
- (w, Y). Wages (and the returns to old capital) fall, and the burden is assigned as income is earned.

Table 9–1 presents a distributional analysis of a 5 percent broad-based consumption tax using each of the four methods. Figure 9–1 graphs the results. Measured as a percentage of expanded income, the burden is most regressive if measured using the (p, C) method. Individuals in the lowest income class (those with economic income of less than $10,000) are hit hard when prices rise, since most of their transfers, particularly AFDC, are not indexed. They are less severely affected if factor returns fall. Because low-income individuals dissave only a very small amount, the burdens measured under the (p, C) and (p, Y) methods coincide, as do those using the (w, C) and (w, Y) methods because the only difference between the income- and consumption-based methods of allocating burdens over time is their treatment of savings, and if savings are very low, the difference is negligible. The most important determinant of the burden on the poor is thus whether prices rise or factor returns fall. The poor are generally much worse off

FIGURE 9–1

BURDEN OF A 5 PERCENT BROAD-BASED CONSUMPTION TAX ON VARIOUS
INCOME GROUPS

Burden as percentage of expended income

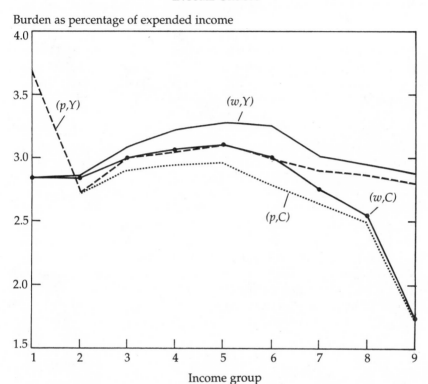

SOURCE: See table 9–1.

if prices rise, and the method of burden allocation over time is relatively unimportant.

The role of savings in distinguishing between the two methods of temporal allocation is significant in the highest income group. There, the (p, C) and (w, C) methods yield approximately equal burden measures, as do the (p, Y) and (w, Y) methods. The consumption-based methods, however, show a much smaller burden than the income-based measures, since much of total saving is done by individuals with incomes above $200,000. Under the consumption-based method, these individuals effectively receive a deduction for the full amount of their savings when they occur, while the income method attributes a deduction only for the annuitized value of the new savings.

In the central income range, the burden is relatively flat as measured by all methods. Using either the consumption- or the income-

159

based method, the burden is generally less when prices rise than when factor returns fall, since the burden is measured net of any other reductions in taxes. In particular, income tax brackets (including the exemption and standard deduction) are indexed to the general price level, so that when prices rise the amount of income tax paid falls. Due to the phase out of the personal exemption at high income levels, this indexation does not significantly change the income tax liability of individuals in the highest income classes. Similarly, for a given type of nominal price adjustment, the consumption-based method measures a lower burden than the income-based method since savings in these groups are positive. The small degree of progressivity observed around the second income class for all methods derives from the fact that these individuals receive proportionately more indexed social security payments (as well as other nonindexed benefits) than those with higher incomes.

In general, consumption taxes appear less regressive as measured by the income methods than by the consumption methods. In fact, the (w, Y) method is relatively flat over the income spectrum. Many researchers have recently contested the traditional view that consumption taxes are very regressive. One approach taken by some authors is to calculate present values of consumption as a fraction of permanent income.[12] Others have looked at consumption taxes paid as a fraction of consumption[13] rather than as a fraction of pretax income. These researchers have pointed out that consumption taxes paid as a fraction of current income may overstate the regressivity of consumption taxes because people smooth their consumption—those in their high earning years will save to finance consumption in retirement, and those with temporarily high or low income (large capital gains or temporary unemployment) will have disproportionately low or high consumption relative to income. A lifetime perspective significantly reduces the regressivity of the consumption tax. The method used by the JCT staff also implicitly uses a lifetime perspective, because while it does not calculate lifetime income, it does apply the lifetime budget constraint to convert consumption taxes into taxes on certain types of income.

A further advantage of the (p, Y) method is its consistency with the method of distributing certain other tax changes. The benefits of

---

12. See James Davies, France St. Hilarie, and John Whalley, "Some Calculations of Lifetime Tax Incidence," *American Economic Review*, vol. 74 (September 1984).

13. See, for instance, James Poterba, "Lifetime Incidence and the Distributional Burden of Excise Taxes," *American Economic Review*, vol. 79 (May 1989), pp. 325–30; and U.S. Congressional Budget Office, "Federal Taxation of Tobacco, Alcoholic Beverages, and Motor Fuels," June 1990.

investment incentives, either expensing or investment tax credits, for example, are assumed to accrue over time as a reduction in taxes paid on earnings on new investment.[14] The benefit of the up-front deduction for IRA contributions is also distributed as the reduction in tax payable on the return to such savings. Finally, the distributional effects of savings-exempt income taxes, or "consumed income taxes" similar to that proposed by Senators Sam Nunn and Pete Domenici, are calculated as a reduction in taxes on earnings from savings.

Less comprehensive consumption taxes. Narrowing the base of a consumption tax has two main effects on distributional analysis. First, by leaving some goods untaxed, the scope for significant behavioral responses is widened. Under a broad-based tax, the only margin at which behavioral responses are important is the work/leisure decision. With a narrower base, however, more substitution possibilities are available for partially avoiding the tax. Second, by narrowing the base, the share of taxable consumption can differ across income groups, depending on income elasticities of demand, whereas under a broad-based tax it is unity for all consumers.

As discussed above, the JCT staff assumes no behavioral response for most distributional analyses. This is not problematic when elasticities are small. Even when demand elasticities are thought to be relatively large, however, they are seldom reported by income class. Faced with these data constraints, the JCT staff chose the most workable alternative.[15] But this approach also makes it easy to ensure consistency of treatment between narrow and broad-based consumption taxes. In assuming low (compensated) demand elasticities, we implicitly assume that indifference curves are close to Leontief (right angle). This means that a tax on a certain share of consumption has approximately the same effect on welfare as a tax on all consumption at the same rate, adjusted for that share. A 10 percent tax on half of an individual's consumption, for example, has approximately the same effect on that person's well-being as a 5 percent tax on all consumption. We then analyze this equivalent broad-based tax using the same method as before.

Of course, one reason narrow-based consumption taxes have distributional consequences potentially different from broad-based taxes

---

14. To see this, recall that in the expensing case, full deductibility of investment expenditures is equivalent to exemption of the earnings of such investment from tax.

15. The use of pretax consumption ahead of after-tax consumption can also be justified by the fact that the compensated elasticity is less than the observed uncompensated value.

TABLE 9–2

DISTRIBUTIONAL EFFECTS OF A 5 CENT PER GALLON MOTOR FUELS TAX,
1993 LEVEL

Expanded Income Class	Present Law Federal Taxes (billions)	Present Law Average Tax Rate (percent)	Proposed Changes in Tax Burden (millions)	Burden Change as a Share of Income (percent)
Less than $10,000	$ 9	10.4	$ 230	0.26
10,000– 20,000	39	11.9	478	0.15
20,000– 30,000	72	17.0	609	0.14
30,000– 40,000	86	19.1	573	0.13
40,000– 50,000	93	20.9	567	0.13
50,000– 75,000	201	22.3	953	0.11
75,000–100,000	120	24.8	499	0.10
100,000–200,000	142	22.8	397	0.07
200,000 and over	168	30.2	283	0.05
Total, all taxpayers	$930	22.1	$4,589	0.11

SOURCE: See table 9–1.

is that individuals in different income classes may consume proportionately more or less of the taxed goods. This important aspect is incorporated into the analysis by treating individuals in each income class as if they faced a broad-based tax at a rate equal to the nominal rate (10 percent in the example above) multiplied by their share of consumption of the taxed goods. If, for example, the consumption of the taxed goods makes up one-half of total consumption of one income group but only one-tenth of that of another, the first group is treated as facing a broad-based tax of 5 percent, and the second as facing a broad-based tax of 1 percent. The burden on each group is then calculated separately, using the appropriate effective broad-based tax rate.[16]

Table 9–2 presents the distribution of the change in burden resulting from an increase in the motor fuels excise tax of 5 cents per gallon. Such a proposal was enacted as part of the Omnibus Budget Reconciliation Act of 1990, and a similar proposal (4.3 cents per gallon on a slightly different base) was enacted as part of OBRA 1993.

---

16. When the tax applies to business use as well as to final consumption, a similar conversion procedure is adopted. The burden associated with final consumption of the taxed goods is computed as above. For the portion of taxed goods that are consumed by businesses, burdens on final consumers of products from such businesses are assigned, data permitting.

Conclusions

The JCT distribution methodology represents a compromise. While the JCT always strives to provide good economic analysis, the staff prepares its analyses subject to constraints. The staff is asked to provide many distributional analyses, often on the extremely tight schedule imposed by congressional consideration of legislative proposals. In addition, good economics does not help produce informed policy decisions if it is not understandable to the policy maker. The need to provide comprehensible as well as comprehensive analysis has guided recent decisions regarding the classification of individuals (that is, in defining the income classifier) and the time horizon over which the analysis is performed. In contrast, in an attempt to be more consistent and accurate, a new methodology of distributing the burden of consumption taxes has been devised, despite the fact that it is not necessarily coincident with intuitive notions held by some policy makers. As the JCT staff's ability to impute confidently more information grows, as policy makers' appreciation of economic analysis increases, or as the needs of policy makers change, it would be appropriate to reassess the compromises that have been made to arrive at the present JCT methodology.

10
Tax Incidence Analysis for Policy Makers
Edgar K. Browning

This chapter presents commentary on specific aspects of the publication of the Joint Committee on Taxation, *Methodology and Issues in Measuring Changes in the Distribution of Tax Burdens*, hereafter referred to as *JCT*. The critical nature of these comments should not, however, be interpreted as a generally negative reaction to *JCT*. Indeed, there is much more that I agree with than that I disagree with. But I will focus on those important areas of disagreement.

Economic Burden of Tax Changes

JCT describes procedures intended to estimate the economic burden of tax changes. The economic burden is not the same as the additional tax revenue collected; instead, it is the additional tax revenue plus the additional excess burden produced by the tax change. The approach adopted to estimate economic burden is to use the static-revenue change (the amount of additional revenue if there is no behavioral response). *JCT* claims that "this methodology overestimates the loss of economic well-being [the economic burden] due to a tax increase and understates the improvement in economic well-being due to a tax reduction" (p. 28). As a matter of theory, this is untrue: the static-revenue change of a tax increase can understate, overstate, or equal the economic burden. In a critically important area, however—the taxation of labor income—the static-revenue change of a tax increase always underestimates the economic burden (in direct contrast to the position of *JCT*), and the underestimate is substantial, as I will explain.

In the analysis of the effect of taxes on labor income, *JCT* assumes that labor supply does not change at all in response to tax changes. In this case, the static-revenue change is equal to the actual revenue change, and that is the measure of economic burden. But the economic burden (of a tax increase) is clearly larger than this because the economic burden is the sum of the additional tax revenue and the additional excess burden. There will always be a positive additional excess burden from a higher tax as long as the *compensated* labor-supply elasticity is positive, even if the actual labor-supply response is zero. The uncompensated labor-supply response governs the actual revenue change, and with opposing income and substitution effects it is possible that there will be no change in labor supply so that the static-revenue change equals the actual revenue change. The compensated labor-supply response (including only the substitution effect), however, determines the change in excess burden, and with a positive compensated elasticity higher tax rates always produce an additional excess burden.

In the case of an excise tax, from the analysis of which JCT deduces the above incorrect generalization, it is possible that the economic burden is smaller than the static-revenue change, as stated. The difference between this tax and a labor income tax is that for an excise tax the income effect of the tax tends to reduce consumption of the taxed good (assuming it is a normal good) and therefore to reduce tax revenue from a preexisting tax. With a labor income tax, however, the income effect tends to increase supply of the taxed good and therefore to increase tax revenue. As a result, the use of the uncompensated product demand curve (as in figure 1, JCT) overstates the additional excess burden of a tax increase for an excise tax, while the uncompensated labor supply curve understates the additional excess burden of a tax increase for a labor tax. But even in the case of an excise tax, the static-revenue change will not necessarily be larger than the economic burden. The reason is that an excise tax also affects labor supply (in addition to the consumption of the taxed good), and JCT does not take into account the effect on labor supply (implicitly assuming that the compensated effect on labor supply is zero). Generally, a higher excise tax will increase the excess burden of preexisting labor income taxes, and adding this to the excess burden in the product market makes it possible (in my view, likely) that the economic burden will be larger than the static-revenue change.

Taxes on labor income (principally, the federal individual income tax and payroll taxes) produce the overwhelming bulk of federal revenue, so it is important to recognize that in this case JCT's proposed measure of economic burden (the static-revenue change, assuming no change in actual labor supply)[1] always understates the true economic

---

1. The static-revenue change can overstate the economic burden if there is a large enough reduction in actual labor supply.

burden of a tax increase. Moreover, the magnitude of understatement is substantial, as the following examples suggest.

Consider the case of a one-percentage-point increase (from 15 to 16 percent) in the first-bracket rate of the federal individual income tax, and let us examine the effect on a family with an income of $25,000 (assumed to be entirely labor income). Assume that the sum of the standard deduction and personal exemptions is $15,000. Then if there is no change in actual labor supply, additional tax revenue will be $100, and this is also the static-revenue estimate. The economic burden on the family is this $100 plus the additional excess burden produced by the increase in the marginal tax rate.

The additional excess burden depends primarily on two factors: the initial effective marginal tax rate and the compensated labor supply elasticity. For the tax rate, it is important to include all tax rates that fall on labor income, not just federal taxes; the rate must also incorporate any implicit marginal tax rates in transfer programs, if applicable. To get an idea of the magnitude involved, assume this family has two children and so is eligible for the earned-income tax credit (EITC) as it will apply in 1996 (the cutoff point for eligibility will then be $27,000). Initially, the family will be subject to a 21 percent marginal tax rate from the EITC, a 15 percent rate from the federal income tax, a 15.3 percent rate from the social security payroll tax, a 3.5 percent rate from state income taxes,[2] and a rate of approximately 5 percent from sales and excise taxes. Thus, the initial effective marginal tax rate is about 60 percent. For the compensated labor supply elasticity, I will assume a value of 0.3; this is approximately a weighted average of empirical estimates of different demographic groups.

The one-percentage-point increase in the federal tax rate therefore increases the effective marginal rate from 60 to 61 percent, which implies that the net-of-tax wage rate falls by 2.5 percent (from 40 to 39 percent of the market wage). A compensated elasticity of 0.3 implies that the compensated reduction in labor supply is 0.75 percent, so (with a given market wage) the compensated reduction in earnings is $187.50 (0.75 percent of $25,000). The difference between the compensated reduction in earnings and the value of additional leisure from the reduction in work is the additional excess burden. Additional leisure can be valued at the average net-of-tax wage rate, 39.5 percent, so

---

2. State income tax revenue was about 23 percent of federal income tax revenue in 1992. I assume that on average the applicable rate is 23 percent of the federal rate of 15 percent.

the compensated value of additional leisure is $74 and the additional excess burden is $113.50.[3]

In this example, the true economic burden on the family is $213.50, more than double the static (and actual) revenue change that JCT proposes as an estimate of the economic burden.

As a second example, consider a tax on the wealthy similar to that enacted in the budget bill in 1993. Suppose that the marginal tax rate increases by one percentage point on income in excess of $140,000. Since about half of all families with incomes above $140,000 have incomes below $180,000, let us consider a family with this median income of $180,000. Assume the same elasticity of 0.3 as before, but in this case the initial effective marginal tax rate is taken to be 45 percent.[4] Making the same calculations as above, we find that the additional excess burden is 112 percent of the static revenue increase, so the true economic burden is more than double the JCT estimate of economic burden in this case also.

Of course, I have chosen examples where the true economic burden is much larger than the static-revenue increase, and in many, perhaps most, instances the true economic burden is likely to be smaller than in these examples. (It would be easy, however, to use examples where the economic burden is even larger: in the above two examples, the true economic burden for families at $20,000 and $160,000 is more than three times the static revenue increase.) In general, the economic burden will be substantially larger than the static-revenue increase. Elsewhere, for example, I have examined the case of a proportionate increase in all federal individual income tax rates and estimated that on average the true economic burden would be 45.8 percent larger than the static revenue increase. By contrast, for an increase in the payroll tax rate, the corresponding figure is 22.9 percent.[5] These are average

---

3. The additional excess burden (as a percentage of tax revenue) can be calculated from equation (10) given in Edgar K. Browning, "On the Marginal Welfare Cost of Taxation," *American Economic Review*, vol. 77 (March 1977), pp. 11–23: $(m + 0.5dm)/(1 - m)$ times η times dm/dt. In this formula, m is the initial effective marginal tax rate, η is the compensated labor supply elasticity, dm is the change in the marginal tax rate of the tax change, and dt is the change in the average tax rate, evaluated at the initial earnings level. In the example, $dm = 0.01$ and $dt = 0.004$—since the $100 tax is 0.4 percent of the $25,000 income.

4. This is roughly the sum of the federal income tax rate (36 percent) and the Medicare payroll tax rate (2.9 percent) plus an allowance for state income taxes and sales and excise taxes.

5. See table 2 in Browning, "On the Marginal Welfare Cost of Taxation." These estimates are based on the same compensated elasticity assumed here (0.3).

figures, and in some cases there is wide variation among income classes, an important consideration in distributional analysis.

This analysis suggests a serious problem with *JCT*'s approach to the estimation of economic burden. There are two fairly obvious ways to deal with the issue. The first is to continue to use the static-revenue response as an estimate of burden but no longer claim that it approximates true economic burden. This method would be in keeping with most previous studies of tax incidence, which have traditionally ignored excess burden in their estimates of tax burdens. The problem with this solution, as *JCT* recognizes and as the above examples make clear, is that when attention is focused on tax changes in the presence of high preexisting tax rates, the additional excess burden is likely to be quite large relative to additional tax revenue, and for labor taxes that means the true economic burden is much larger than the static revenue change.

Obviously, a second way to handle this issue is to develop estimates of true economic burdens along the lines suggested by the above discussion. There are, however, a great many practical problems with implementing this solution. Foremost among these are data requirements. Estimates of initial marginal tax rates would be necessary for each family, and these rates *must* incorporate all federal, state, and local programs that impose explicit or implicit marginal tax rates. In addition, estimates of compensated labor-supply elasticities (and other elasticities for different taxes) are required, and there is no consensus in the literature about the appropriate values to use. Developing accurate estimates would clearly be no easy task.

I do think that it is important for policy makers to understand that the true economic burden of raising taxes is often substantially larger than the revenues raised. Some method of communicating that idea would be desirable.

Another issue related to the treatment of labor taxes deserves brief mention, that is, the assumption that there will be a zero change in actual labor supply in response to tax changes. *JCT* bases this assumption on the empirical literature on labor supply that generally finds quite small (uncompensated) labor-supply elasticities. I have two problems with this assumption. First, it is probably reasonable to assume that the uncompensated wage elasticity of labor supply for prime-age males is close to zero based on this literature, but this is not so for females. Empirical studies generally find positive, and often quite large, elasticities for women. For the labor force as a whole, the uncompensated elasticity is almost certainly positive, although it can still be argued that it is small enough to ignore in some cases.

Second, *JCT* seems to equate a zero uncompensated wage elasticity with a zero response to a change in the labor tax, but the two are not the same. A zero wage elasticity implies that the income and substitution effects of a change in the wage rate are equal and offsetting, but when this is the case, any progressive change in taxes on labor income will reduce labor supply. A progressive tax change results in a substitution effect that is larger relative to the income effect than does a change in the wage rate. In the example dealing with the taxation of the wealthy, suppose the household has a zero uncompensated wage elasticity that results from a positive compensated elasticity of 0.3 and a negative total income elasticity of 0.3. Because the tax change we examined changes the marginal tax rate (governing the substitution, or compensated, effect, leading to a reduction in labor) 4.5 times as much as it does the average tax rate (governing the income effect that increases labor supply), actual labor supply would fall by 78 percent as much as the compensated reduction in labor supply.

For these two reasons, in some cases it is important to consider the possibility of actual reductions in labor supply from increases in labor tax rates.

Incidence of Consumption Taxes

JCT's treatment of consumption taxes represents a bold departure from most previous work. Three specific aspects of the procedure are particularly noteworthy. First, *JCT* recognizes that many government transfers are indexed to the price level, and so recipients of these transfers will bear no burden from general consumption taxes. (Recipients of nonindexed transfers continue to bear a burden in this analysis; I will discuss this issue further.) Second, when consumption is the basis for allocation of the tax, the data set commonly used to measure consumption—the Consumer Expenditure Survey—is not employed. Instead, estimates are based on the Survey of Consumer Finances, and these estimates display much less dissaving in lower income groups. Third, consumption tax burdens are allocated not when consumption occurs but when the income that finances the consumption is earned.

JCT reports estimates illustrating the pattern of incidence produced using these assumptions in its table 3. For those not familiar with previous work in this area, let me contrast these results with those of Joseph Pechman, who followed the conventional procedure of allocating consumption taxes to annual consumption.[6] In *JCT*'s preferred approach (the [p,Y] approach), the tax burden of a hypothetical general

---

6. Joseph A. Pechman, *Who Paid the Taxes, 1966–85?* (Washington, D.C.: Brookings Institution, 1985).

consumption tax is estimated to be 3.69 percent of income for the lowest income class and 2.78 percent for the highest income class. Generally, the tax is nearly proportional to income, but with the tax rate for the lowest income class 1.33 times as great as for the top class. By contrast, for comparable low and high income classes in 1985, Pechman estimates that the tax rate of sales and excise taxes for the lowest income class is more than *six times* as great as for the top income class.[7] Moreover, Pechman finds the taxes to be strongly regressive throughout the income distribution.

These striking differences are due almost entirely to the differences in approach. If the *JCT* approach is correct, much of what has been written and is believed about the incidence of consumption taxes is simply wrong. These taxes are not highly regressive; at best, they are mildly regressive, and over most of the income distribution they are best described as proportional.

Before I comment on the *JCT* approach, I will briefly discuss the importance of this issue. For purposes of federal tax research by the JCT staff, the incidence of consumption taxes is relatively unimportant. As *JCT* points out, there is no federal general consumption tax, although the same procedure can be extended to federal excise taxes and to the evaluation of proposals for federal general consumption taxes, such as a value-added tax. Where the proper incidence of the consumption tax becomes important is in the analysis of the distributional effects of a multitude of other policy issues. Accepting the *JCT* analysis, for example, immediately means that state and local sales and excise taxes are far less regressive than they are widely believed to be. Indeed, state and local tax systems would be quite progressive if this approach is used. But the importance of the issue extends well beyond tax incidence analysis per se. Consider the incidence of the burden of pollution controls. The effects of pollution controls in specific industries are quite similar to those of excise taxes. Economists often hold that pollution controls raise consumer prices and are therefore regressive. But the *JCT* approach applies here as well and would hold pollution controls to be much less regressive than previous estimates (using annual consumption as the basis for burden distribution) have found. Indeed, it is clear that the *JCT* approach, if correct for consumption taxes, is also correct for a multitude of public policies and market phenomena, including farm price supports, trade restrictions, safety requirements, monopoly, labor unions, and so on.

---

7. See ibid., table A–4. The two income classes are the lowest decile and the top 1 percent of the population, which will roughly correspond to the lowest and highest income classes in *JCT*.

In short, our understanding of the distributional implications of a multitude of important phenomena depends on whether the *JCT* analysis is correct. I happen to believe that it is largely correct and represents a significant improvement over the conventional analysis, which will not surprise those familiar with some of my earlier work where I have advocated a similar approach.[8] My major area of disagreement with *JCT* concerns the treatment of nonindexed government transfers. *JCT* claims that recipients of nonindexed transfers bear a burden from consumption taxes, while I think these transfers should be treated as if they were indexed and therefore immune to any burden. (We agree, of course, that indexed transfers bear no tax burden.)

In a somewhat oblique approach to the argument, I begin by considering the claim by *JCT*: "A broad-based consumption tax is equivalent to a tax on wages plus a tax on income from existing capital" (p. 52). Is this statement correct when there are nonindexed government transfers? To simplify, assume there is no capital; all market earnings are wage income. *JCT* holds that the consumption tax increases the total price level by the amount of the tax and therefore results in a burden on those receiving nonindexed transfers (as well as wage earners, whose real wages decline). But does the allegedly equivalent wage tax also place a burden on nonindexed transfers? It could, but only if the wage tax results in a price level increase (that is exactly equal in magnitude to the price increase of the consumption tax). Fine—in that event the two taxes are then equivalent. But if this is the model, then the analysis of labor taxes in *JCT* is incorrect. With labor taxes, the entire burden is placed on wage earners, presumably reflecting the view that labor taxes do not increase the price level.

Consider the possibilities. If neither tax raises the price level, the *JCT* analysis of labor taxes is correct, its analysis of consumption taxes is incorrect (nonindexed transfers bear no burden if prices do not rise), and the equivalence proposition holds. If both taxes raise the price level by exactly the amount of the tax, the analysis of labor taxes is incorrect, the analysis of consumption taxes is correct, and the equivalence proposition holds. If the consumption tax raises prices and the labor tax does not, the analysis of both taxes is correct, but the equivalence proposition does not hold. Finally, if the labor tax raises

---

8. See Edgar K. Browning, "The Burden of Taxation," *Journal of Political Economy*, vol. 86 (August 1978), pp. 649–71; Edgar K. Browning and William R. Johnson, *The Distribution of the Tax Burden* (Washington, D.C.: American Enterprise Institute, 1979); and Edgar K. Browning, "Tax Incidence, Indirect Taxes, and Transfers," *National Tax Journal*, vol. 38 (December 1985), pp. 525–34.

prices and the consumption tax does not, the analysis of both taxes is wrong, and the equivalence proposition does not hold.

The only way to salvage the analysis as it stands is to hold that the consumption tax raises prices and labor taxes do not (which implies that the equivalence proposition is wrong). Is this really a satisfactory methodology? We must assume that consumption taxes raise the total price level by exactly the amount of the tax, while other indirect taxes collected from businesses do not raise the price level at all. (It must also be assumed that corporate taxes, property taxes, payroll taxes collected from employers, and so on do not affect the price level—or else the analysis of these taxes is wrong.) This is a consistent position, but it seems decidedly arbitrary. *JCT* seems to recognize this, for it states: "These assumptions are valid only if the Federal Reserve reacts differently to economically equivalent tax changes" (p. 53). To my knowledge, there is little theoretical reason or empirical evidence that supports this position.

The basic problem is that *JCT* is using a model in which the incidence of all taxes depends on what happens to the general price level. This is unavoidable once it is assumed that nonindexed transfers are constant in nominal terms, for then they bear a tax burden if the price level rises and do not if the price level does not rise, regardless of the tax being examined. Although it is not mentioned, the *JCT* analysis represents a major deviation from the accepted methodology of the analysis of tax incidence. All the seminal writers in this field—Musgrave, Harberger, Mieszkowski, Pechman, McLure, and others—have held that tax incidence depends on what happens to relative prices, not absolute prices.[9] The formal models supporting this conclusion, however, did not include government transfers, so perhaps it is time to reevaluate whether tax incidence really should be held to depend on absolute as well as on relative price changes.

As a point of departure, consider the statement by *JCT*: "When [absolute] prices rise, the value of all income falls, unless the income is specifically indexed to changes in the price level." That this is not exactly correct can be seen by considering a pure monetary inflation in a competitive economy with no government. Then, incomes rise *pari passu* with the price level even though wages, profit rates, and so on

---

9. Qualifications to this position have been noted, but they were generally thought to be of minor importance. Government transfers are not, however, of minor importance. I should also mention that, while most analysts have claimed to be using a methodology in which incidence depends only on relative prices, in actual practice they often employ tax burden allocation rules that implicitly violate this precept.

are *not* "specifically indexed to changes in the price level." Wages do not have to be specifically indexed; competitive markets lead to higher nominal wages when nominal prices rise. In other words, the institutions determining wages produce the same result *as if* wages were indexed.

Now consider nonindexed government transfers. Political institutions determine these transfers. We know much less about how political institutions work than about how competitive markets work, but it is certainly possible that during inflationary periods government will increase nonindexed transfers to preserve their real value. Indeed, it is easy to stipulate several public choice models with that outcome. All that is necessary is to assume that political decision makers care about the real value of the transfers. If decision makers make transfers adequate to raise people to the poverty line, which rises with inflation, for example, they will increase nonindexed transfers in line with increases in the price level. If so, it would be appropriate in analyzing tax incidence to treat nonindexed transfers *as if* they were indexed.

This argument is far from conclusive since it is based on models of a poorly understood political process. By way of contrast, it could be argued that when decision makers increase consumption taxes, they intend for a burden to fall on nonindexed transfers and so will not increase their nominal values when the price level rises. This is a possibility, but it raises a number of troubling issues. Because the decision makers do not control the Federal Reserve, for example, they cannot be certain of imposing a burden on nonindexed transfers with a consumption tax. If they want to be sure of placing a burden on nonindexed transfers, they could just cut the nominal benefits as part of the tax bill. Moreover, if the *intentions* of decision makers are relevant in determining the effects of a tax policy, we would have great difficulties identifying the incidence of any tax.

Thus, there is a reasonable theoretical basis for treating all government transfers as if they were indexed. This rationale would also be in line with the methodological position advocated in much of the theoretical literature, which holds that *all* government spending should be considered constant in real terms when conducting analyses of tax incidence, acknowledging that transfers are just one component of government spending. Implicitly, when the price level rises with a consumption tax, *JCT* assumes that all government spending *except* nonindexed transfers is constant in real terms. A price level rise, for example, will reduce the real value of unchanged nominal spending on schools, defense, highways, and so on in ways with important distributional implications. Since *JCT* does not mention any changes in real spending on these other nonindexed government programs, it is implicitly taking them as unchanged. I am arguing only that the same assumption be made with regard to nonindexed government transfers as is already made with respect to all other government spending.

I conclude that a reasonable, but not conclusive, theoretical basis exists for treating nonindexed transfers as indexed. But what of the empirical evidence? It is difficult to marshal empirical evidence that would directly test the approach. But several pieces of evidence are suggestive. JCT cites a study that concludes, for example, that absolute prices go up following introduction of consumption taxes (principally, value-added taxes) in other countries but that prices did not rise by the amount of the tax. This partially contradicts the JCT assumption about the price-level adjustment to consumption taxes. But presumably the study does not identify what happened to the nominal value of government transfers.

Several relevant studies have investigated the distributional impact of general inflation. Typically, these studies find that lower income classes do not lose, and may even gain slightly, during inflationary periods, suggesting that nonindexed transfers are increased at least as much as prices.[10] But these studies do not distinguish general inflation from one-shot tax-induced price increases, so they are not conclusive.

When I have discussed this issue, the most common objection I have heard is based on the well-known fact that Aid to Families with Dependent Children (AFDC) benefits, which are not indexed, have declined significantly in real terms over the past two decades. Yet properly interpreted, I believe this experience supports my position. Robert Moffitt concludes in a recent article:

> A statistical analysis of the trend suggests that real welfare benefits [that is, AFDC] have declined not because of a conservative shift in voter preferences but because state legislatures have allowed federally-financed Food Stamp benefits and federally-subsidized Medicaid benefits to substitute for AFDC. The data reveal that the total transfer, including all benefit types, has grown in real terms directly in line with income growth.[11]

---

10. See John L. Palmer, "Inflation, Unemployment, and Poverty" (Ph.D. diss., Stanford University, 1971); and Joseph J. Minarik, "Who Wins, Who Loses from Inflation," *Brookings Bulletin*, vol. 15 (Summer 1978), pp. 6–10. That these studies covered periods before social security benefits were indexed strengthens their relevance.

11. Robert Moffitt, "Has State Redistribution Policy Grown More Conservative?" *National Tax Journal*, vol. 43 (June 1990), p. 123.

In short, inflation did not lead to lower real AFDC benefits; the introduction and expansion of other federal transfers are responsible for state governments' reducing these benefits. Political decision makers have increased the total benefit package in line with price increases, consistent with the type of political model I mentioned earlier. Of course, the federal government did not introduce a general consumption tax in this period, so how state governments would have responded to that is not clear. But the federal government did impose a variety of regulations, from pollution controls to safety regulations, which are closely analogous to consumption taxes, and yet the real benefit package for recipients of nonindexed transfers did not decline.

My conclusion is that *JCT* should treat all government transfers as indexed. One very important methodological benefit of that approach is that it makes tax incidence independent of absolute price effects (with some remaining, but relatively unimportant, qualifications), so it would not be necessary to make different, and largely arbitrary, assumptions regarding the effects of different taxes on the general price level.

Many people balk at treating all government transfers as indexed because of the implications of that assumption. The disquieting implication for many is that consumption taxes are progressive in their incidence when all transfers are treated as indexed (and the consumption data used by *JCT* are employed). But *JCT* has already traveled far down the road leading to this conclusion, and I hope that it will take the final step and can convince others of the essential correctness of this analysis.

Distributional Analysis and Equity

Why should we be concerned about the distributional effects of tax changes? According to *JCT*: "Distributional analysis shows policy makers the equity effects of a proposal" (p. 2). Of course, distributional analysis does not *show* the equity effects: it only provides information that may be helpful to individuals in making judgments about equity. To serve that role, the tax incidence estimates must not only be based on the best theory and data available but also be presented with enough information about the characteristics of the people affected that meaningful equity judgments can be made. Thus, *JCT* devotes a lot of space to considering the best definition of income (the "income classifier," discussed in chapter IV) and the type of household unit (the "reporting unit," discussed in chapter V) to serve as a basis for the presentation of the results.

In the end, I do not think that the way *JCT* has chosen to present the results is as illuminating as it could be. Consider a simple example where we are examining the effects of a tax change on two households, A and B. In the *JCT* format, we would be told that A has an expanded income of $10,000, that B has an expanded income of $30,000, and that the tax change places a burden of 1 percent on A ($100) and 2 percent on B ($600). Is the tax change equitable?

Would your judgment about equity be different if you also know the following? Household A is a single graduate student in engineering (making straight A's) with a fellowship of $10,000 (which is, I assume, included in adjusted gross income (AGI) and hence in expanded income) and a government-subsidized loan of $10,000 (which is not counted in expanded income, even though according to the Congressional Budget Office about 40 percent of such "loans" are really outright grants). Household A has $20,000 in consumption. Household B is composed of four persons, two middle-aged adults working full time and two children. Its labor earnings are $27,000 (which by including employer payroll taxes and other additions yields $30,000 in expanded income), which after taxes and work-related expenses leaves it with $20,000 in consumption. Is it fair for household A to pay an additional tax of $100 and household B to pay an additional tax of $600?

This is an extreme example, of course. But the basic point is valid: we require enormously more information than simply "expanded income" to make a reasonably informed equity judgment. When confronted with tabular presentations of the sort contained in *JCT*, with households grouped into different income classes, there is a strong temptation to assume that the households in different classes are similar in all relevant respect except for the differences in income. If that were true, the table would contain enough information for an informed equity judgment. But of course it is not true; there are systematic and large differences in characteristics of households within and among income classes that most people would consider highly relevant in making an equity judgment. It could be argued that the users of the *JCT* estimates already know this, so it is unnecessary to present this information. But I doubt if this is so. Although one might optimistically think that policy makers are familiar with distributional information, individual taxpayers are not, and they are part of the intended audience (p. 107).

What information is necessary to make an informed equity judgment? We can never have enough information to make a fully informed decision, and people will certainly differ on what sort of information is the most important. But a reasonable short list might include, for each income class: family size and composition, age, market earnings, government transfers, initial tax burden, and hours of work per year.

.In making equity judgments, for example, I think it is helpful to know that the top quintile of households works about six times as many hours per year as the bottom quintile. It is also instructive to know that 70 to 90 percent of the total income of the bottom quintile is in the form of government transfers and that the top 10 percent of federal income taxpayers already pay 60 percent of total federal income taxes.

While *JCT* provides helpful estimates of initial average federal tax rates by income class in one table (see table 1, *JCT*), it should also include initial government transfers. I do not think it is possible to make an informed equity judgment of a tax *change* without knowing the existing effect of taxes *and* transfers. Indeed, a knowledge of the incidence of transfers by income class can lead to the conclusion that for the lowest income class, taxes and tax changes are relatively unimportant, because total transfers (federal, state, and local) are perhaps five times as large as the total tax burden for the lowest quintile. The distributional outcome for this class is therefore much more affected by transfer policy than by tax policy.

The *JCT* definition of expanded income also suffers from one enormous defect, in my view. *Expanded income does not include any government welfare transfers.* (It does include social insurance transfers.) This means that expanded income greatly understates the economic resources available to the lower income classes. To gain an idea of the magnitudes involved, consider that government spending on welfare programs in 1993 was approximately $250 billion.[12] Most of the benefits from this spending go to households in the lowest quintile (using the Census Bureau definition of households). In contrast, the total expanded income of the lowest quintile in *JCT* tabulations is $162 billion (see table 10–11). Thus, it is possible that the actual income for the lowest quintile is twice as much as *JCT* records. This fact is relevant not only in judging the neediness of these households but also in determining the tax burdens reported by *JCT.* Since tax burdens are reported as a percentage of expanded income, tax burdens if expressed as a percentage of total income including welfare transfers would be much smaller.

In its discussion of the definition of income, *JCT* approvingly re-

---

12. See Edgar K. Browning and Jacquelene M. Browning, *Public Finance and the Price System* (New York: Macmillan Publishing Company, 1994), chap. 8. I have extrapolated based on estimates of 1991 spending levels. The spending figure is based on the six major welfare programs (AFDC, Supplemental Security Income, EITC, housing assistance, Medicaid, and food stamps) plus fifteen smaller programs (including Head Start, Pell grants, and low-income energy assistance).

fers to the Haig-Simons definition and suggests that it is attempting to approximate this definition (p. 83). But every writer of whom I am aware interprets the Haig-Simons concept to include government welfare transfers. After all, government transfers either provide consumption to recipients or add to their net worth and therefore seem to satisfy this definition. Certainly the major studies of tax incidence have included transfers in their measures of income, insofar as data availability permitted.

JCT offers two reasons for not including welfare transfers in its income definition. First: "Transfers can be interpreted as negative taxes; they do not, therefore, belong in a pre-tax income concept" (p. 94). Although this pretax concept of income is not the Haig-Simons concept or that used in other incidence studies, it is possible to view transfers consistently as negative taxes. But if they are not included in the income concept, they must be included in the measure of preexisting tax burden as negative elements, and it becomes all the more important to show the preexisting tax burden in every table investigating a tax change. Consider a household with $5,000 in expanded income, $10,000 in government transfers, and $1,000 in initial tax burden. This could be reported, faithful to the above quotation, as pretax income of $5,000 and initial tax liability of $-\$9,000$. But consider a tax change that places an additional burden of $1,000 on the household. *JCT* would report the tax change as imposing an additional tax burden of 20 percent on the household with an income of $5,000. While consistent, I believe it is misleading; it is certainly misleading unless the initial $-\$9,000$ tax burden is identified, since readers would assume that the household had only $5,000 out of which to pay the additional tax. Most studies have treated this household as having a pretax (but after-transfer) income of $15,000, an initial tax liability of $1,000, and the tax change as imposing an additional burden of 6.7 percent. I think this is far more revealing of what is actually going on.

Thus, this argument does not provide a reason for neglecting transfers altogether; it means only that it is possible to be consistent by including them as negative taxes in the initial tax burden. I do not believe *JCT* actually does this in table 1 where it identifies the initial tax burden. Welfare transfers appear to be ignored altogether rather than included as negative taxes, but I could be mistaken. The important point, however, is that the transfers must be included as negative initial taxes if any meaningful equity judgment is to be made. I prefer, in line with previous studies, to view transfers as part of pretax income.

JCT's second argument for not including government transfers in expanded income is that the transfers go largely to nonfilers of tax returns (p. 94). This raises another issue concerning whether meaningful equity judgments can be made: apparently, the population of households covered in most of the tables includes only those who file federal individual income tax returns. This means that millions of low-income households are not represented at all; the lowest income class does not include those with the lowest incomes but only those tax filers with the lowest incomes. Data considerations aside, this seems to me to be totally unacceptable. With some exceptions (where special attention is explicitly given to subsamples of the population), I think all tabulations should cover the entire population.

Actually, *JCT* does apparently base estimates on the entire population in some cases (p. 96). (It uses Current Population Survey data to augment the tax return data by statistical matching.) It does this in analyzing proposals "that would affect persons not currently required to file tax returns" (p. 96). Apparently, this was done in the case of table 3 dealing with a general consumption tax. (Note that income is identified as "adjusted income" in this table, whereas it is identified as "expanded income" in other tables.) I wonder how many readers of *JCT* were aware that the under-$10,000 income class in table 3 represented a totally different group of households than does the same income class in other tables and that income was measured using a different definition.

Clearly, in distributional analysis of taxes affecting nonfilers, there is no argument for not counting government welfare transfers; it is all the more important to recognize them in this case. I am not sure which, if any, are counted in table 3; but they are not all counted, and if they are incorporated as negative taxes, the results of table 3 are misleading.

Thus, *JCT* is able to develop estimates for the entire population. I suggest that this should be done for every tax change, even if there are no direct effects on nonfilers. When there are no direct effects on nonfilers, this is pertinent information. Moreover, it would be difficult to make comparisons among different tax policies if some tabulations covered only filers and others covered the entire population. If the entire population is covered in the tabulations, however, counting all government welfare transfers and presenting the results in an understandable fashion are especially important.

I now return to *JCT*'s second argument for not including welfare transfers—that when analyzing tax changes affecting filers it is legitimate not to count government welfare transfers because filers receive none (or almost none) of these transfers. Is it factually true that filers receive almost none of the $250 billion in government welfare transfers? I do not know, but I have significant doubts. While a case along these lines could have been made before the advent of the earned-income tax credit, now households with very low earnings are required to file federal income tax returns to receive EITC benefits. Moreover, many of these households are also eligible to receive food stamps, Pell grants, and a number of other smaller programs. Nor is it even clear that the entire AFDC population does not file tax returns. Although 94 percent of that population does not work while receiving benefits from this program, there is a lot of turnover in the program. Consider this possibility: a female-headed household is on AFDC the first six months of the year (also receiving food stamps, Medicaid, and housing assistance); the head of household then goes to work the last six months of the year, during which time the household receives EITC and food stamp benefits. This household files a tax return to receive EITC benefits. In the JCT methodology, this household's expanded income includes only its wage earnings, potentially ignoring 80 percent or so of its real income.

My general conclusions are that the entire population should be represented in every analysis and that all government welfare transfers should be counted as income. I recognize that the data problems associated with allocating all government welfare transfers to persons are likely to make it impossible to do this accurately at an individual level. Given the sheer magnitude of these transfers, however, it would be better to make a rough imputation to entire income classes (for example, assume that 70 percent of the $250 billion goes to the bottom quintile) than to ignore them altogether. In addition, I reiterate that it would be useful to provide information on age, work effort, and so on for each income class.

Finally, I will make a few remarks on the use of lifetime relative to annual measures of income in the analysis of the tax incidence. JCT recognizes that a lifetime analysis offers many advantages and is often a better basis for making equity judgments. I tend to concur. The major problem is that the data are not available to do an accurate lifetime analysis. I would like to offer an alternative: present the results of the analysis for a subset of the population containing only married-couple families aged thirty-five to forty-five. This is not suggested because married-couple families are in themselves an interesting subsample but because I believe the results will more closely approximate the true lifetime effects for the entire population. Looking at a single age group removes at least part of the normal life-cycle variation in incomes, and looking at a particular and common household type removes much of the systematic variation in household types that complicates the making of equity judgments. There would also be less variation in work effort among income classes than is found in the full population. While the results would still differ from a true lifetime analysis, they will be closer to the lifetime effects than when the entire population is included in the analysis.

11

Using Generational Accounting to Assess Fiscal Sustainability and Generational Equity

Alan J. Auerbach, Jagadeesh Gokhale, and Laurence J. Kotlikoff

The intergenerational distribution of fiscal burdens is probably the single most important aspect of fiscal policy. It determines not only how the government uses taxes and transfers to redistribute directly between the old, the young, and the unborn but also how the government indirectly redistributes across generations, by changing the economy's time path of wages and interest rates. Generational policy affects these time paths by altering the amounts that current generations can afford to consume and thereby altering current aggregate consumption and saving. When aggregate saving changes, aggregate domestic investment typically changes as well. This changes the amount of capital per worker, which alters the returns to labor and capital—namely, the wage and interest rate.

The intergenerational distribution of fiscal burdens is also intimately connected to the sustainability of current fiscal policy and the feasibility of alternative fiscal policies. A fiscal policy that envisions burdening future generations to the same degree as current generations may not produce enough net taxes (taxes paid net of transfer payments received) to balance the government's intertemporal budget constraint. In this case, the policy will not be sustainable. The government may respond to the knowledge that its current policy is unsustainable by proposing to begin dealing with the problem at some future date. But, as generational accounting will show, such temporiz-

This chapter draws heavily on Office of Management and Budget (1994). We thank Robert Kilpatrick, Barry Anderson, Robert Anderson, Bruce Baker, and other economists at OMB for their collaboration. The opinions expressed herein are the authors' and not necessarily those of the Federal Reserve Bank of Cleveland or of the Federal Reserve System.

181

ing may be infeasible, because it implies impossibly high fiscal burdens on future generations.

Notwithstanding its importance, the explicit documentation of generational policy is a relatively recent phenomenon. Indeed, *generational accounting*—the direct measurement of the fiscal burdens placed on different generations—is only five years old.[1] Absent direct measures of generational policy, governments have relied on their official debts as a proxy for the burden being passed to the next generation. The problem with this practice is that what governments classify as official debts is fundamentally a matter of language, not economics.[2] As such, the size of the government's official debt, and its changes over time—the deficit—need bear no necessary relationship to the government's underlying generational policy. In fact, during the postwar period, most generational policy in the United States and other countries in the Organization for Economic Cooperation and Development has been conducted through the expansion of so-called pay-as-you-go social security systems, which have had no direct effect on officially reported government debt.

This chapter describes generational accounting and uses it to understand the generational effects of the 1993 Omnibus Budget Reconciliation Act, to assess the current stance of U.S. generational policy, to assess the generational implications of President Clinton's health reform proposal, to compare the lifetime net tax treatment of different generations, and to compare U.S. generational policy with that of Norway. These analyses illustrate the range of potential uses of generational accounting. Indeed, it can be used to examine the generational implications of any and all fiscal policies, including so-called revenue neutral changes in the tax base. The larger question with respect to generational accounting is not its capacity to gauge generational policies, but rather whether politicians in the United States and abroad will begin to use it in a systematic manner in formulating their fiscal policies.

---

1. Alan J. Auerbach, Jagadeesh Gokhale, and Laurence J. Kotlikoff, "Generational Accounts: A Meaningful Alternative to Deficit Accounting," in David Bradford, ed., *Tax Policy and the Economy*, vol. 5 (Cambridge, Mass.: MIT Press, 1991), pp. 55–110; Laurence J. Kotlikoff, *Generational Accounting—Knowing Who Pays, and When, for What We Spend* (New York, Free Press, 1992).

2. See Laurence J. Kotlikoff, "Deficit Delusion," *The Public Interest*, no. 84 (June 1986), pp. 53–65; Alan J. Auerbach and Laurence J. Kotlikoff, *Dynamic Fiscal Policy* (Cambridge: Cambridge University Press, 1987); and Laurence J. Kotlikoff, "From Deficit Delusion to the Fiscal Balance Rule—Looking for an Economically Meaningful Way to Assess Fiscal Policy, *Journal of Economics*, supplement 7 (1993), pp. 17–41.

The Nature of Generational Accounts

Government cash-flow budgets normally measure receipts and outlays for one year at a time, and they usually show these estimates for only a few years into the future. Generational accounts, in contrast, look many decades ahead; they classify taxes paid and transfers received—such as social security, Medicare, and food stamps—according to the generation that pays or receives the money. For an existing generation, they estimate its taxes and transfers year by year over its entire remaining lifespan. They summarize these amounts for that generation in terms of one number—the present value of its entire annual series of average future tax payments, net of transfers received.

For future generations, generational accounts estimate the net payments based on the proposition that the government's bills will have to be paid either by people who are now alive or by future generations. They calculate how much future generations will have to pay on average to the government, above the amounts they will receive in transfers, if the government's total spending is not reduced from the projected path and if the people now alive do not pay more than projected.

Defined more precisely, generational accounts measure, as of a particular base year, the present value of the average future taxes that a member of each given generation is estimated to pay to the government, minus the present value of the average future transfers that a member is estimated to receive. This difference is called the "net payment" in the following discussion. A generation is defined as all the males or females born in a given year.

Generational accounts can be used to make two types of comparison. First, they can be used to compare the lifetime net payments by future generations with those by the generation of people just born and with those by different generations of people born in the past. The lifetime net payments by generations born in the past are based on estimates of actual taxes paid and transfer payments received in past years up through 1992, as well as projections of taxes to be paid and transfer payments to be received in the future. Second, generational accounts can be used to compare the effects of actual or proposed policy changes on the remaining lifetime net payments of generations currently alive and on future generations.

Generational accounts include the taxes and transfers of all levels of government alike—federal, state, and local. But they reflect only taxes paid to the government and transfers received. They do not impute to particular generations the value of the government purchases of goods and services made to provide them with education, highways, national defense, and other services. Therefore, they do not show the full net benefit or burden that any generation receives from government fiscal policy as a whole, although they can show a generation's net benefit or burden from a particular policy change that affects only taxes and transfers. In the future, it may be feasible to impute the value of certain types of government purchases, such as education, to specific generations.

Generational accounting does not, as yet, incorporate any feedback of policy on the economy's growth and interest rates. Feedback effects can be significant, but they generally occur slowly, so their impact on the discounted values used in the generational accounts may be small. Moreover, their inclusion would simply reinforce the conclusions derived here. The reason is that policies that decrease the net payment by current generations and increase the net payment by future generations raise current consumption and reduce current saving and investment. This in turn means lower real wage growth and higher real interest rates, which on balance harm future generations.

Generational accounting divides the people born in the same year into only two categories, males and females, each designated a "generation." This is an important distinction, for males and females differ significantly in characteristics such as lifetime earnings and longevity. It does not reveal differences with respect to other characteristics, however, such as income level or race. Nor does it reveal the wide diversity among individuals within any grouping. The categories would be expanded if more data were available.

Construction of Generational Accounts

Generational accounting is based on the present value budget constraint of the government sector. In simple terms, this constraint says that the government must ultimately pay for its purchases of goods and services with resources it obtains from current and future generations or with its current assets (net of debt). If current generations pay less in taxes (net of transfers received) to finance government purchases, future generations will have to pay more.

More precisely, the government's present value constraint says that, at any given time, the present value of the government's future purchases of goods and services cannot exceed the sum of three items: (1) the present value of future taxes to be paid (net of transfers received) by existing generations (that is, the sum of their generational accounts multiplied by the number of people in each generation); (2) the present value of taxes to be paid (net of transfers received) by future generations; and (3) the value of government assets that yield income, less the government debt. Generational accounting estimates the present value of the government's purchases of goods and services and the amounts (1) and (3). Amount (2), the present value of taxes to be paid by all future generations (net of transfers received), is calculated as the present value of future government purchases minus amounts (1) and (3).

The generational accounts for future generations are derived from the aggregate amount (2). The aggregate present value net payment by future generations is divided on an even basis among all future generations in such a way that the average net payment by the members of each generation keeps pace with the economy's growth in productivity. Thus, one single (growth-adjusted) average figure stands as the generational account for all future generations of a given sex. Because the generational account is calculated indirectly from the above aggregates, it can be shown only as a single number and cannot be divided among specific taxes and transfers.

The Underlying Calculations

The calculation of the generational accounts is a three-step process. The first step entails projecting each currently living generation's average taxes and transfers to each future year in which at least some member of the generation will be alive. The second step converts these projected average taxes and transfers into an actuarial present value, using assumptions for the discount rate and the probability that the generation's members will be alive in each of the future years. The sum of these present values, with transfers subtracted from taxes, is the generational account or "net payment" for existing generations shown in the first column of tables 11–1 and 11–2. The third step is to estimate the other terms of the present value constraint explained in the previous section so as to derive the average net payment by future generations. The calculations are based on projections to the year 2200.

Projection of Taxes and Transfers. The projection of average future taxes and transfers begins with the national totals of all federal, state, and local taxes and transfers, as reported by the national income and product accounts (NIPA) for calendar year 1992. (All years in this section are calendar years, unless otherwise stated.) Employee retirement and veterans' benefits paid by government are considered a form of employee compensation and are classified as the purchases of a service rather than as transfer payments.

The base-year NIPA totals are distributed to all existing generations, as defined by age and sex, based on the corresponding distribu-

TABLE 11-1
Generational Accounts for Males at Present Value of Taxes and Transfers
(in thousands of dollars)

Generation's Age in 1992	Net Tax Payment	Taxes Paid				Transfers Received		
		Labor income taxes	Capital income taxes	Payroll taxes	Excise taxes	Social security	Health	Welfare
0	78.4	32.2	7.9	34.7	30.2	6.8	16.2	3.6
5	89.3	41.3	10.1	44.6	36.8	8.6	19.1	4.6
10	124.8	52.6	12.9	56.9	41.3	10.3	22.7	5.9
15	157.2	67.1	16.6	72.8	47.4	11.9	27.3	7.6
20	187.7	80.8	21.0	86.2	51.4	13.3	31.0	9.2
25	203.0	86.2	25.2	96.7	52.2	16.4	33.0	9.9
30	201.6	87.8	30.2	98.5	51.4	20.1	34.7	9.4

Age								
35	192.4	84.5	36.1	83.2	50.4	25.2	37.9	8.7
40	170.9	77.2	40.8	86.4	49.4	31.7	42.3	8.0
45	132.5	64.9	43.5	72.0	46.7	39.8	47.5	7.2
50	81.0	49.6	44.0	56.2	42.8	50.4	53.6	6.5
55	19.5	32.7	42.2	36.6	37.8	63.7	60.2	5.8
60	−43.9	17.5	38.9	19.6	32.2	80.4	86.7	5.1
65	−94.1	6.2	34.3	6.9	26.9	80.6	73.4	4.4
70	−96.5	2.5	27.1	2.9	21.5	82.7	86.1	3.8
75	−92.9	1.2	18.2	1.3	16.4	89.0	57.8	3.2
80	−79.4	0.6	9.2	0.7	11.5	52.0	47.2	2.2
85	−89.4	0.3	—	0.3	7.9	39.4	37.5	1.0
90	−11.6	—	—	—	1.7	6.9	6.4	—
Future generations	177.1	—	—	—	—	—	—	—
Percentage difference in net tax payment: future generations and age zero	126.0	—	—	—	—	—	—	—

SOURCE: Authors' calculations.

TABLE 11-2

GENERATIONAL ACCOUNTS FOR FEMALES AT PRESENT VALUE OF TAXES AND TRANSFERS
(in thousands of dollars)

Generation's Age in 1992	Net Tax Payment	Taxes Paid				Transfers Received		
		Labor income taxes	Capital income taxes	Payroll taxes	Excise taxes	Social security	Health	Welfare
0	44.1	16.6	8.4	18.0	29.2	6.4	13.1	8.6
5	54.8	21.3	10.8	23.0	34.2	8.1	15.5	11.0
10	67.3	27.1	13.8	29.4	39.3	9.7	18.6	14.0
15	82.5	34.4	17.7	37.5	44.5	11.1	22.6	17.9
20	96.9	40.7	22.3	44.6	48.0	12.4	25.8	20.5
25	101.5	42.1	27.3	46.2	49.1	15.4	29.4	18.5
30	96.9	39.5	32.2	43.5	49.0	18.9	33.4	15.0

35	87.8	36.3	37.3	40.0	46.9	23.7	39.1	11.9
40	69.1	31.5	40.5	34.9	47.8	29.9	46.6	9.1
45	39.7	25.1	41.4	27.8	45.4	37.9	55.3	6.8
50	2.4	18.1	40.2	20.2	41.5	46.4	64.1	5.2
55	−40.2	11.8	36.1	13.0	37.0	62.0	73.9	4.1
60	−86.3	8.0	34.9	6.8	31.8	79.2	83.2	3.5
65	−122.5	2.2	29.5	2.4	26.6	88.4	91.6	3.1
70	−124.6	0.9	20.7	1.0	21.7	81.4	84.6	2.8
75	−117.9	0.4	11.4	0.5	16.5	89.1	75.2	2.4
80	−100.5	0.2	4.3	0.2	12.1	54.1	61.2	2.0
85	−79.3	0.1	—	0.1	9.2	39.9	47.1	1.6
90	−11.3	—	—	—	1.6	5.9	6.7	0.3
Future generations	99.6	—	—	—	—	—	—	—
Percentage difference in net tax payment: future generations and age zero	126.0	—	—	—	—	—	—	—

SOURCE: Authors' calculations.

tions in cross-section survey data. These surveys include the Survey of Income and Program Participation by the Bureau of the Census, the Survey of Consumer Expenditures by the Bureau of Labor Statistics, the Survey of Consumer Finances by the Federal Reserve, and the Current Population Survey by the Bureau of the Census. Those taxes not directly paid by persons and so not appearing in these surveys, such as the corporation income tax, are allocated. Since generational accounting attributes taxes and transfers to individuals, household taxes and transfers are attributed to the individuals in the household. No special imputations are made to children, but the cross-section surveys impute some consumption to children, and the taxes on that consumption would be attributed to the children. The attribution rules affect the values of the baseline accounts but are not likely to alter the generational implications of policy changes.

The distribution of average taxes and transfers by age and sex in the future is adjusted for growth and projected policy. In the case of federal taxes and non-Medicare transfers for 1993–2004, projected aggregate amounts are distributed by age and sex. These projected amounts correspond to the current service estimates of taxes and transfers in the midsession review of the 1994 budget, extended beyond 1998 and updated for the actual fiscal year 1993 results. In the case of state and local taxes and non-Medicaid transfers for 1993–2004, the amounts are based on the gross domestic product assumptions in the midsession review, and on the assumption that the ratios of state and local tax and transfer aggregates to GDP remain constant at the 1992 levels. After 2004, the average federal, state, and local non–social security payroll taxes and transfers (excluding social security, Medicare, and Medicaid) by age and sex are assumed to increase at the assumed rate of productivity growth. Productivity (both labor and multifactor productivity) is assumed to increase at 0.75 percent a year, which is close to the average annual rate of labor productivity growth since 1970.

Projected social security transfers and payroll tax receipts after 2004 are based on special calculations made by the Social Security Administration, assuming a productivity growth rate of 0.75 percent. Projected Medicaid transfers from 1993 through 2030 and projected Medicare transfers from 2005 through 2030 are calculated using the Medicaid growth rates in the Health Care Financing Administration's middle scenario estimates published in 1991.[3] After 2030, health care transfers are assumed to stabilize as a percentage of GDP apart from

---

3. This scenario is discussed in Sally Sonnefeld et al., "Projections of National Health Expenditures through the Year 2000," Health Care Financing Review, vol. 13 (Fall 1991).

the effect of changes in the composition of the population by age and sex.

Assumptions for Forming Present Values. The appropriate discount rate for calculating the present value of future amounts depends on whether these amounts are known with certainty. Future government receipts and expenditures are risky, which suggests that they be discounted by a rate higher than the real rate of interest on government securities. Nevertheless, government receipts and expenditures appear to be less volatile than the real return on capital, which suggests that they be discounted by a rate lower than that. The baseline calculations assume a 6 percent real discount rate, which is intermediate between the roughly 2 percent average real return available in recent years on short-term Treasury securities and the roughly 10 percent real return available in recent years on capital.

The present values of future average taxes and transfers are also discounted for mortality probabilities to derive actuarial present values. The demographic probabilities through 2066 are those embedded in the social security trustees' intermediate projection in 1992 (alternative number 2) of the population by age and sex. The fertility, mortality, and immigration probabilities in 2066 were used for later years. Immigration is treated as equivalent to a change in mortality.

Other Projections. Federal purchases of goods and services through 2004, like federal taxes and transfers, are from the latest midsession review extended beyond 1998 and updated for the actual fiscal year 1993 results. State and local purchases through 2004 are kept at the same ratio to GDP as in 1991. Federal, state, and local purchases after 2004 were divided between those made on behalf of specific age groups, such as educational expenditures on the young, the middle aged, and the elderly and those that are more nearly pure public goods, such as defense and public safety. Purchases per person in each of the three age groups, and purchases of public goods per capita, all increase at the assumed rate of productivity growth.

The economic value of the government's assets that yield income, less the government debt, was estimated to be the cumulative amount of the NIPA deficit since 1900 converted to constant dollars by the GDP deflator. The average growth-adjusted net payment to be made by future generations was determined using the aggregate present value of the net payment (as derived through the present value budget constraint), the assumed productivity growth, and the projected size of future generations. The size of future generations was estimated using the social security alternative number 2 projection through 2066 and the demographic assumptions for 2066 applied to later years.

Historical Lifetime Net Tax Rates. Lifetime net tax rates for generations born between 1900 and 1992 were calculated by dividing the generational account of each generation at birth by its human wealth—the present value at birth of its future labor earnings. The calculation of a generation's human wealth requires knowing its average labor earnings in each future year. The average labor earnings received by particular generations in particular years were determined by distributing aggregate labor income by age and sex using cross-section distributions of labor income found in cross-section survey data. The lifetime generational accounts for generations born between 1900 and 1992 are based on actual taxes and transfers between 1900 and 1992 and projected taxes and transfers in years after 1991.

Aggregate labor earnings, taxes, and transfers were obtained from the national income and product accounts for 1929 and later years. Pre-1929 aggregate labor earnings were obtained from series in *Historical Statistics of the United States, Colonial Times to 1970*. Pre-1929 taxes and transfers were obtained from the 1982 *Census of Governments, Historical Statistics on Government Finances and Employment*. Various cross-section surveys were used to distribute aggregate labor earnings, taxes, and transfers by age and sex. Cross-section surveys before the early 1960s were not available for this study, so surveys from years after 1960 were used for earlier years. The Current Population Surveys, for example, were used for labor earnings and taxes on labor earnings in 1964 and later years, and the 1964 survey was used for earlier years.

The Remaining Net Payments by Existing Generations

Tables 11–1 and 11–2 show U.S. generational accounts as of calendar year 1992 for every fifth generation of males and females alive in that year. The first column, "net payment," is the difference between the present value of taxes that a member of each generation will pay, on average, over his or her remaining life and the present value of the transfers he or she will receive. The other columns show the average present values of the different taxes and transfers. All federal, state, and local taxes and transfers are included in these calculations. Because of the time needed to prepare these estimates, federal spending and receipts are based on the baseline in the midsession review of the 1994 budget rather than the projections in more recent documents.

The present value of the future taxes to be paid by the young and middle-aged generations is much more than the present value of the future transfers they will receive. For males who were age forty in 1992, for example, the present value of future taxes is $170,900 more than the present value of future transfers. The amounts are large because these generations are close to their peak tax-paying years. For newborn males, conversely, the present value of the net payment is much smaller, $78,400, because they will not pay much in taxes for a number of years.

The older generations, who are largely retired, will receive more social security, Medicare, and other future benefits than they will pay in future taxes. That is, they have negative net payments. Females have smaller net payments than males, mostly because they earn less income and therefore pay less income and social security taxes.

Since the figures in these tables show the remaining lifetime net payments of particular generations, they do not include the taxes a generation paid in the past or the transfer payments it received in the past. This should be kept in mind in considering the net payments by those now alive. The portion of a generation's remaining lifetime net payments depends on whether it is ten, forty, or sixty-five years old. The fact that forty-year-old males can expect to pay more in the future than they receive, in present value terms, while the reverse is true for sixty-five-year-old males, does not mean the federal, state, and local governments are treating forty-year-old males unfairly. Males who are now sixty-five paid considerably higher taxes when they were younger, and these past taxes are not included in the remaining lifetime net payments shown in their generational accounts. Therefore, the remaining lifetime net payment by one existing generation cannot be directly compared with that of another. The lifetime net payments of different generations can be compared only by using the lifetime net tax rates discussed below.

The Net Payments by Future Generations

Future generations—those born in 1992 and later—are estimated to make a 126 percent larger net payment to the government, on average, than those born in 1992. The $177,100 average net payment by future males and the $99,600 average net payment by future females are calculated by assuming that the ratio of net payments by males to that of females is the same for future generations as for those born in 1992. The calculations also assume that all people of a particular sex born in the future will make the same average net payment over their lifetimes after adjusting for economic growth.

A growth adjustment must be made to the average payment be-

TABLE 11–3

PERCENTAGE DIFFERENCE BETWEEN NET PAYMENTS OF FUTURE GENERATIONS
AND THOSE OF THE NEWLY BORN, USING THREE
ASSUMPTIONS FOR INTEREST RATES

Interest Rate	Growth Rate		
	0.25	0.75	1.25
3.0	137.3	101.9	73.4
6.0	159.5	126.0	97.3
9.0	263.8	220.4	181.5

SOURCE: Authors' calculations.

cause future generations will pay more in taxes, net of the transfers they receive, simply because their incomes will be higher. To assess properly the net payment by future generations relative to the newly born, we must calculate the net payment they would make above and beyond the amount due to economic growth. The generational accounts assume that all future generations pay the same net amount apart from the adjustment for growth. This net amount is the number shown in the table for all future generations of the same sex.

A generational imbalance, as defined before, is calculated in such a way that the generations now alive, including the newly born, do not pay any more taxes (or receive any fewer transfers) than projected in the baseline. This assumption is an analytical device for determining the size of the nation's fiscal imbalance; it is not meant to suggest that future generations will in fact close the gap all by themselves. Any actual policy change is almost certain to bear in some degree on generations now living as well as those to be born in the future. If such a policy change is made, the percentage difference in net payments between the newly born generations and future generations would be less than shown in this table. Policy changes of this kind are illustrated below.

The size of the imbalance between future generations and the newly born is sensitive to the assumptions about the interest rate used for discounting and the growth rate of the economy. Table 11–3 shows the percentage differential under alternative assumptions. It considers interest rates of 3, 6, and 9 percent and productivity growth rates of 0.25, 0.75, and 1.25 percent. The central assumptions used in this chapter were an interest rate of 6 percent and a growth rate of 0.75 percent. This led to a 126 percent larger net tax payment by future generations than by the newly born. Under the alternatives in table 11–3, the difference ranges from 73 percent to 264 percent. While this range is large, the basic conclusion holds for all alternatives. Future generations are estimated to make a much larger payment of taxes to the government, net of transfers received, than those just born.

Effect of the 1993 Omnibus Budget Reconciliation Act

Through a combination of spending reductions and tax increases, the 1993 Omnibus Budget Reconciliation Act reduced projected federal deficits between 1993 and 1998 by $500 billion. Table 11–4 shows the change in generational accounts resulting from the enactment of the agreement. It raised the generational accounts of all but the very oldest existing generations. The accounts of forty-year-old males, for example, rose by $5,600, the accounts of fifteen-year-old females rose by $2,200, and the accounts of seventy-year-old males rose by $3,300. As a consequence of existing generations' paying more, net payments by future generations were reduced by $25,300 for males and $14,200 for females. Without the enactment of the budget agreement, the net payment of future generations, on a growth-adjusted basis, would be 165 percent larger than that for 1992 newborns—significantly larger than the current 126 percent baseline imbalance.

Health Care Reform

The president's health care reform proposal would further reduce the outstanding generational imbalance primarily by slowing the growth in health care spending after the turn of the century. Table 11–4 shows the change in generational accounts associated with enacting the president's proposal. The growth-adjusted burden on future generations is reduced by $32,400 in the case of males and $19,900 in the case of females, leaving future generations with a net tax payment that is 74 percent, rather than 126 percent, larger than that of 1992 newborns. Thus, the president's health care reform proposal eliminates more than two-fifths of the generational imbalance. In combination, the passage of the 1993 budget agreement and the proposed enactment of health care reform eliminate almost half the pre-agreement generational imbalance of 1992.

Enactment of the president's health reform proposal is shown to raise the generational accounts of all existing generations. This result reflects the treatment in the accounts of government health care spending as a transfer payment. To the extent that the proposed reduction in government health care spending reflects reduction in waste and improvement in efficiency, the increase in generational accounts of existing generations indicated in table 11–4 overstates the effect of health

TABLE 11-4
CHANGE IN GENERATIONAL ACCOUNTS DUE TO 1993 OBRA AND HEALTH CARE REFORM, AS OF 1992
(thousands of 1992 dollars)

Generation's Age in 1991	OBRA93		Health Care Reform		Health Care Reform Pessimistic Growth	
	Males	Females	Males	Females	Males	Females
0	2.0	1.1	4.9	1.8	0.9	−1.8
5	2.5	1.4	5.5	1.8	1.0	−2.3
10	3.2	1.8	6.0	1.7	1.2	−2.7
15	4.0	2.2	6.6	1.8	1.5	−2.9
20	4.7	2.7	7.0	3.1	1.8	−1.9
25	5.2	3.2	7.3	5.0	2.0	−0.5
30	5.4	3.5	7.7	6.9	2.3	0.9

35	5.6	3.9	8.5	8.9	2.8	2.4
40	5.6	4.1	9.5	11.0	3.5	3.9
45	5.4	4.3	10.1	12.4	4.6	5.4
50	5.1	4.4	10.1	12.8	5.9	7.0
55	4.8	4.6	9.8	12.8	8.0	9.3
60	4.6	4.9	8.8	12.0	8.4	10.1
65	4.0	4.6	6.5	9.3	7.1	9.1
70	3.3	3.8	4.4	6.6	5.4	7.6
75	2.5	3.0	2.5	3.9	3.5	5.4
80	1.6	2.1	1.4	2.3	1.9	3.1
85	1.1	1.4	0.5	0.8	0.5	0.8
90	0.0	0.0	0.0	0.0	0.0	0.0
Future generations	−25.3	−14.2	−32.4	−19.9	−11.6	−11.4

SOURCE: Authors.

reform on their accounts, although the benefit to future generations will remain essentially unchanged.

Table 11–4 also shows the importance of implementing the cost-containment measures in the president's proposal. It shows the change in generational accounts associated with enacting health reform, but permitting health care costs to grow, from the year 2000 through the year 2020, at a rate that is 2 percent higher than would be warranted by demographic change and economywide productivity growth. In this case the generational imbalance is 109 percent, rather than 126 percent—the imbalance under baseline policy. While the generational accounts of all existing males and middle-aged and older females increase under this scenario, those of young females actually decline, reflecting the higher female than male longevity and the timing of the growth in health care benefits compared with the baseline projection of growth in government health care benefits.

Historical and Future Lifetime Net Tax Rates

The analysis so far has been prospective, considering only the present value of future taxes and transfers as of 1992 for existing generations and generations yet to be born. A prospective analysis can compare policy changes, and it can compare the lifetime fiscal burdens of the newly born and future generations, because their entire lifetimes are in the future. But it cannot compare the lifetime fiscal burden on one existing generation with the lifetime fiscal burden on another existing generation born in a different year, or with future generations, because part of any living generation's taxes and transfers were in the past and therefore are not taken into account.

A comparison of one existing generation with another must be based on its entire lifetime taxes and transfers. The lifetime net tax rate of a generation is defined as the present value of its lifetime net taxes (taxes paid less transfer payments received) divided by the present value of its lifetime income. The present values are calculated as of the generation's year of birth, so that each generation can be compared from the standpoint of when it was born. The lifetime net taxes are the same as the generational account for a generation in the year of its birth. (As shown in tables 11–1 and 11–2, the lifetime net taxes of males and females born in 1992 were $78,400 and $44,100, respectively.) Since lifetime taxes, transfers, and income have trended upward and have fluctuated to some extent, it is more appropriate to compare the relative fiscal burden on different generations in terms of lifetime net tax rates rather than in terms of absolute amounts.

The lifetime net tax rates are calculated from historical data on taxes, transfers, and income up to 1992 and projections of future data as described for the previous sections. Historical data, however, are not available to the same extent as the data for recent years that underlie the projections, and in some cases they are not available at all. A technical note at the end of this section summarizes the methods of constructing the historical series.

Lifetime calculations also introduce a number of conceptual issues. How should lifetime income be measured, for example? Lifetime income is defined as a present value, like lifetime taxes and transfers. The present value calculation should include all income that increases a generation's resources: labor earnings, inherited wealth, and capital gains over and above the normal return to saving. The normal return to saving is not itself included in income, because that would be double counting. Saving and earning a normal rate of return do not increase the present value of a household's resources. Data do not exist on the share of each generation's income that has come from inherited wealth or supernormal capital gains, so labor earnings are used to represent income.[4]

Table 11–5 shows baseline lifetime net tax rates for different generations born since 1900 and future generations. Males and females are combined for purposes of these and subsequent lifetime net tax rate calculations. The lifetime net tax rate in the base case exhibits a strong upward trend, rising from 24 percent for the generation born in 1900 to 36 percent for existing generations born since 1970.[5] The lifetime net tax rate for future generations is 82.4 percent.[6]

Table 11–5 also breaks down the net tax rates between gross tax rates and transfer rates. To calculate these rates, the present value of a generation's lifetime taxes (or transfers) is divided by the present value of its lifetime income. This breakdown reveals the expanded role of government transfer payments during the past century. The lifetime transfer rate for males and females taken together nearly quadrupled

---

4. The error due to this omission is relatively small in the aggregate, given that labor income has long accounted for approximately four-fifths of all income and that only part of the remaining income from capital should be included. The errors for different generations could vary, however, depending on trends and fluctuations in asset values and bequest behavior.

5. In the fiscal year 1994 budget baselines, the lifetime net tax rate reported for generations born in 1900 was 22 percent. The 24 percent figure reported here is larger primarily because of revision in the estimation of human wealth—the denominator of the lifetime net tax rate. This revision in the calculation of human wealth also raises the lifetime net tax rates of generations born after 1900, as well as future generations, by roughly 10 percent.

6. The baseline generation imbalance can also be calculated as the ratio of the lifetime net tax rate of future generations divided by that of newborns.

TABLE 11-5
Baseline and Pre-1993 OBRA Lifetime Net Tax Rates for Generations Born since 1900, 1900–1992
(thousands of 1992 dollars)

Year Generation Was Born	Baseline			Pre-OBRA93		
	Net tax rate	Gross tax rate	Gross transfer rate	Net tax rate	Gross tax rate	Gross transfer rate
1900	23.6	27.3	3.7	23.6	27.3	3.7
1910	27.2	33.0	5.8	27.2	33.0	5.8
1920	29.0	35.9	6.9	29.0	35.9	6.9
1930	30.6	38.8	8.1	30.5	38.7	8.2
1940	31.9	41.0	9.1	31.6	40.9	9.2
1950	33.2	44.0	10.8	32.8	43.7	10.9
1960	35.0	47.2	12.2	34.4	46.7	12.3
1970	36.5	50.6	14.1	35.7	49.8	14.1
1980	36.9	51.9	15.0	36.0	51.5	15.0
1990	36.5	52.4	15.9	35.5	51.5	16.0
1992	36.3	52.4	16.1	35.4	51.5	16.2
Future generations	82.0			93.7		

Source: Authors.

TABLE 11–6

Effects of Health Care Spending and Health Reform, 1900–1992, on
Lifetime Net Tax Rates for Generations Born since 1900
(thousands of 1992 dollars)

Year Generation Was Born	Baseline	Health Care Reform	
		As projected	Pessimistic growth
1900	23.6	23.6	23.6
1910	27.2	27.2	27.2
1920	29.0	29.1	29.1
1930	30.6	30.9	30.9
1940	31.9	32.4	32.2
1950	33.2	34.0	33.5
1960	35.0	35.9	35.2
1970	36.5	37.6	36.6
1980	36.9	38.2	36.7
1990	36.5	38.3	36.2
1992	36.3	38.3	36.0
Future generations	82.0	66.5	75.2

Source: Authors' calculations.

between the generations born in 1900 and those born in 1992, starting at 3.7 percent and increasing each decade to a rate of 16.1 percent. The increase was more rapid, in both relative and absolute terms, for the generations born before World War II than afterward.

Because of the growth in the transfer rate, the gross tax rate has not leveled off in the past two decades to the same extent as the net tax rate. The gross tax rate nearly doubled between the generations born in 1900 and 1992, starting at 27.3 percent and increasing each decade to a rate of 52.4 percent. A generation's lifetime taxes pay for the purchases of goods and services as well as transfers and pay for transfers to other generations as well as its own.

Table 11–5 also shows the impact of the 1993 budget agreement on the lifetime net tax rates of different generations. For future generations, the agreement reduced the lifetime net tax rate from 93.7 percent to 82.4 percent. It raised the lifetime net tax rate of existing children by roughly 1 percentage point, of the baby boom generations by 0.3 to 0.6 percentage points, and of older generations by fewer than 0.3 percentage points.

Table 11–6 shows the effect of health reform on the lifetime net tax rates of different generations. Health reform, as projected, reduces the lifetime net tax rate of future generations from 82.4 percent to 66.5 percent. In combination, the actual passage of the budget agreement and the passage of health care reform would reduce the lifetime net tax rate of future generations from 93.7 percent to 66.5 percent. Health reform raises the lifetime net tax rates of all existing generations. For 1992 newborns, the increase is from 36.3 percent to 38.3 percent. For 1992 forty-two-year-olds (those born in 1950), the increase is from 33.2 to 34.0 percent. For 1992 seventy-two-year-olds (those born in 1920), the increase is from 29.0 percent to 29.1 percent. As indicated above, much of these increases reflect the assumption that reductions in government health care spending are properly measured as a decline in transfer payments to the public. To the extent that the proposed reduction in health care spending simply reduces waste and improves the efficiency of the health delivery system, the lifetime net tax rates of existing generations will be largely unaffected by health reform.

Comparing U.S. with Norwegian Generational Accounts

The Norwegian government has also prepared generational accounts to examine the long-term sustainability of its fiscal policy.[7] Norway's generational accounts provide an interesting comparison with those of the United States. Because of its considerable petroleum and hydro-electric wealth, the Norwegian government has positive net wealth, roughly equal to 20 percent of GDP. Norway is aging at roughly the same rate as the United States. Relative to its GDP, Norwegian government purchases are almost 40 percent greater than U.S. government purchases, and its transfer payments are almost 60 percent greater. Nevertheless, relative to its GDP, Norway's net tax payments are about 50 percent greater than U.S. net tax payments. The difference between Norwegian and U.S. government purchases, government transfers, and taxes can be summarized in terms of the primary deficit—government purchases plus transfer payments less taxes. Relative to its GDP, the Norwegian primary deficit is smaller than the U.S. primary deficit. In 1992, the ratio of the Norwegian primary deficit to GDP was 1.7 percent—71 percent of the corresponding U.S. ratio of 2.4 percent.[8]

The fact that Norway has positive government net wealth and a

---

7. Alan J. Auerbach, Jagadeesh Gokhale, Laurence J. Kotlikoff, and Erling Steigum, Jr., "Generational Accounting in Norway: Is Norway Overconsuming Its Petroleum Wealth?" Report to the Norwegian Research Council for Applied Social Science (October 1993). Boston University Department of Economics: Ruth Pollack Working Paper Series on Economics, no. 18, October 1993.

8. These figures are based on OECD estimates.

TABLE 11–7
U.S. AND NORWEGIAN GENERATIONAL ACCOUNTS, 1991
(thousands of dollars)

Age in 1991	United States		Norway	
	Males	Females	Males	Females
0	78.4	44.1	104.7	47.7
5	99.3	54.8	127.6	52.6
10	124.8	67.3	154.6	57.4
15	157.2	82.5	186.1	63.6
20	187.7	96.9	214.5	66.1
25	203.0	101.5	237.9	67.3
30	201.6	96.9	241.0	62.0
35	192.4	87.8	225.6	59.7
40	170.9	69.1	198.8	54.1
45	132.5	39.7	157.5	35.1
50	81.0	2.4	105.4	6.8
55	19.5	−40.2	46.6	−24.7
60	−43.9	−86.3	−14.2	−60.3
65	−94.1	−122.5	−57.8	−71.6
70	−98.6	−124.6	−61.1	−71.1
75	−92.9	−117.9	−68.3	−66.8
80	−79.4	−100.5	−50.4	−54.0
85	−69.4	−79.3	−36.0	−43.2
90	−11.6	−11.3	−26.1	−34.8
Future generations	177.1	99.6	178.2	81.2
Percentage difference for future generations versus age zero	126.0	126.0	68.9	68.9

SOURCE: Authors' calculations.

lower primary deficit relative to GDP suggests a smaller intergenerational imbalance in Norwegian than U.S. fiscal policy. Table 11–7, which compares U.S. with Norwegian generational accounts for 1992, confirms this to be the case. The Norwegian imbalance is 69 percent, just over half the U.S. imbalance of 126 percent. While the percentage imbalance is larger in the United States, the absolute fiscal burdens on future Americans and future Norwegians are very similar—$177,100 for future American males and $178,200 for future Norwegian males; $99,600 for future American females and $81,200 for future Norwegian females. The smaller Norwegian and U.S. imbalance primarily reflects the higher net tax burden on existing Norwegians. The generational accounts of forty-year-old Norwegian males is $198,800, for example, compared with $170,900 for forty-year-old American males; the generational accounts of seventy-year-old Norwegian females is—$71,100, compared with—$124,600 for seventy-year-old American females.

Conclusions

This chapter has described a new long-term fiscal planning tool, called generational accounting, that can and should be used to measure and evaluate generational policy. The chapter has also applied generational accounting to a number of issues, reaching the following major conclusions. First, the lifetime net tax rates paid by Americans in the "baby boom" and successive generations are much higher than the net tax rates paid by Americans born earlier. Second, despite a significant reduction in the fiscal burden facing future generations as a result of the enactment of the 1993 Omnibus Budget Reconciliation Act, the net tax rates to be paid by future generations will be substantially higher than those paid by the baby boom and other current generations, unless policy actions are taken now to mitigate this increase. Third, the president's health reform proposal, had it been enacted, would further have significantly lowered the lifetime net tax rates facing future generations. The combined effect of the agreement and the enactment of the president's health reform proposal would be to lower future generations' lifetime net tax rates by almost one-third. Nevertheless, the remaining fiscal burden on future generations is immense. Finally, Norwegian fiscal policy, like that of the United States, suggests a severe imbalance in the treatment of current and future generations. Norway's generational imbalance reflects a high level of government expenditures, which more than offset its large stock of public wealth in terms of the implications for the lifetime net tax rates of future Norwegians.

Methodological Issues
of Generational Accounting

A Commentary by Jane G. Gravelle

Laurence Kotlikoff and the coauthors of "Using General Accounting to Assess Fiscal Sustainability and Generational Equity" are to be commended for calling attention to our need to look at the effects of government policy over time and recognize the tax burdens that different generations will face. This focus on generational accounting, which includes questions about the meaning and measurement of deficits, has met with some resistance. The approach, however, has merit, and it is time for others to weigh in with ideas of how to adapt this method as a policy-making tool. My comments will address some general methodological issues rather than the specifics of policy.

Generational Accounting

As a distributional tool, generational accounting must be considered in broad terms. I see three implications of generational accounting that need to be sorted out in designing an analytical tool that will be accepted by and useful to policy makers.

First is the issue of defining the deficit for purposes of stabilization policy. When Kotlikoff refers to incorrect measures of the deficit and to fiscal policy, stabilization policy comes to mind—and this is where generational accounting has the most difficult time finding acceptance. That may be for good reason. The current deficit is problematic as a measure for the effect of government policy on short-run aggregate demand only if policies somehow alter private savings behavior. Given the lack of consensus about behavioral responses and the question of how quickly people will respond to future changes as opposed to current income, particularly as a result of government policies they do not

---

The views in this comment do not reflect those of the Congressional Research Service.

understand, economists and policy makers are reluctant to embrace generational accounting fully. What measure of the deficit will guide us in understanding effects of policy on short-term aggregate demand is very much up in the air. I suspect that this reservation has made acceptance of generational accounting more difficult.

Second is the issue of how future deficits are being affected by current policy, an issue crucial to policy making. Examples abound in tax policy of actions taken today that will have very different revenue consequences in the future. Examples include perhaps deliberate attempts to frame policies that look cheap in the short run—the most obvious example may be the proposal to use back-loaded rather than front-loaded individual retirement accounts. Consequences of policies may also be unintended, such as the different effects of subsidies enacted through accelerated depreciation, investment credits, or partial expensing.

What is the best mechanism to handle this issue? Is it generational accounting, or is it something else? Should we increase the budget accounting horizon, or should we graph the time path? Should we provide present values? I have suggested, for example, taking the present value of revenue effects over a time horizon (an infinite one for permanent tax changes) and turning it into an annuity that is constant relative to output as the most consistent method of revealing the true deficits emerging from tax changes.

Third is the issue of general intergenerational redistribution, which itself can include several components. It can include direct transfers of income—taking from the young to give directly to the old (for example, expansion of social security). The transfers of income go beyond tax effects to include tax capitalization (as, for example, those that would occur with expensing). It can include changes in the deficit—that is, any policy that standing alone violates an intertemporal government budget constraint—which in one way or another shift income from the young and new generations to the old. It can include various induced behavioral changes, such as changes in savings behavior that alter the capital stock and labor productivity.

It is important to separate out some of these effects. First, let us ask the question, What is the analog to income distribution tables in intergenerational accounting? I think that the direct (and directly induced) distributional effects explicitly imposing taxes and payments on individuals of different age groups would be the generational analog to income distribution tables. Tables of this sort could be developed and introduced into the policy-making process without great difficulty. Generational accounting would be more meaningful if it separated these direct effects from the consequences of the deficit.

Generational accounting and its distribution are embodied in the policy; the distributional consequences of the deficit are still up in the air. Combining them causes people to distrust results because some assumption is made about how the deficit is resolved.

Similar reservations might be expressed about any aggregate, essentially macroeconomic policies that derive, say, from changes in savings behavior, since these are the subject of some controversy. Thus, if I were concerned with the consequences of the 1993 budget legislation, I would want to know how the direct tax increases affected different age groups, as a separate issue from how the deficit change affected them. In income distributional tables, we do not allocate the changes in deficits to incomes; a similar policy should be considered in preparing intergenerational distribution tables.

Of course, deficit policy itself is clearly an intergenerational policy and is of vital import. But the uses of the accounting might be best served by isolating this policy and also by thinking very carefully about how it is likely to be resolved. One might present more than one possibility—amortizing it, carrying part of it permanently, and paying off the rest, and applying it proportionally to all generations.

This issue is so important that I would like to elaborate on it with an example. If an income distributional table had a set of tax increases and decreases that netted to zero, we could do a standard distributional effect. The same would be true in an intergenerational redistribution table if the present value of taxes and payments netted out to zero. But suppose we had simply a tax cut. In an income distribution table, everyone would get a tax cut. The intergenerational tables have an offsetting tax increase that takes care of the deficit. It is as if in the income distribution table we imposed a tax cut and then decided some particular group or groups would pay for it. Whom we decided on would radically affect the distributional pattern.

The generational accounts prepared by Kotlikoff and his coauthors follow a method of allocating the deficit (allocating it to unborn generations), and it may be a reasonable method—but it is still arbitrary. It is embodied in no policy other than their own. At the same time, the creation of a deficit *is* a generational policy, and the deficit must be considered. That leads to two conclusions: separate the two effects, and think very hard about how to allocate the deficit. It could be argued, for example, that a more neutral policy would be an amortization of the deficit.

The Distributional Analog

I would now like to turn directly to the distributional analog itself and discuss some of the problems. First, just as I prefer to see income distri-

207

bution tables done as a percentage of after-tax income, I would prefer to see intergenerational tables done the same way. It would be easy enough to compute them, but they should also be presented that way.

Second, some very tough problems of analyzing certain tax provisions in a generational context are far from being resolved. Even if we did not have the problems of debt finance and double taxation of corporate income, for example, adoption of expensing of capital goods is completely different from shifting to a consumption tax base. To shift to consumption would require eliminating current depreciation deductions; as long as they remain, the effects on the value of firms will be different. Adopting an investment credit equivalent in present value with current depreciation deductions added to expensing is yet another policy—different from a consumption tax and different from adopting expensing while maintaining depreciation. I have argued, for example, that an investment credit for equipment is more like a rate cut than a movement to a consumption base.

Third, we must use the intergenerational tables with a great deal of caution, perhaps even more caution than with income distribution tables. For one thing, the data may be more uncertain. For another, while with income distribution data, the concepts are hard to interpret, with generational distribution data, the concepts are reasonably clear, but income is difficult to measure. Our information is still very poor about the patterns of income, consumption, work, and the like over the life cycle. Even if we had good data on past patterns, new patterns might be quite difficult to determine as tastes, technology, longevity, and many other factors are changing. Our data with respect to bequests and gifts are even more weak. More work is obviously needed to gather this information, including long panels that track individuals for many years, but there is no question that we have very imperfect data.

A relative difficulty with intergenerational distribution tables is that the effects of private transfers—and of policy-induced private transfers—are much greater than they are in income distribution data (where the effects of these transfers can be considered minor). Our lack of information on intergenerational transfers is complicated not only by lack of calibrating data but also by lack of information on motivation. Truth presumably lies somewhere between no transfers and Ricardian equivalence.

One example of this problem can be illustrated with introduction of social security. Did it redistribute, or did it substitute social for private interfamily transfers?

A related problem is that people feel differently and interpret differently generational redistribution from cross-income distribution. If

I am paying higher taxes but my mother is gaining, that is different from my paying higher taxes with a stranger gaining. It is harder to know how to interpret these effects. Moreover, there has not been a consensus on the desirable distributional effects. What does the present older generation—who lived through the depression and World War II—deserve? What do our children deserve? Does it depend on whether we think their standard of living is growing because of technology so that, absent transfers, they will be better off? There has been little attempt to grapple with these issues.

There is also a need to combine generational and income distribution. Don't we want to distinguish between the rich old and the poor old? Distributing income from the well-off young to the poor old is an entirely different proposition from distributing income from the poor young to the well-off old. We need more work that identifies income categories within each age group.

Finally, we need to remind ourselves that this type of generational accounting is an incomplete accounting for the intergenerational distribution consequences of government policy. Just as distribution tables across incomes, even if they included direct transfers, would tell an incomplete story because they do not include the value of other government-provided goods, generational distribution tables will not tell the whole story. Government spending on capital goods benefits future as well as current generations. Other expenditures may also have effects that accrue to future generations. Did the expenditures on World War II, for example, provide benefits only during the years of the war? As with distribution tables across incomes, it is important to remember that generational accounting is not a complete accounting of government distribution policy.

What Questions Are Answered by Generational Accounting?

A Commentary by Carolyn L. Weaver

In the space of a decade, Laurence Kotlikoff's work on generational accounting has grown from a theoretical idea in academic papers into a concrete alternative for presenting budget data that is now in use by the federal government. This transformation is testimony to the power of good ideas in the hands of capable (and persistent) researchers.

In response to the observation that changes in distributional analysis that may make good economic sense may not be well received politically without a good deal of advance work, few would question Mr. Kotlikoff's commitment to doing that advance work.

Generational accounts spring from the simple observation that official budget deficit numbers are inherently flawed. The government can run any fiscal policy and, depending on how particular policies are labeled, generate a surplus or deficit of any size. In Mr. Kotlikoff's words (and those of his coauthors Alan Auerbach and Jagadeesh Gokhale), "from the perspective of economic theory, the deficit is an arbitrary accounting construct whose value has no necessary relation to the question of generational burdens." The authors have set out to construct an alternative measure that is less influenced by labels and that answers the underlying conceptual question, How do changes in government policy affect the intergenerational distribution of welfare? Generational accounts attempt to show, in present value terms, how much people in different generations must pay over their remaining lifetimes to finance government consumption and to subsidize each other.[1]

As the charts in the chapter make clear, enormous imbalances in fiscal burdens now exist between current and future generations. The

---

1. Alan J. Auerbach, Jagadeesh Gokhale, and Laurence J. Kotlikoff, "Generational Accounts—A Meaningful Alternative to Deficit Accounting," National Bureau of Economic Research Working Paper 3589, pp. 1–2.

introduction and expansion of unfunded social security and public employee retirement programs have been the major culprits behind this redistribution of resources toward older generations from younger and unborn generations—a redistribution that has been largely obscured by government bookkeeping. The charts also help illuminate the extent to which major new policy initiatives, such as health care reform, can perpetuate if not aggravate these imbalances across generations. The hope, of course, is that the availability of this type of data will help refocus public debate on economically relevant issues and bring about policies that are more neutral across generations.

One can hope. Generational accounts are a major advance in distributional analysis and in the measurement of the intergenerational consequences of fiscal policy. Policy making would be enhanced by their routine use in the evaluation of major changes in fiscal policy, particularly as the data and underlying techniques are further developed and refined.

Having said this, I would caution that generational accounts do not answer all or even most of the important questions we would wish to have answered about federal policy. Consider, for example, the tabular data on the Clinton health care package. These data assume, among other things, that the rate of growth of federal health spending will stabilize at the rate of productivity and population growth. Who believes that spending *will* stabilize at that rate? Alternatively, who believes that it *could* stabilize at this rate without resulting in significant economic distortions affecting the well-being of future generations? Indeed, these numbers assume that the health care package—with massive new government regulations and employer mandates—would have no significant effects on output or employment. Surely there would be such effects, and their impact on the well-being of future generations could easily dwarf those arising from the direct effects of any particular tax and spending provision in, say, the Clinton budget agreement.

Importantly, generational accounts do *not* show us what lifetime fiscal burdens *will be* based on the best available knowledge but what they *would be* under a carefully selected set of assumptions—in this case, the administration's (or the Office of Management and Budget's) assumptions—and ignoring any offsetting policy responses or economic feedbacks such as lost employment and output.

As a general matter, it is worth reflecting on how much meaningful economic information *can* be captured in—and how much can be accomplished by—an improved accounting system. Suppose we had had a system of generational accounts in place in the 1960s, when Medicare was enacted, or in the early 1970s, when Congress increased social security benefits by a whopping 20 percent and then indexed them to changes in the cost of living. Would generational accounts have reflected the opportunity cost of these actions—that is, the income and wealth forgone as a result of unfunded expansions of these programs—which is critical to rational, informed decision making? No less important, would a better set of accounts have altered the election year politics that brought us these policies?

I do not mean to suggest that revising accounts is unimportant. To the contrary, improving the information upon which citizens and legislators base decisions can have only salutary effects. But it would be easy to overstate the ability of accounting measures to capture all, or even most, economically relevant information or to alter fundamentally the political incentives and constraints facing policy makers.

Consider another example involving social security. As is well known, as a result of the 1983 reform legislation, social security tax collections will exceed annual benefit payments for the next one or two decades, during which time the trust funds will amass large balances of government IOUs. Meeting benefits in the next century will require the rapid depletion of these balances. The system is not projected to be solvent in the long run.[2]

The question for accounting reformers is this: Does the advance funding of social security (as compared with pay-as-you-go financing) reduce the burden of the debt for future generations, increase national saving, and help secure benefits for baby-boom retirees? Or does advance funding underwrite an expansion in the rest of the budget, or in social security and Medicare, that undermines the attainment of these goals? Either outcome is possible; each has dramatically different implications for the real indebtedness of the federal government and the well-being of future generations. To the best of my knowledge, generational accounting cannot inform us on this important fiscal policy question—but it gives us an answer anyway!

As noted in Alan Auerbach's chapter, in any revenue or distributional analysis many assumptions must be made about the nature of the "experiment" under consideration.[3] Here the question is the extent to which accounting surpluses in the social security trust funds induce policy responses in the rest of the budget. As I understand them, generational accounts—like official budget deficit numbers—assume no

2. Board of Trustees of the Federal Old-Age and Survivors Insurance and Disability Insurance Trust Funds, *Annual Report* (Washington, D.C.: U.S. Government Printing Office, 1993).

3. Alan J. Auerbach, "Public Finance in Theory and Practice," Unpublished manuscript, University of Pennsylvania, 1993.

policy responses, resulting in the most favorable (but probably not the most realistic) assumption about the impact of advance funding on the well-being of future generations. A social security surplus is assumed to result in a dollar-for-dollar reduction in the government's net indebtedness. This is by no means a noncontroversial assumption.[4]

More generally, a number of the criticisms leveled at distributional analysis can be leveled at generational accounting, too. In particular, these data carry an "illusion of precision." They tend to obscure the uncertainty surrounding empirical estimates. While many would be skeptical of the value of more such analyses, a good argument can be made for presenting a range of estimates for generational accounts or using modern statistical techniques, such as stochastic simulation, to quantify some of the uncertainty. With this said, generational accounts still would not answer the questions noted above or help us answer questions relating to which policies are best suited for particular economic or social problems—should we, for example, rely on the tax system, on regulation and employer mandates, or on private markets for meeting the retirement income needs of future generations?

I would conclude by noting that getting a handle on the costs and benefits of government within and between generations undoubtedly requires improved measures of government activity. But getting a handle on debt creation undoubtedly requires more. In my view, basic changes in the rules of the fiscal policy game are in order. I would be interested in hearing Mr. Kotlikoff's views on revising budget enforcement rules to incorporate generational accounts or imposing requirements on the degree of generational neutrality that must be embodied in our fiscal policies. Beyond that, a hefty dose of competition for many of the activities the government now undertakes would be constructive. There is not a bookkeeping device around that can compare to the competitive process in producing useful information on the price and quality of alternative programs and policies. One need look no further than the postal service and public education for illustrations of this simple point.

---

4. Carolyn L. Weaver, ed., *Social Security's Looming Surpluses: Prospects and Implications* (Washington, D.C.: AEI Press, 1990).

12

Individual Marginal Tax Rates under the U.S. Tax and Transfer System

Andrew B. Lyon

The burden of taxation is generally expressed in terms of the revenue raised from affected taxpayers. Policy makers have an immense interest in knowing the distributional analysis of a proposed tax change based on these revenue collections. Frequently, this interest comes at the expense of an understanding of the behavioral effects of taxation. These behavioral effects can affect the well-being of taxpayers as much as the direct revenue effects of a tax, but unfortunately these effects cannot be gleaned from most distributional analyses.

Textbooks in economics explain the notion of the "excess burden" created by a tax—that is, the burden borne by taxpayers through changes in their behavior in an attempt to avoid the tax. This excess burden reduces the well-being of the taxpayer beyond the dollar amount of revenue raised from the tax. An excise tax on a particular good set at a sufficiently high level, for example, may yield no revenue, because the tax drives purchases to zero. Such a tax is burdensome because consumers would have preferred, in the absence of the tax, to purchase that particular good over other goods.

At times, the behavioral effects of taxation have been ignored by policy makers even when an analysis of these effects could have supported their objectives. During the debate on President Clinton's 1993 budget package, for example, some economists questioned whether the proposed higher marginal tax rates would bring in the amount of revenue estimated by the Treasury Department and Joint Committee on Taxation. These analysts noted that if the higher marginal tax rates on upper-income taxpayers discouraged work effort, a large fraction

I have benefited from the comments of David Bradford, Gary Burtless, Karla Hoff, Joe Richardson, and Eugene Steuerle on an earlier version of this chapter. I thank Sharon Hoke for research assistance.

of the estimated revenue could vanish.[1] Republicans in Congress opposed to the budget package generally did not adopt this argument. Some have suggested that Republicans found it more persuasive to argue that the higher tax rates would result in overly large increases in tax payments borne by these upper-income taxpayers—a statement that would not be precisely true if taxpayers reduced their incomes to avoid the taxes.[2] Many economists, however, recognizing that the changed behavior imposes a cost on the taxpayer in reduced well-being and at the same time lowers tax revenues collected by the government, might have found an argument about excess burdens more compelling.

The behavioral response to many types of tax changes cannot be estimated from the information on tax payments usually contained in distributional tables. The reason is that the incentive to undertake an additional amount of an activity depends on the marginal tax rate, while burden tables generally show data relating to the average tax rate. Excess burden is the result of changes in the relative prices for different goods (or changes in the relative returns to different activities). Relative prices, in turn, are affected directly by the marginal tax on the last unit. Therefore, it is the marginal tax rate and not the average tax rate that affects the excess burden of a tax. Consider, for example, a tax system with a constant marginal tax rate on income over some exemption amount, say, $5,000. An increase in the exemption amount to $10,000 would lower average tax rates for any worker with more than $5,000 in income, but it would have no effect on the after-tax wage of an additional hour worked (or the after-tax return to an additional dollar saved) for someone with more than $10,000 in income. Since the marginal tax rate is unchanged, so is the reward to working and saving additional amounts.[3]

---

1. Martin Feldstein and Daniel Feenberg, "Higher Tax Rates with Little Revenue Gain: An Empirical Analysis of the Clinton Tax Plan," *Tax Notes*, March 22, 1993, pp. 1653–57.

2. David Wessel, "It's the Argument Neither Party Wants to Hear: Increasing Tax Rates on Rich Won't Work," *Wall Street Journal*, April 27, 1993.

3. Of course, in determining changes in incentives, we must distinguish between two effects of a tax change: the substitution effect and the income effect. Changes in the relative price of an activity or in the marginal return from an activity change the relative attractiveness of the activity even if the individual were somehow compensated to hold his income level or level of satisfaction constant. This effect is identified as the substitution effect. Changes in the total amount of income exert another force that generally will change the relative attractiveness of one activity over another. For example, it is generally believed that holding everything else unchanged, people with higher incomes would choose to work fewer hours than if their incomes were lower. In the preceding

This chapter examines the marginal tax rates arising from the individual income tax and transfer programs and considers their potential effects on behavior. The next section examines how the Tax Reform Act of 1986 changed individual marginal income tax rates. The third section examines the changes in marginal income tax rates arising from the 1993 budget act. The fourth section evaluates the potential effects of the 1993 tax changes on labor supply and tax revenue from high-income individuals. The fifth section provides an analysis of the combined marginal tax rates resulting from the major tax and transfer programs applying to lower-income individuals. The final section provides some brief conclusions on the goal of minimizing the efficiency cost of tax and transfer programs.

Recent Changes in Marginal Income Tax Rates, 1986–1990

The Tax Reform Act of 1986 continued the trend toward lower marginal income tax rates begun with the 1981 tax cuts. Under the act, the tax rate applying to the highest-income individuals fell from 50 percent to 28 percent, increasing the after-tax share on additional income by 44 percent.[4] The act was also estimated to remove 6 million individuals from any tax liability through increases in the standard deduction and personal exemptions.[5] For these individuals, marginal tax rates generally fell from 11 percent to zero.

Changes in the Distribution of Marginal Tax Rates. The magnitude of the rate cut resulting from the 1986 tax act can be seen by examining changes in the distribution of returns across marginal tax rates from 1986 to 1990.[6] The following comparison of marginal tax rates in 1986

---

example in the text, the increase in the exemption amount from $5,000 to $10,000 would result in an increase in after-tax incomes, holding labor effort unchanged. This higher after-tax income then might induce individuals to work fewer hours.

4. The percentage change in the after-tax share of additional income is $(1 - .28)/(1 - .50) - 1$.

5. Joint Committee on Taxation, *General Explanation of the Tax Reform Act of 1986* (Washington, D.C.: Government Printing Office, 1987); and Jerry A. Hausman and James M. Poterba, "Household Behavior and the Tax Reform Act of 1986," *Journal of Economic Perspectives*, vol. 1, no. 1 (1987), pp. 101–19.

6. Tax return information is from various issues of the annual publication 1304, Internal Revenue Service, *Statistics of Income, Individual Income Tax Returns* (Washington, D.C.: Government Printing Office). Data for tax year 1990 are the latest available at the time of this writing. See Jon Bakija and Eugene Steuerle, "Individual Income Taxation Since 1948," *National Tax Journal*, vol. 44, no. 4,

and 1990 is based on the tax rate applying to an additional dollar of fully taxable income. The effects of the phaseout of the benefit of the 15 percent tax bracket and the phaseout of personal exemptions for high-income taxpayers introduced by the 1986 act are included in the analysis. The analysis here, however, omits the special treatment of certain income. The 1986 act, for example, fully includes long-term capital gains in income, rather than including only 40 percent as existed before the act. Similarly, the repeal of the two-earner deduction may increase the marginal tax rate on wage income of the secondary earner. While changes in the marginal tax rate on these sources of income are not explicitly considered, the full inclusion of this income affects the level of taxable income reported and may therefore affect the marginal tax rate on other fully taxable income.[7] The effects of certain special phaseouts of deductions on marginal tax rates are considered in the section on marginal rates under the 1993 act.

Because changes to the standard deduction and personal exemption changed the income threshold at which an individual becomes subject to tax, it is necessary to adjust the actual distribution of taxable returns for changes in the number of taxpayers facing no tax liability between 1986 and 1990. The analysis below considers filers of joint returns and single returns separately.[8]

The actual number of joint returns filed with positive taxable income in 1990 decreased by about 1.8 percent from 1986, while the number of married couples in the population is estimated by the Bureau of the Census to have increased by 2.6 percent over this period.[9] The decrease in returns is mostly due to the sizable increase in the standard deduction and personal exemptions that eliminated all income tax liability for many low-income families.[10] Under the assumption that in

---

pt. 2 (1991), pp. 451–75; and Robert J. Barro and Chaipat Sahasakul, "Measuring the Average Marginal Tax Rate from the Individual Income Tax," *Journal of Business*, vol. 56, no. 4 (1983), pp. 419–52, for historical analyses.

7. The individual alternative minimum tax (AMT) is also not considered. In 1990, 0.1 percent of taxpayers paid AMT. In that year, a taxpayer subject to the AMT faced a 21 percent marginal tax rate on taxable income. Certain deductions are deferred under the AMT or disallowed entirely.

8. In 1990, the distribution of taxable returns by filing status was: joint (46.0 percent), single (42.3 percent), head of household (9.7 percent), and married filing separate (2.0 percent).

9. Positive taxable income for 1986 is defined as taxable income in excess of the zero bracket amount. Data on joint filers discussed here also include returns of surviving spouses.

10. The standard deduction (formerly the zero bracket amount) increased from $3,670 in 1986 to $5,450 in 1990. The personal exemption increased from $1,080 in 1986 to $2,050 in 1990.

the absence of the 1986 act the ratio of taxable returns to married couples would have remained constant between 1986 and 1990, it is estimated that the actual effect of the 1986 act was to reduce the number of taxable joint returns by 1.94 million (3.88 million married adults and their dependents), or approximately 4.4 percent of the joint returns that would otherwise have been filed in 1990.[11]

Figure 12–1 compares the distribution of joint returns across marginal tax rates for 1986 and 1990. As described above, an estimated 4.4 percent of returns that would have paid positive taxes in 1986 benefits from a zero marginal tax rate in 1990. Taxpayers in the upper end of the 15 percent and 28 percent brackets in 1990 also benefit from sizable marginal tax rate reductions relative to the distribution in 1986. Taxpayers in the lower ranges of the 15 percent and 28 percent tax brackets in 1990 face slightly higher tax rates, generally from one to three percentage points higher. Taxpayers in the 33 percent bracket in 1990 (resulting from phaseout provisions) experience a reduction in marginal tax rates from five to sixteen percentage points. The net effect of these changes is to lower the return-weighted average marginal tax rate by more than 16 percent, from 23.14 percent in 1986 to 19.30 percent in 1990. If the marginal tax rate of each return is weighted by taxable income, the percentage decline is slightly larger. The income-weighted average tax rate declines from 30.50 percent in 1986 to 24.51 percent in 1990, a nearly 20 percent decline.

Taxpayers receiving reductions in marginal tax rates exceed the number experiencing slight increases in the marginal tax rate. Almost

---

11. Some of the reduction in joint returns is the result of an increase in the number of married couples filing separate returns. The number of couples choosing the married-filing-separate status increased by 0.5 million more than predicted by population growth over this time period. Each marginal tax rate on the married-filing-separate tax schedule begins at half the level of income as for the joint schedule. Before 1987, couples generally benefited from filing joint returns because of the slower rate progression under this filing status. The 1986 act removed the penalty many couples faced when filing separate returns, because the wider tax brackets potentially resulted in the same marginal tax rate (and total tax liability) under either filing method. Further, if the couple has special itemized deductions limited by adjusted gross income (for example, miscellaneous deductions are only deductible to the extent they exceed 2 percent of AGI), the allocation of the deductions to a single person may increase the total amount of itemized deductions (if one return filer itemizes, the other must also itemize). However, over 70 percent of the additional separate returns filed between 1986 and 1990 were filed by nonitemizers, suggesting that this latter reason was not the motivation for most of the increase in separate returns.

FIGURE 12–1
DISTRIBUTION OF MARGINAL TAX RATES FOR JOINT INCOME TAX RETURNS,
1986 AND 1990
(percent)

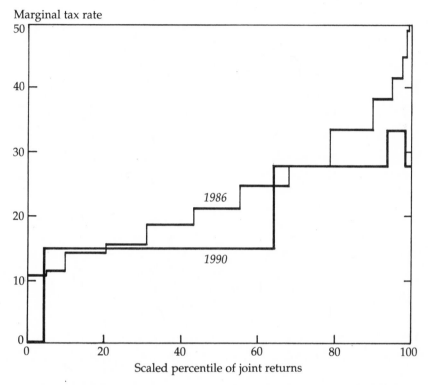

SOURCE: Internal Revenue Service, *Statistics of Income, Individual Income Tax Returns*, 1986 and 1990.

70 percent of joint filers receives a rate reduction. Figure 12–2 summarizes the data in terms of the percentage change in the after-tax share (one minus the marginal tax rate). The reduction in marginal tax rates increases the after-tax share on additional income by up to 10 percent for nearly half the distribution of joint filers. An additional 21 percent of the distribution benefits from an increase in the after-tax share of more than 10 percent. Ten percent of the distribution faces no change in the after-tax share, and 21 percent (9.4 million returns) receives a small reduction in the after-tax share of less than 5 percent.[12]

12. These results are very similar to those in simulations by Hausman and Poterba, "Household Behavior and the Tax Reform Act of 1986" (especially

FIGURE 12–2

PERCENTAGE CHANGE IN AFTER-TAX SHARES FOR AGGREGATE JOINT INCOME
TAX RETURNS, 1986 AND 1990

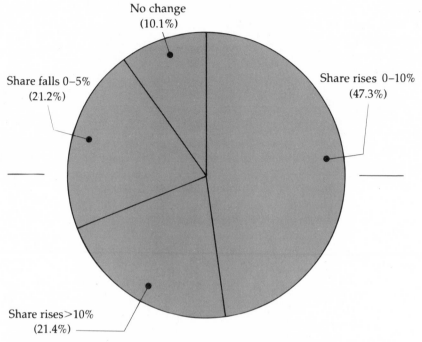

No change
(10.1%)

Share falls 0–5%
(21.2%)

Share rises 0–10%
(47.3%)

Share rises>10%
(21.4%)

NOTE: After-tax share defined as $(1 - t)$, where t is the marginal tax rate.
SOURCE: Internal Revenue Service, *Statistics of Income, Individual Income Tax Returns*, 1986 and 1990.

The above analysis is repeated for single returns. Perhaps surprisingly, the number of single returns with positive taxable income increased greatly between 1986 and 1990, beyond the increase arising from population growth. The change appears to be due to the 1986 act. Between 1986 and 1987 alone, the number of single returns grew by 10.7 percent, while the nonmarried adult population expanded by only

when the effect on joint filers only is considered). One difference in methodology is that the current analysis compares marginal tax rates at equal points of the distribution of returns. The Hausman and Poterba study examined the marginal tax rates of the same taxpayers before and after simulating the effects of the 1986 act. Because taxpayers could change their relative position in the distribution of returns, a greater absolute magnitude of tax rate changes is possible in their study.

1.25 percent. Between 1986 and 1990, the number of single returns expanded by 20 percent, while the nonmarried adult population grew by 6.2 percent.

The large increase in taxable single returns appears surprising because single filers also received the benefit of an increase in the standard deduction and personal exemption. In real terms, however, a single filer with no dependents is able to shelter only an additional $1,055 in 1990 relative to 1986. Further, under the 1986 act, children or other dependents who are claimed as exemptions by other taxpayers cannot claim a personal exemption for themselves. Other base-broadening measures of the act that may have disproportionately affected low-income single filers include the full taxation of unemployment benefits (formerly nontaxable for low-income taxpayers and only partially includable in income if adjusted gross income exceeded $12,000 for singles or $18,000 for joint returns) and the changes in the taxation of scholarships, fellowships, and stipends of students.[13] Better compliance may also have resulted in a small increase in taxable returns.[14]

Figure 12–3 shows the distribution of marginal tax rates for single returns in 1986 and 1990. A slightly larger number of returns actually face a marginal tax rate increase rather than a decrease. Under the assumption that in the absence of the 1986 act the ratio of taxable single returns to nonmarried adults would have remained constant between 1986 and 1990, then about 8.1 percent fewer returns (3.2 million returns) would have been filed in 1990 than were actually filed. These returns are shown to have an increase in the marginal tax rate from zero to 15 percent under the 1986 act. Only by the forty-seventh percentile in the distribution of returns do single taxpayers experience a reduction in marginal tax rates. As found for joint filers, taxpayers in the upper end of the 15 percent and 28 percent brackets in 1990 receive sizable marginal tax rate reductions. For single filers as a group, the

---

13. The effect of these minor provisions may be significant. Between 1986 and 1987, for example, an additional 1.1 million taxable returns with AGI under $20,000 reported unemployment benefits in AGI (all filing statuses combined). Of taxable returns with AGI over $20,000, 50,000 fewer returns reported unemployment benefits in AGI in 1987 than in 1986.

14. John Szilagyi notes that 7 million fewer dependents were claimed on tax returns of all filing statuses in 1987 relative to projections. Beginning in 1987, a social security number needed to be reported for dependents five years and older. Although only about 3 percent of single filers claimed dependent exemptions in 1986, the number claimed by a sample of single filers who filed in both 1986 and 1987 was found to have dropped 48 percent. See Szilagyi, "Where Have All the Dependents Gone?" *Trend Analyses and Related Statistics—1990 Update.* Internal Revenue Service, Washington, D.C., 1990.

FIGURE 12–3

DISTRIBUTION OF MARGINAL TAX RATES FOR SINGLE INCOME TAX RETURNS,
1986 AND 1990
(percent)

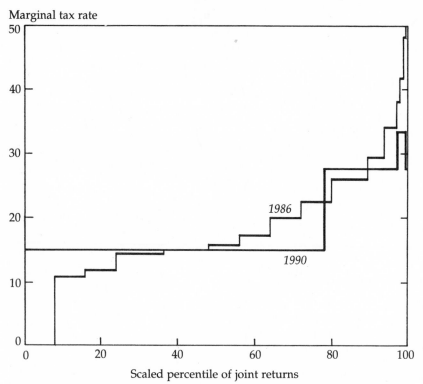

SOURCE: Internal Revenue Service, *Statistics of Income, Individual Income Tax Returns,* 1986 and 1990.

return-weighted average marginal tax rate actually increases, from 17.56 percent in 1986 to 18.07 percent in 1990.[15] Because the largest declines in the marginal tax rate occur in the highest income groups, however, the taxable-income-weighted average tax rate falls from 25.82 percent in 1986 to 23.46 percent in 1990, a 9 percent decline.

Figure 12–4 summarizes this information for single filers. Forty-

15. If one calculates the average tax rate on the basis of the actual distribution of taxable returns in 1986 (rather than using the scaled distribution of returns that applies a marginal tax rate of zero to 8.1 percent of the returns), the return-weighted average marginal tax rate falls between 1986 and 1990 from 19.12 percent to 18.07 percent.

FIGURE 12–4
PERCENTAGE CHANGE IN AFTER-TAX SHARES FOR SINGLE INCOME TAX RETURNS, 1986 AND 1990

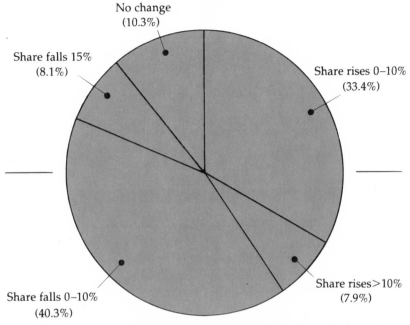

NOTE: After-tax share defined as $(1-t)$, where t is the marginal tax rate.
SOURCE: Internal Revenue Service, *Statistics of Income, Individual Income Tax Returns*, 1986 and 1990.

eight percent of single filers, or 19 million taxpayers, receives a reduction in the after-tax share on additional income (that is, an increase in the marginal tax rate), while only 41.3 percent receives an increase in the after-tax share on additional income. A better understanding of the reasons leading to the increase in single returns with positive taxable income seems essential to a full appreciation of the efficiency consequences of the 1986 act on these taxpayers. The increase, for example, in the number of taxable returns filed by dependents due to the loss of their personal exemption could apply primarily to investment income on wealth given to children by their parents. The efficiency effects of this tax, in turn, depend on whether such wealth transfers represent a marginal source of net savings or are simply inframarginal transfers designed to minimize tax liability on a given amount of wealth.[16] The

16. A separate provision taxes investment interest of a child under fourteen

taxation of unemployment benefits, as another example, could lead to efficiency improvements if it reduced the length of time that individuals were unemployed.

Based on a simulation of the reduction in marginal tax rates under the 1986 act, Jerry Hausman and James Poterba estimated a less than 1 percent increase in the number of hours worked for the average married full-time worker. High-income workers and secondary workers were estimated to have a larger labor supply response, ranging from 2.5 percent to less than 3 percent. Although these responses seem small in percentage terms, they amount to an additional supply of labor of twenty to sixty hours per year for a full-time worker. Further, the reduction in excess burden from the 1986 act is estimated by Hausman and Poterba to be larger, on the order of 8 to 20 percent. Barry Bosworth and Gary Burtless, using data through 1989, also find evidence consistent with the view that the combined effect of the 1981 and 1986 tax cuts was to slightly increase the labor supply of men and women.[17] Martin Feldstein, using tax return data on a panel of taxpayers between 1985 and 1988, finds substantial increases in reported income for taxpayers facing the largest reductions in tax rates.[18] Feldstein emphasizes that the increased income may not be just a response to increased work effort but may also reflect a change in compensation patterns from tax-preferred fringe benefits to fully taxable cash income.[19] This dimension of behavioral change is also welfare enhancing to the extent that the individuals derive greater satisfaction from the cash income and, at the same time, tax collections of the government increase.

The Movement toward a Flat-Rate Tax System. While marginal tax

---

years old at the parent's marginal tax rate. Investment income in excess of $1,000 in 1990 ($1,200 in 1994) is taxable at the higher of the child's or parents' marginal tax rate. To the extent parents use the ability to shelter investment income in the child's name as a marginal source of saving, savings incentives are affected by this provision as well. (Note, however, even under prior law, amounts of investment income in excess of the personal exemption were taxable. This provision affects the rate of tax paid on the investment income but does not increase the number of dependent returns.)

17. Barry Bosworth and Gary Burtless, "Effects of Tax Reform on Labor Supply, Investment, and Saving," *Journal of Economic Perspectives*, vol. 6, no. 1 (1992), pp. 3–25.

18. Martin Feldstein (1993) "The Effects of Marginal Tax Rates on Taxable Income: A Panel Study of the 1986 Tax Reform Act," Working paper no. 4496, National Bureau of Economic Research, Cambridge, Mass., 1993.

19. Lawrence Lindsey also focuses on the incentives for individuals to change the form of their compensation in response to lower marginal tax rates. See Lawrence Lindsey, *The Growth Experiment* (New York: Basic Books, 1990).

rates fell for most individuals over the 1986–1990 period, this result should not be surprising. After all, the 1986 Tax Reform Act was estimated to reduce individual tax liability on the order of $15 billion per year.[20] Perhaps a more meaningful question is to ask whether, for a similar revenue loss, greater efficiency gains were possible.

One possible concern is that movement toward a rate structure with only several tax brackets leaves fairly large jumps between marginal tax rates. These jumps in marginal tax rates produce kinks in individuals' budget constraints. A worker may be willing to work additional overtime at a 15 percent marginal tax rate, for example, but be unwilling to work the overtime at a marginal tax rate of 28 percent. If the same worker were given an alternative marginal tax rate schedule of, say, 18 percent, he might be willing to work overtime, increasing well-being and government revenue relative to the 28 percent bracket. In one study, David Altig and Charles Carlstrom show that a smoothly increasing marginal tax rate structure can yield welfare gains relative to a tax schedule approximating the U.S. tax schedule.[21]

Perhaps more surprisingly, a totally flat rate tax structure or even a two-bracket tax system with a *lower* marginal tax rate in the higher income bracket can yield greater welfare gains than an increasing marginal tax rate. Joel Slemrod and others show that the optimal two-bracket tax system for a wide range of parameter values features a lower marginal tax rate for the highest income tax bracket.[22] This tax system offers slight efficiency gains over a flat-rate tax system.

Although the model of Altig and Carlstrom differs from that of Slemrod and others, together they indicate an interesting possibility. Even in the case where a flat-rate tax system provides welfare gains relative to a graduated rate structure, movement toward the flat-rate system achieved simply by reducing the number of tax brackets might not be efficiency enhancing.

These models abstract from costs of tax administration by the government and costs of tax planning, decision making, and uncertainty

---

20. The estimate of revenue loss is from the Joint Committee on Taxation, *General Explanation of the Tax Reform Act of 1986*. The act was estimated to be revenue neutral when tax increases on the corporate sector are included. While clearly individuals ultimately bear the entire burden of corporate taxes, the focus of this chapter is on taxes paid directly by individuals.

21. David Altig and Charles T. Carlstrom, "The Efficiency and Welfare Effects of Tax Reform: Are Fewer Tax Brackets Better than More?" Discussion paper 78, Federal Reserve Bank of Minneapolis, Minneapolis, 1992.

22. Joel Slemrod, Shlomo Yitzhaki, Joram Mayshar, and Michael Lundholm, "The Optimal Two-Bracket Linear Income Tax," *Journal of Public Economics*, vol. 53 (1994), pp. 269–90.

to individuals. It might be argued that movement from the prior-law 14 percent bracket system to a several-bracket system reduces these costs. For taxpayers near the threshold between the 15 percent and the 28 percent tax brackets, however, these costs may actually increase given that a relatively small change in income can significantly change their marginal tax rates. A large number of taxpayers are near this threshold. In 1990, the 28 percent tax bracket for a married couple filing a joint return was for taxable income between $32,450 and $78,450, with 24 percent of the joint filers in this group in the lowest $5,000 of this bracket. An additional number of joint filers, equal to 27.8 percent of this bracket, had taxable income between $27,450 and $32,450, placing them just short of the 28 percent bracket.[23] If these two groups of taxpayers experienced a slight amount of unexpected income fluctuation, it is possible that a number of taxpayers exceeding half of those who actually faced the 28 percent tax bracket could have underestimated their marginal tax bracket by nearly 50 percent or overestimated their tax bracket by 85 percent. In 1986, an equivalent movement in income ($8,400 in 1986 dollars) would generally have resulted in an increase or a decrease in marginal tax rates of only three percentage points.

The efficiency effects of such a misunderstanding of tax rates are fairly complex. Individuals who underestimate their marginal tax rate may work more than they would choose to work given their true tax rate. For these individuals, the miscalculation has no efficiency cost, however, just a loss in well-being equal to the additional amount of tax paid. More problematic in terms of efficiency are those who overestimate their tax liability only to reduce work effort. The reduction in hours worked creates an efficiency loss since individuals achieve a level of well-being below that achievable had they correctly perceived their tax rate, and this loss in well-being comes with a decrease in tax revenues. The net efficiency cost depends on the mixture of over- and under-estimates of tax rates.[24]

---

23. I am grateful to John O'Hare of the Joint Committee on Taxation for supplying these data.

24. An additional source of uncertainty in estimating tax liability and the tax consequences of alternative activities is due to the alternative minimum tax (AMT). Originally set at a marginal tax rate of 21 percent in 1987, and later increased to 24 percent, the Omnibus Budget Reconciliation Act of 1993 increased the tax to a two-tiered rate of 26 percent on the first $175,000 and 28 percent on amounts in excess of that threshold. Uncertainty of the AMT extends beyond marginal tax rate uncertainty. Certain types of investment that are favored under the regular tax rules treated significantly worse under the AMT. For example, interest on "private activity" bonds that is exempt from

As an example of the magnitude of the uncertainty faced by taxpayers in gauging their marginal tax rates, one can estimate the number of taxpayers who held tax-exempt bonds in recent years who would have received a higher after-tax return by holding fully taxable bonds.[25] In 1989, yield spreads between taxable and tax-exempt bonds would generally have made it economical only for taxpayers with a marginal tax rate above 20 percent to hold tax-exempt bonds. It is estimated that between 29 and 35 percent of all recipients of tax-exempt interest would have received a higher after-tax return by at least marginally substituting taxable bonds for tax-exempt bonds. Perhaps even more surprising, approximately 25 percent of all recipients of tax-exempt interest would have received a higher after-tax return if they had substituted their *entire* tax-exempt portfolio for a taxable portfolio.[26] Calculations for 1987 and 1988 show an even greater percentage of these noneconomic holdings.[27]

One might speculate that the large number of taxpayers concentrated near the break point between the 15 percent and the 28 percent brackets is the outcome of taxpayer attempts to minimize tax liability. The large percentage of taxpayers who mistakenly hold tax-exempt bonds suggests that many taxpayers do not correctly anticipate their tax rate. For different reasons, then, either to reduce the direct disincentive to earning additional income or to reduce the costs of taxpayer decision making, there may be efficiency gains from a more gradual increase in marginal tax rates.

Marginal Income Tax Rates under the 1993 Act

The Omnibus Budget Reconciliation Act of 1993 instituted new higher marginal tax rates on high-income taxpayers and made permanent a

---

taxation under the regular tax rules is fully taxable under the AMT. Thus, an AMT taxpayer would never wish to hold these bonds, regardless of the AMT marginal tax rate. As noted earlier, only 0.1 percent of taxpayers paid AMT in 1990. The number is likely to increase as a result of the 1993 changes.

25. I am grateful to Bill Trautman of the Office of Tax Analysis for supplying the data in this paragraph. For more details, see William B. Trautman and Gerald E. Auten, "The Efficiency Cost of the Tax-exempt Bond Subsidy to State and Local Governments," U.S. Treasury, mimeo, 1993.

26. These recipients account for about 10 percent of the tax-exempt interest received by taxpayers.

27. The large number of these noneconomic holdings of tax-exempt securities greatly reduces the efficiency cost of tax-exempt securities, where the cost is defined as the difference between the forgone tax revenue collected on the interest otherwise earned by the bondholders less the implicit subsidy to tax-exempt borrowers.

phaseout of personal exemptions and a limitation on itemized deductions that were introduced on a temporary basis in 1991 as part of the 1990 budget agreement. The 1993 act added a 36 percent and a 39.6 percent bracket to the 31 percent tax bracket put in place in 1991. The 1993 changes in income tax rates were made effective retroactively to January 1, 1993. Under the new rate schedules, joint filers with taxable income between $140,000 and $250,000 are subject to the 36 percent bracket, and a 39.6 percent bracket applies to income in excess of $250,000. For single filers, the 36 percent bracket starts at taxable income of $115,000, and the 39.6 percent bracket applies to taxable income in excess of $250,000.[28]

Almost as important as the explicit new tax brackets are the effects of the personal exemption phaseout (PEP) and the limitation on itemized deductions. For joint and single filers in 1994, itemized deductions are reduced by three cents for each dollar of adjusted gross income (AGI) in excess of $111,800. Thus, each dollar of additional earnings effectively increases taxable income by $1.03. For these taxpayers, this increases the 28, 31, 36, and 39.6 percent marginal tax rates to 28.84, 31.93, 37.08, and 40.79 percent, respectively. Itemized deductions may not be reduced to less than 20 percent of the initial amount claimed. At the point at which this floor is reached, this provision no longer affects marginal tax rates. A couple facing state income tax rates in excess of 4 percent is virtually assured of being continually subject to this provision, since each dollar of income increases the deduction for state taxes by four cents, of which three cents are disallowed at the margin, allowing more than 20 percent to remain.[29]

The PEP creates another hidden marginal tax rate. For joint filers in 1994, all exemptions are reduced by 2 percent for each $2,500 (or fraction thereof) of AGI in excess of $167,700.[30] Exemptions are totally phased out at an AGI of $290,200. In 1994, each exemption is $2,450.

---

28. The breakpoints for the new higher tax brackets were not indexed for inflation between 1993 and 1994. Taxable income below these amounts is subject to the following rate schedule in 1994 for joint filers: $0–38,000 (15 percent), $38,000–91,850 (28 percent), and $91,850–140,000 (31 percent). For single filers in 1994: $0–$22,750 (15 percent), $22,750–55,100 (28 percent), and $55,100–115,000 (31 percent). The 1994 rate schedule is from James Young, "Inflation Adjustments Affecting Individual Taxpayers in 1994," *Tax Notes* (October 1993), vol. 4, pp. 109–14.

29. A couple with a fixed $40,000 in itemized deductions reaches the minimum floor on deductions once AGI exceeds about $1.2 million. For a couple with a fixed $120,000 in itemized deductions, the floor is reached at an AGI of $3.3 million.

30. The AGI threshold for single filers is $111,800 in 1994.

Thus, for a family of four claiming exemptions of $9,800, each $2,500 in additional AGI increases taxable income by an additional $196. For couples with AGI between $167,700 and $290,200, the marginal tax rate in the 31 percent and 36 percent bracket effectively increases by 2.43 and 2.82 percentage points.[31]

Because the 39.6 percent bracket begins at *taxable income* of $250,000 and the PEP is concluded at an *AGI* of $290,200 on joint returns, only returns with below-average itemized deductions or couples claiming the standard deduction can be simultaneously subject to both the 39.6 percent tax bracket and the PEP. If itemized deductions exceed 16 percent of AGI, for example, the PEP will be concluded before taxable income reaches $250,000.[32] For couples with fewer itemized deductions, there will be a small region where the PEP overlaps with the 39.6 percent bracket. A family of four with itemized deductions totaling only 10 percent of AGI, for example, would be subject to the PEP and the 39.6 percent bracket for AGI between $273,900 and $290,200. Taking into account the additional effect of the limitation on itemized deductions, the marginal income tax rate in this interval would be 43.89 percent.

Figure 12–5 shows the effect of all these provisions on the marginal income tax rate for a representative family of four at various levels of AGI.[33] The marginal tax rate is shown to be uniformly increasing throughout the first $290,000 of AGI. At an AGI of $290,200, the PEP is concluded, and the marginal tax rate falls slightly. The 39.6 percent bracket, however, begins shortly after the conclusion of the PEP, resulting in a further increase in the marginal tax rate.[34]

---

31. These rates are calculated as .31 × (196/2500) = .0243 and .36 × (196/2500) = .0282. Strictly, these marginal rates hold only if additional income is earned in increments of $2,500. Because $196 in exemptions are lost for each $2,500 increment by which AGI exceeds $167,700, the unfortunate couple who reports AGI an additional $1 beyond such an increment (for example, from $167,700 to $167,701) increases its tax liability by at least $60 (.31 × $196).

32. Average itemized deductions for joint filers in this income category approximate 17 percent of AGI.

33. Because the 15, 28, 31, 36, and 39.6 percent tax brackets are a function of taxable income, while the limitation on itemized deductions and the PEP are a function of AGI, it is necessary to assume the amount of itemized deductions claimed. The family is assumed to have gross itemized deductions equal to 16 percent of AGI, slightly less than the average amount claimed in the income category affected by the PEP.

34. As noted above, for taxpayers with itemized deductions less than 16 percent of AGI, a higher tax rate of 43.89 percent will apply in a narrow interval before the PEP is concluded.

FIGURE 12–5

EFFECT OF THE PERSONAL EXEMPTION PHASEOUT AND THE LIMIT
ON ITEMIZED DEDUCTIONS ON MARGINAL INCOME TAX RATES FOR A FAMILY
OF FOUR FILING JOINT RETURNS, 1994

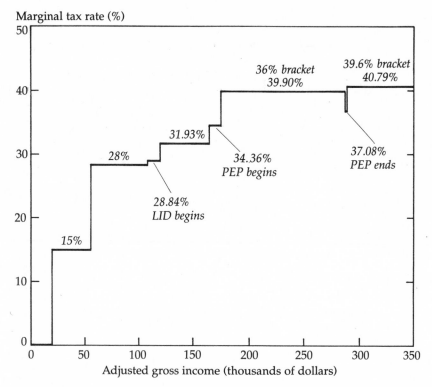

Marginal tax rate (%)

NOTES: PEP = personal exemption phaseout; LID = limitation on itemized
deductions.
SOURCE: Author.

Most elements of the tax schedule are indexed for inflation for
years after 1994. Because personal exemptions are indexed for inflation
while the dollar interval over which personal exemptions are phased
out is fixed at $122,500, however, the marginal tax rate created by the
PEP will increase by approximately 0.10 percentage points per year for
a family of four, assuming 4 percent annual inflation. Marginal tax
rates outside the range of the PEP will not be affected by inflation.

The discussion of marginal tax rates has focused on the income tax
provisions affecting a representative family. Other taxpayers, facing
separate limitations on certain itemized deductions for medical ex-

penses, casualty losses, or miscellaneous deductions, can experience higher tax rates.[35] In addition, payroll taxes must be paid for social security (Old-Age, Survivors, and Disability Insurance and Hospital Insurance) at a rate of 7.65 percent on the first $60,600 of wages in 1994 and at a rate of 1.45 percent on additional wages. Employers contribute an equal amount, although the incidence of this payment is understood to fall on the wage earner. Depending on one's lifetime earnings, the OASDI portion of the payroll tax generally results in higher retirement benefits, reducing the net burden of the payroll tax.[36]

The 1993 act maintains a provision ostensibly setting the maximum tax rate on capital gains at 28 percent. The provision operates by taxing capital gains included in taxable income at a 28 percent rate when the taxable income would otherwise subject the taxpayer to the 31, 36 or 39.6 percent tax brackets. The provision is slightly misleading, because the inclusion of capital gains in AGI reduces itemized deductions that may be claimed and reduces personal exemptions by taxpayers subject to the PEP. The loss of these deductions and exemptions has an after-tax cost that depends on the marginal tax rate on ordinary income. Consider a family of four in the 36 percent bracket with AGI of $250,000 and taxable income of $200,000 in the absence of capital gains. The realization of $40,000 in capital gains will reduce itemized deductions by $1,200 and cause a loss in exemptions of $3,136. The loss

---

35. For example, a taxpayer simultaneously facing the limitation on medical expenses (which must exceed 7.5 percent of AGI), casualty losses (which must exceed 10 percent of AGI), and miscellaneous deductions (which must exceed 2 percent of AGI) increases taxable income by 19.5 percent of additional AGI reported. In the 36 percent tax bracket, this would increase the marginal tax rate by seven percentage points. Under the Tax Reform Act of 1986, taxpayers with income between $100,000 and $150,000 face a phaseout on the use of certain passive losses. These denied losses are claimed when the underlying asset is sold. As a result, the effective rate of tax resulting from the phaseout should reflect only an acceleration of tax payments, not a permanent increase in tax liability. The efficiency effects of this provision should also reflect the change in the composition of investment from activities with low pretax returns to activities with higher pretax returns.

36. Martin Feldstein and Andrew Samwick present calculations of the net marginal tax rate from social security, which take into account future benefits, for a range of characteristics. There is great variation in these tax rates. For example, for middle-income earners, they find that the effective tax rate can range from between the full statutory rate to a net subsidy, depending on age, marital status, and earnings of the spouse. Variation is also significant across income groups. See Martin Feldstein and Andrew Samwick, "Social Security Rules and Marginal Tax Rates," *National Tax Journal*, vol. 45, no. 1 (1992), pp. 1–22.

of these deductions and exemptions directly increases tax liability by $1,561 (.36 × $4,336), or 3.9 percent of the gain realized. The $40,000 capital gain taxed at 28 percent results in an additional $11,200 in taxes. The actual marginal tax rate on capital gains is therefore 31.9 percent for this family, rather than the frequently mentioned cap of 28 percent.

The next section focuses specifically on labor supply responses to the higher tax rates, but a frequently discussed side-effect of the graduated rate schedule is its effect on marriage incentives. In general, two earners with approximately the same income will be taxed less favorably if married than if both filed single returns. For two earners with disparate income, total taxes may be lower if married than if both filed separate returns as single individuals.[37] Consider, for example, two earners with no dependents whose total AGI sums to $60,000 in 1994. If they are married, their tax liability will be $8,710. If they are single, their tax liability depends on the particular division of their income. If they both earn $30,000, the sum of their tax liability would be $7,385, about 15 percent less than if married. But if their AGI were divided $45,000 and $15,000, the sum of their tax liability would be $9,205, or $500 more than if the two were married.[38]

Much was written in the press about how the 1993 act increases the marriage penalty for high-income earners.[39] This increase occurs because the income levels at which the new marginal tax rates begin are relatively close together for single and joint filers. The 36 percent tax bracket for single filers, for example, begins at 82 percent of the income level for joint filers. The 39.6 percent bracket begins at $250,000 for both single and joint filers. Further, the limitation on itemized deductions begins at the same AGI for both single and joint filers. Let us consider two individuals each with $150,000 in AGI and $25,000 in itemized deductions. If single, the sum of their tax liability is $68,905. Assuming they married, their tax liability would increase to $77,540. While this is an $8,635 absolute difference in tax liability, it represents about the same percentage change in after-tax income as for the two individuals each earning $30,000.[40]

---

37. The earned income tax credit (EITC) creates different incentives for marriage and separation. For a discussion of the EITC's possible effects on family structure, see John Karl Scholz, "Tax Policy and the Working Poor: The Earned Income Tax Credit," *Focus,* vol. 15, no. 3 (1993).

38. The example assumes the standard deduction is claimed.

39. For example, see Tom Herman, "Marriage Will Cost More for Some Couples If the Tax Bill Passes," *Wall Street Journal,* July 28, 1993.

40. Daniel Feenberg and Harvey Rosen provide a comprehensive analysis of the marriage tax under the 1993 act. They estimate that the mean marriage tax increased by about $250. The mean marriage tax for those with incomes in

As Harvey Rosen has shown, the marriage penalty and marriage bonus are the inevitable result of a graduated income tax schedule and a belief that a married family should pay the same total tax, irrespective of the division of its income.[41] It is not known how much marriage behavior is affected by these incentives. A more likely effect is on the labor supply behavior of the secondary earner. If single, a low-income earner may be taxable only at the 15 percent bracket. If the earner marries a high-income earner in the upper ranges of the 28 percent bracket, the two could face a marginal tax rate of over 31 percent. The reduction in the after-tax wage of the secondary worker could easily lead to a reduction in labor supply, or complete withdrawal from the labor market.[42]

Labor Supply and Revenue Effects of the 1993 Act

The increase in tax rates occurring as part of the 1993 act has rekindled arguments over how responsive income-generating activities are to changes in marginal tax rates. Supporters of the 1981 rate reductions point to large increases in taxable income reported by higher-income taxpayers as evidence that these taxpayers are quite responsive to tax rates. Others suggest that the increases in income received by the highest-income groups may more fundamentally reflect changes in the opportunities available to these taxpayers that were not the result of the tax changes but reflected larger economywide and worldwide trends. In reference to the 1993 act, the debate has taken the form of whether taxpayers will change their behavior to reduce significantly the revenues forecast by the Treasury.[43]

---

excess of $200,000 was estimated to increase from − $3,667 to $7,451. See Daniel R. Feenberg and Harvey S. Rosen, "Recent Developments in the Marriage Tax," Working paper no. 4705, National Bureau of Economic Research, Cambridge, Mass., 1994.

41. See Harvey S. Rosen, *Public Finance*, 3d ed. (Homewood, Ill.: Richard D. Irwin, 1992).

42. Social security taxes may increase the likelihood of a reduction for secondary workers. A single worker may face a smaller disincentive from the social security tax since his or her benefits are a function of tax payments. The social security taxes paid by a secondary worker do not increase retirement benefits if the primary worker's earnings are sufficiently high relative to the secondary worker's.

43. See Feldstein and Feenberg, "Higher Tax Rates with Little Revenue Gain"; and Feldstein, "The Effects of Marginal Tax Rates on Taxable Income." Laura Tyson provides an administration response; see Laura Tyson, "Higher Taxes Do So Raise Money," *Wall Street Journal*, August 3, 1993.

Without examining all the ways in which taxpayers can alter their behavior in response to higher tax rates, it is instructive to examine the potential changes in behavior along a single dimension. The following analysis considers how changes in the labor supply of high-income taxpayers can affect tax revenue under a range of alternative elasticities.

Let us consider the effects of the introduction of the 36 percent tax bracket for a family of four whose income would subject them to the higher rate in the absence of behavioral response. In 1994, given the PEP and the limitation on itemized deductions, a family of four with AGI of $175,200 and gross itemized deductions of $28,032 (16 percent of AGI) would have taxable income of $140,000, the point at which additional income would be subject to the higher 36 percent bracket. At this income level, the family's marginal tax rate would increase from 34.36 percent to 39.90 percent.[44]

The effects of the tax change will depend on the labor supply elasticity. Consider an uncompensated labor supply elasticity of zero, where a positive compensated wage elasticity is assumed to be offset by a negative income effect. Under a proportional tax system, such an elasticity would predict that an increase in the tax rate would leave an individual's labor supply unchanged. The reduced incentive to undertake additional work through the reduction in the marginal return to labor is exactly offset by an income effect, under which the loss in after-tax income from the tax induces the individual to work additional hours.

Given the actual graduated rate schedule, however, the assumption of a zero uncompensated labor elasticity will cause a family with an AGI just slightly over the $175,200 threshold, say, $100 over the threshold, to reduce earnings until AGI falls to $175,200. This occurs because the family experiences the same substitution effect as under a hypothetical proportional income tax increasing from 34.36 to 39.90 percent, but the *income effect* is substantially smaller. Under a proportional income tax, the higher tax rate would reduce income by $(.3990 - .3436) \times (\$140,100)$, holding labor supply fixed. Under the actual graduated tax schedule, the higher tax rate applies to only $100, resulting in virtually no income effect to offset the substitution effect.

---

44. For simplicity, the effects of the HI payroll tax, a combined marginal tax rate of 2.9 percent on employees and employers, are ignored. Under prior law, the tax would not have been collected on labor earnings in excess of approximately $140,000 in 1994. State tax payments are also omitted. The analysis below assumes that gross itemized deductions do not change if labor income changes.

Further, the tax change would cause an actual loss in tax revenue. Relative to its initial tax collections, the government would lose $34 of tax on the $100 increment of taxable income.

To derive the implications for all taxpayers in the new 36 percent tax bracket requires more explicit assumptions on the magnitude of the *compensated* wage elasticity, not the *uncompensated* elasticity. The following formula can be used to examine the amount by which AGI would be reduced for a family whose entire income is from labor earnings and that is now subject to the new 39.90 percent tax rate:

$$\Delta\,AGI \;=\; AGI_0\left\{\frac{t_1-t_0}{1-t_0}(-\eta_c) \;-\; \frac{(Y_0-Y_1)}{Y_0}M\right\} \tag{13-1}$$

where, AGI_0 is the family's initial earnings, t_0 and t_1 are the initial and new marginal tax rates, and η_c is the compensated labor supply elasticity. The first term within the braces is the percentage change in AGI resulting from the substitution effect. In the second term, Y_0 is initial after-tax income (AGI less taxes), Y_1 is after-tax income holding labor supply fixed but assuming the higher marginal tax rate applies to taxable income in the new tax bracket, and M is the income elasticity of labor. The second term is the percentage change in labor arising from the income effect. Multiplying both terms by initial earnings gives the change in earnings resulting from the new marginal tax rate.[45] Because the percentage change in after-tax income is smaller than the percentage change in marginal tax rates, the change in earnings will be negative even for a zero uncompensated labor supply elasticity.

The change in tax revenues can also be calculated by comparing the revenue on income subject to the new higher rate, after accounting for the behavioral response, with the revenue that would have been collected at the initial tax rate on the higher initial increment of earnings in excess of the threshold.

Unfortunately, econometric research on labor supply shows little consensus on precise estimates of labor supply elasticities. Mark Killingsworth notes that a simple-minded reading of the literature on female labor supply would suggest an uncompensated wage elasticity anywhere between -0.89 and $+15.24$.[46] Even the compensated wage elasticity, which should in theory be of an unambiguous positive sign, is estimated in his survey to be between -0.05 and 1.00 for males.

---

45. The new level of AGI cannot be lower than the AGI that would return the family to the old marginal tax rate ($175,200 in this example).

46. Mark R. Killingsworth. *Labor Supply* (Cambridge: Cambridge University Press, 1983).

Jerry Hausman shows that studies that fail to control for taxes can give incorrect estimates of the magnitude of the compensated wage elasticity.[47] The literature reviewed by him as properly controlling for taxes suggests an elasticity of about 0.2 for men and on the order of 1.00 for wives. James Heckman contends that the estimates cited by Hausman suffer from other econometric problems that result in overestimates of the compensated elasticity.[48] Future research will undoubtedly provide better estimates of these parameters. The following analysis examines the implications of the tax change by considering several estimates of the compensated elasticity intended to be within the range of plausible values.

Table 12–1 examines the changes in labor earnings and tax revenue using two alternative assumptions on the compensated labor supply elasticity. In both cases, the uncompensated elasticity is assumed to be zero. In the upper panel of table 12–1, a compensated elasticity of 0.2 is assumed. This estimate is based on Hausman's review of compensated elasticities for men. The lower panel uses a higher compensated wage elasticity of 0.4 that is intended to give some weight to the higher estimated elasticities for wives. The first column in each panel shows AGI (labor earnings) in the absence of the higher tax rate. The next column shows the loss in AGI arising from the substitution effect given the higher marginal tax rate. Column 3 shows the increase in AGI resulting from the income effect of the higher tax rate. The fourth column is the net change in AGI. The change in tax revenue from the higher rate is shown in the fifth column. Finally, the last column shows the change in tax revenue as a percentage of a naive revenue estimate based on an unchanged labor supply.

Under the lower estimate of the compensated elasticity, tax collections fall for taxpayers with AGI less than $197,000. Under the 0.4 compensated elasticity, tax collections fall on all taxpayers with AGI less than $220,000. For taxpayers with initial incomes higher than these amounts, the reduction in labor supply in response to the higher tax rate is not sufficient to reduce tax collections.

It is notable that taxpayers with incomes $20,000 to $40,000 above the level at which the higher tax rate begins, by reducing their incomes only $3,000 to $6,000, actually pay a smaller amount of tax than in the absence of the tax change. Of course, the lower tax payment does not

---

47. Jerry A. Hausman, "Taxes and Labor Supply," in Alan Auerbach and Martin Feldstein, eds. *Handbook of Public Economics* (Amsterdam: North-Holland, 1985).

48. James J. Heckman, "What Has Been Learned about Labor Supply in the Past Twenty Years?" *American Economic Review*, vol. 83, no. 2 (1993), pp. 116–21.

TABLE 12-1
SIMULATED EFFECTS OF LABOR INCOME AND TAX REVENUE
(dollars)

Initial AGI (1)	Substitution Effect (2)	Income Effect (3)	Change in AGI (4)	Change in Tax Revenue (5)	Percentage of Static Estimate (6)
			Compensated Wage Elasticity = 0.2		
175,200	—	—	—	—	—
185,200	(3,126)	140	(2,986)	(637)	−115.0
195,200	(3,295)	283	(3,012)	(94)	−8.4
205,200	(3,464)	428	(3,035)	451	27.1
215,200	(3,633)	575	(3,057)	996	45.0
225,200	(3,801)	724	(3,077)	1,542	55.7
235,200	(3,970)	874	(3,096)	2,089	62.8
245,200	(4,139)	1,026	(3,113)	2,636	68.0
255,200	(4,308)	1,178	(3,130)	3,183	71.8
265,200	(4,477)	1,332	(3,145)	3,731	74.8
275,200	(4,645)	1,486	(3,159)	4,280	77.2
			Compensated Wage Elasticity = 0.4		
175,200	—	—	—	—	—
185,200	(6,252)	281	(5,971)	(1,829)	−330.1
195,200	(6,590)	567	(6,023)	(1,295)	−116.9
205,200	(6,928)	857	(6,071)	(760)	−45.7
215,200	(7,265)	1,151	(6,114)	(224)	−10.1
225,200	(7,603)	1,448	(6,155)	314	11.3
235,200	(7,940)	1,748	(6,192)	853	25.7
245,200	(8,278)	2,051	(6,227)	1,393	35.9
255,200	(8,616)	2,356	(6,259)	1,935	43.6
265,200	(8,953)	2,664	(6,290)	2,476	49.7
275,200	(9,291)	2,973	(6,318)	3,019	54.5

SOURCE: Author.

mean that these households are better off than before. At the lower tax rate, households would have worked more and paid more in tax to the government. The higher tax rates result in a pure efficiency loss for these households—the well-being of these households declines *and* government revenues fall.

The efficiency loss on these taxpayers is one price of collecting positive amounts of revenue on taxpayers with even greater incomes. What is striking here, however, is the small amount of revenue collected from these highest-income taxpayers as a percentage of a naive estimate that assumes no behavioral response. Not until households earn $50,000 to $100,000 more than the $175,200 threshold do additional revenues exceed half of a naive forecast from these taxpayers. Total revenue collections over the income ranges shown will be a significantly smaller percentage of the naive forecast, since it reflects a weighted average of the income earned at each income level represented. Because the number of taxpayers in the highest end of the earnings distribution drops off rapidly, most taxpayers affected by the higher rates will be in the first $100,000 of this distribution.[49]

Finally, it should be emphasized that in contrast to labor supply, total income might be even more responsive to taxation than reflected in traditional labor supply elasticities. Feldstein notes that self-employment, partnership, and other business income may change, as well as the composition of employment compensation between taxable wages and other fringe benefits that are excluded from taxation.[50]

Individual Marginal Tax Rates and Government Transfer Programs

The "safety net" provided by government transfer programs, such as Aid to Families with Dependent Children (AFDC) and food stamps, is intended to provide assistance to those who are most in need. To reduce the cost of these transfer programs, the largest benefits are generally given to those with the lowest income, and benefit levels are reduced as market income rises. The range over which additional income reduces benefits is referred to as the *phaseout* or *clawback* range. The phaseout of these benefits as additional market income is earned is economically equivalent to an additional tax on income. Incentives for transfer recipients to earn additional income may be impaired because additional earnings will reduce their benefits. The incentive ef-

---

49. The analysis assumes that all taxable income is from labor earnings. To the extent that a portion of earnings is from investment income, the substitution effect on labor earnings will be proportionally reduced. Note, however, that capital gains income is subject to tax at a maximum rate of 28 percent (plus the effects of the PEP and limitation on itemized deductions). As a result, only investment income from sources other than capital gains affects revenue collections.

50. Feldstein, "The Effects of Marginal Tax Rates on Taxable Income." He estimates elasticities of taxable income from all sources with respect to the after-tax share on income ranging between 1.0 and 3.0, based on a panel of returns filed in 1985 and 1988. Using the lower elasticity, he calculates that the 1993 act would cause a couple with $180,000 in taxable income to reduce income by about $21,000 (rather than than the $3,000–6,000 amount assumed above).

fects from phaseouts therefore have to be considered equally with those arising from direct taxes on income.

The primary assistance program for low-income families with children is AFDC. State rules define need standards and benefit levels by family size. In 1992, AFDC benefit payments were $22.2 billion.[51] An average of 13.6 million recipients (4.8 million families) received benefit payments each month in 1992. In January 1993, the median state maximum AFDC benefit for a three-person family was $367 per month ($4,404 annual benefit).

AFDC recipients also generally qualify for food stamps. Food stamp benefit payments in fiscal year 1992 were approximately $21.9 billion. An average of 25.4 million recipients received benefits each month in 1992. The maximum food stamp allotment for a three-person family receiving the median state maximum AFDC benefit in 1993 was $220 per month ($2,640 annual allotment). This combined annual value of AFDC and food stamp benefits was 59 percent of the poverty level in 1993 for a three-person family.[52]

One additional important benefit program aimed at lower-income working families is the earned income tax credit. The EITC is a refundable tax credit tied to earnings. The 1993 act significantly increased the maximum amount of the credit for 1994 and later years and made the credit available for the first time to workers without children. In 1996, when the credit is fully effective, a maximum credit of $306 will be available for workers without children, $2,040 for families with one child, and $3,370 for families with two or more children (all dollar amounts are in 1994 dollars; the legislation provides for these amounts to be indexed for inflation). The credit available to a taxpayer is a fixed percentage of earnings until the maximum credit is reached. For a family with two children, for example, the credit is equal to 40 percent of the first $8,425 in earnings. After reaching the maximum credit, there is another interval of earnings (the plateau range) over which further earnings have no effect on the amount of credit available. For a family with two children, the maximum credit is available for earnings be-

---

51. Program data in this section are from the *1993 Green Book* (U.S. House of Representatives, Committee on Ways and Means, 1993).

52. Families qualifying for AFDC are also automatically eligible for Medicaid. Medicaid spending in fiscal year 1992 was $118 billion. Medicaid coverage extended to about 26.7 million individuals in 1991. Other programs covering low-income individuals include Supplemental Security Income, serving the elderly and disabled poor, which paid $21.8 billion in benefits to about 5.5 million monthly recipients in 1992, and federal housing assistance, with $18 billion in expenditures for 5.5 million households in 1992.

tween $8,425 and $11,000. After the plateau range, further income *decreases* the credit available to the taxpayer. For a family with two children, each additional hundred dollars of income over $11,000 reduces the available credit by $21.06. The credit is therefore totally phased out at income of $27,000.[53]

The interaction of the phaseouts provided by AFDC, food stamps, and the EITC result in a wide range of effective tax rates for low-income families. For the first four months of earnings while on AFDC, AFDC benefits are reduced by one-third of earnings, after a deduction for a standard disregard and a capped amount of child care expenses. After four months of earnings, AFDC benefits are reduced by 100 percent of earnings, after a deduction for a standard disregard and child care expenses.[54] Food stamp benefits are reduced by 30 percent of countable income. Countable income is derived by computing a household's gross income (including AFDC benefits) and subtracting a standard deduction, 20 percent of earned income, and certain child care expenses.

At very low income levels, the phase-in of the EITC counteracts phaseouts on AFDC and food stamps. At somewhat higher income levels, the phaseout of the EITC can combine with phaseouts of AFDC, food stamps, or both to produce higher effective tax rates. Food stamps are also subject to a gross income eligibility cutoff that may create a significant notch—an additional dollar of income can cause a family to lose over $100 in monthly benefits.

Because AFDC benefits vary by state, two examples are presented to show the effects of these interactions on after-tax income. The examples are based on the state with the median AFDC benefit and on California, a high-benefit state. Benefits are computed for a family with two children and one adult using the 1993 AFDC and food stamp benefit level and the 1996 EITC schedule, indexed to 1993 dollars. It is assumed that the parent has been working for at least four months.

It is necessary to make an estimate of child care expenses to model their exclusion under AFDC and food stamps from earnings (resulting in a larger transfer payment). It is assumed that child care expenses are

---

53. For a thorough analysis of the EITC, see John Karl Scholz, "The Earned Income Tax Credit: Participation, Compliance, and Antipoverty Effectiveness," *National Tax Journal*, vol. 47, no. 1 (1994), pp. 63–87.

54. Eligibility for Medicaid benefits for adults is lost one year after no longer qualifying for AFDC because of an increase in income. (Medicaid benefits for young children up to six years old continue for family income less than 133 percent of the poverty standard and for children born after 1983 for family income up to the poverty standard.)

equal to 20 percent of earnings, up to the maximum permitted by each program ($350 per month for AFDC and $320 per month for food stamps). At higher income levels, it is assumed that the family uses the (nonrefundable) dependent care tax credit. Like other work expenses, child care expenses that increase with hours worked are an expense that reduce the return to work. The direct effect of these expenses on the return to work is not included in the effective tax rates detailed here to distinguish the change in tax and transfer payments from other expenses that affect the return to work effort. If the direct effect of these expenses were considered, the effective tax rates would increase by twenty percent points for child care expenses and an appropriate additional amount to represent other work expenses.[55]

The combined effects of AFDC, food stamps, the EITC, and federal income taxes on effective tax rates are shown in the upper panel of table 12–2 and figure 12–6 for the median benefit state and the lower panel of table 12–2 and figure 12–7 for California.[56] In both states, starting at about $1,800 and extending throughout the range of AFDC eligibility, the AFDC component of the effective tax rate is 80 percent, given the assumption that 20 percent of earnings is devoted to child care costs. Because the food stamp program counts AFDC benefits but exempts 20 percent of earnings as a work expense and in addition excludes the child care costs that are assumed to increase with income, food stamp benefits increase throughout the range of AFDC eligibility. The food stamp program therefore provides a subsidy to work effort over this range; the effective tax rate is −6 percent. Once AFDC eligibility is lost, food stamp benefits decline with earnings at an effective tax rate of 18 percent. At 130 percent of the poverty guideline, a family

---

55. If, alternatively, child care costs were assumed fixed, say at $2,000 per year, effective tax rates (in terms of tax and transfer payments) would increase by an additional 20 percent where both AFDC and food stamps were received simultaneously and by an additional 6 percent where only food stamps were received.

56. Among the tax and program benefits omitted from this computation are social security, Medicaid, and state income taxes. The social security payroll tax, including retirement and survivor benefits and disability insurance, is a combined 12.4 percent tax and Medicare is a 2.9 percent tax, all split equally between the employee and employer. Except for Medicare, social security benefits are a function of lifetime earnings histories. Feldstein and Samwick calculate that for young women without a dependent spouse, effective net tax rates from the retirement portion of social security range from about −7.55 percent for average lifetime annual earnings less than $4,300 to 8.73 percent for those with average lifetime annual earnings between $4,300 and $26,000. See "Social Security Rules and Marginal Tax Rates."

TABLE 12–2

EFFECTIVE TAX RATES OF MEDIAN STATE AND OF CALIFORNIA, INCLUDING
AFDC, FOOD STAMPS, 1996 EITC, AND FEDERAL INCOME TAX
(dollars)

Earnings	AFDC	Food Stamps	EITC	Federal Income Tax	After-Tax Income	Marginal Tax Rate
			Median State			
2,000	4,244	2,328	800	0	9,372	34.00
4,000	2,644	2,448	1,600	0	10,692	34.00
6,000	1,044	2,568	2,400	0	12,012	34.00
7,305	0	2,646	2,922	0	12,873	−22.00
8,000	0	2,521	3,200	0	13,721	−22.00
8,101	0	2,503	3,240	0	13,844	18.00
10,000	0	2,161	3,240	0	15,402	18.00
10,577	0	2,057	3,240	0	15,875	39.06
12,500	0	1,711	2,835	0	17,047	39.06
15,048	0	1,253	2,299	0	18,599	<notch>
15,049	0	0	2,299	0	17,348	21.06
18,750	0	0	1,519	0	20,269	31.06
20,000	0	0	1,256	125	21,131	37.42
22,500	0	0	729	534	22,695	37.74
25,000	0	0	203	951	24,252	n.c.
			California			
2,000	7,328	1,403	800	0	11,531	34.00
4,000	5,728	1,523	1,600	0	12,851	34.00
6,000	4,128	1,643	2,400	0	14,171	34.00
8,000	2,528	1,763	3,200	0	15,491	34.00
8,101	2,447	1,769	3,240	0	15,557	74.00
10,000	928	1,883	3,240	0	16,051	74.00
10,577	466	1,917	3,240	0	16,201	95.06
11,000	128	1,943	3,151	0	16,222	95.06
11,160	0	1,952	3,118	0	16,230	39.06
12,500	0	1,711	2,835	0	17,047	39.06
15,048	0	1,253	2,299	0	18,599	<notch>
15,049	0	0	2,299	0	17,348	21.06
18,750	0	0	1,519	0	20,269	31.06
20,000	0	0	1,256	125	21,131	37.42
22,500	0	0	729	534	22,695	37.74
25,000	0	0	203	951	24,252	n.c.

n.c. = not calculated.
NOTES: Benefits are computed for a one-parent family with two children. The data use the 1993 AFDC and food stamp benefit levels, the federal income tax, and the 1996 EITC, indexed to 1993 dollars. It is assumed that the parent has been working for at least four months.
SOURCE: Same as figure 12–6.

FIGURE 12–6

MARGINAL TAX RATES FOR THE MEDIAN STATE, INCLUDING AFDC, FOOD
STAMPS, AND 1996 EITC

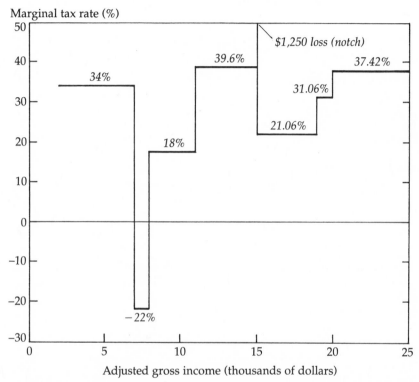

Marginal tax rate (%)

NOTES: Benefits are computed for a one-parent family with two children. The
data use the 1993 AFDC and food stamp benefit levels, the federal income tax,
and the 1996 EITC, indexed to 1993 dollars. It is assumed that the parent has
been working for at least four months.
SOURCE: Constructed by author, based on programmatic data in U.S. House of
Representatives, Committee on Way and Means, *1993 Green Book: Background
Material and Data on Programs within the Jurisdiction of the Committee on Ways and
Means* (Washington, D.C.: GPO).

(without an elderly or disabled member) is ineligible for food stamps,
notwithstanding its countable income. For the three-person family in
this example, the family loses over $100 in monthly food stamp bene-
fits when its gross earnings exceed $1,254 per month in 1993. (Food
stamp eligibility is determined based on monthly earnings; the annual-
ized equivalent is a loss of over $1,250 in benefits when gross income
exceeds $15,048 in 1993.) This extreme notch can cause a family with

FIGURE 12–7

MARGINAL TAX RATES FOR CALIFORNIA, INCLUDING AFDC, FOOD STAMPS, AND 1996 EITC

Marginal tax rate (%)

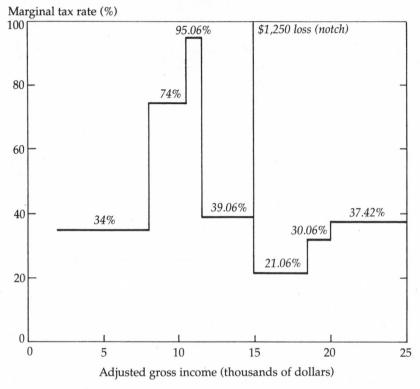

Adjusted gross income (thousands of dollars)

NOTES: Benefits are computed for a one-parent family with two children. The data use the 1993 AFDC and food stamp benefit levels, the federal income tax, and the 1996 EITC, indexed to 1993 dollars. It is assumed that the parent has been working for at least four months.

SOURCE: Constructed by author, based on programmatic data in U.S. House of Representatives, Committee on Way and Means, *1993 Green Book: Background Material and Data on Programs within the Jurisdiction of the Committee on Ways and Means* (Washington, D.C.: GPO).

higher earnings to have less posttax and transfer income than a family with lower earnings.[57]

The interaction of AFDC and food stamps (AFDC-FS) results in tax brackets from these programs of 74 percent, 18 percent, and the

---

57. The food stamp program also provides a shelter deduction to countable income to the extent that rent exceeds 50 percent of countable income. The

$1,250 notch. Because the AFDC benefit levels are state determined, the income cutoff between the first two AFDC-FS tax brackets varies by state. In low-benefit states, the entire 74 percent AFDC-FS bracket and some of the 18 percent AFDC-FS bracket rate are partly offset by the EITC subsidy rate of 40 percent, resulting in net effective tax rates of 34 percent and − 22 percent. In high-benefit states, the EITC subsidy rate extends only through part of the 74 percent AFDC-FS bracket. In high-benefit states, the plateau range of the EITC and the 21.06 percent phaseout rate combine with the 74 percent AFDC-FS bracket to produce net tax rates of 74 percent and 95.06 percent. Once food stamp eligibility is lost, families face only the 21.06 percent tax rate from the EITC phaseout. At higher income levels, federal income tax payments (reduced by the child care credit) add an additional ten to sixteen percentage points to the EITC phaseout rate. Once the EITC is totally phased out, the family returns to the 15 percent marginal tax rate of the federal income tax.[58]

In additional to the income eligibility requirements of AFDC, food stamps, and Medicaid, these programs also have wealth or asset limits. For AFDC, families are allowed only $1,000 in assets, excluding the home and one automobile. For food stamps, there is a $2,000 limit on assets, excluding the home, personal property, and one automobile. For Medicaid, state-established standards may require medically needy families to spend down assets to begin benefits. Glenn Hubbard, Jonathan Skinner, and Stephen Zeldes investigate the effect these program limits may have on savings incentives.[59]

The actual influence of these diverse effective tax rates on work incentives is difficult to evaluate. Robert Moffitt, in his review of the work incentive effects of the U.S. welfare system, finds that while reductions in work appear to be statistically significant, work by AFDC recipients in the absence of these programs would also be at fairly low

shelter deduction is capped at $200 per month. This deduction, if binding, would increase the notch from $1,250 per year to $2,000.

58. Stacy Dickert, Scott Houser, and John Karl Scholz use Survey of Income and Program Participation data to simulate marginal tax rates facing low-income families. They find that initially most individuals receiving AFDC would be subject to fairly low effective tax rates on earnings apparently because their earnings are less than the standard disregard applying to the first $120 in monthly earnings. See Stacy Dickert, Scott Houser, and John Karl Scholz, "Taxes and the Poor: A Microsimulation Study of Implicit and Explicit Taxes," University of Wisconsin-Madison, mimeo, 1994.

59. See R. Glenn Hubbard, Jonathan Skinner, and Stephen P. Zeldes, "The Importance of Precautionary Motives in Explaining Individual and Aggregate Saving," *Carnegie-Rochester Conference Series on Public Policy* (forthcoming).

levels, insufficient to bring most recipient families out of poverty.[60] Estimates by Sheldon Danziger, Robert Haveman, and Robert Plotnick cited in Moffitt's study find AFDC to reduce weekly work effort between one and ten hours. It is estimated that in the absence of AFDC, recipients would work between ten and nineteen hours.[61]

Reducing the disincentive effects of these income support programs would appear to be worthwhile goal. Knowing the direction of reform, however, is difficult. It might seem at first that reducing the phaseout rates would unambiguously increase work effort, but reducing these rates requires the range over which benefits are phased out to become greater. Individuals in the newly extended range of the phaseout face higher effective tax rates than before. Such a reform increases work effort only if the increase in work by those formerly subject to the high phaseout rates is greater than the decrease in work by those higher-income workers now subject to the phaseout who were formerly ineligible to receive benefits. Alan Blinder and Harvey Rosen provide examples where sharp discontinuities in benefit schedules (like the $1,250 food stamp notch in the earlier examples) can be efficiency enhancing.[62]

Finally, as the nation considers the design of a health insurance system, potentially offering universal coverage to all, we might ask what lessons can be drawn from other transfer programs and the income tax system. The dimensions along which behavior can be affected by a new health insurance system are at least as extensive as those under other benefit programs.

Universal coverage would require transfers at low income levels to ensure the affordability of insurance. In an effort to minimize the cost of the transfers, some phaseout of transfers would be required over an extended income range. At low income levels, families could simultaneously confront a reduction in the earned income tax credit, a reduction in medical insurance subsidies, and the 15 percent marginal income tax rate. Depending on how these provisions are designed to interact, a family could potentially face marginal tax rates on the order of 60 percent.

In an effort to reduce the apparent cost to workers of health care

---

60. See Robert Moffitt, "Incentive Effects of the U.S. Welfare System: A Review," *Journal of Economic Literature*, vol. 30, no. 1 (1992), pp. 1–61.

61. See Sheldon Danziger, Robert Haveman, and Robert Plotnick, "How Income Transfers Affect Work, Savings, and the Income Distribution: A Critical Review," *Journal of Economic Literature*, vol. 19, no. 3 (1981), pp. 975–1028.

62. Alan S. Blinder and Harvey S. Rosen, "Notches," *American Economic Review*, vol. 75, no. 4 (1985), pp. 736–47.

coverage, the Clinton administration's proposal required that employers make a contribution for the health insurance benefits of a worker about three times greater than what each employee pays. The division of these payments between employer and employee is unlikely to affect the long-run incidence of the payments. In the long run, health insurance contributions paid by the employer will be one part of a worker's total compensation package. Cash wages will be reduced in the long run by the additional amount an employer pays.

For employees near the minimum wage, however, cash wages cannot be reduced. This is likely to lead to disemployment of low-wage workers if the employer is not otherwise subsidized by the government. The alternative solution is to require workers to pay a larger share of the costs of health insurance. This reduces the amount by which employers reduce cash wages, but it may make the need for low-income subsidies more apparent. The cost of these additional subsidies can be reduced only by increasing the rate at which all subsidies are phased out. A higher phaseout rate, in turn, leads to a higher marginal tax rate on the worker's earnings. The higher tax rate may lead workers in the phaseout range to choose to work fewer hours. The end result for employment of low-income workers may be very similar; the two approaches differ only in whether employment will be reduced at the employers' or at the workers' initiative.

Conclusions

This chapter has demonstrated the wide array of differential incentives provided under the income tax and transfer systems at different income levels. Frequently, taxpayers who have roughly comparable income face very different marginal rates of tax, owing to their marital status, number of personal exemptions, types of deductions, or source of income. The resulting marginal tax rate effects are neither simple nor well understood. Although views on the desired degree of progressivity of the income tax will differ, it is unclear why one would desire a tax system with such widely divergent marginal tax rates. The actual effects of the tax system on behavior must remain partly speculative in a number of areas given our inability to estimate behavioral response precisely. As demonstrated, however, even relatively minor changes in behavior can seriously affect the desirability of a given policy.

Incentives of Marginal Tax Rates

A Commentary by Gary Burtless

Andrew Lyon's chapter on the incentive effects of the tax and transfer system touches on a wide range of issues. Nearly all public finance economists have given some thought to the marginal incentive effects of positive taxes on work effort and employment. Edgar Browning, Charles Ballard, Charles Stewart, and Ingemar Hansson, among others, have written notable analyses of this subject.

Misunderstanding Marginal Tax Rates

Until I read Lyon's treatment, however, I had given little thought to the efficiency effects of "misunderstanding" one's marginal tax rate. Lyon points out that these adverse consequences of the tax system are magnified when the step increase in marginal rates between tax brackets goes up. If true, this suggestion means the Tax Reform Act of 1986 did not improve the efficiency of the tax system as much as advertised at the time. By reducing the number of brackets—but increasing the marginal-tax-rate difference between them—Congress apparently boosted the efficiency losses occurring as a result of tax rate "misunderstanding." This is certainly a novel interpretation of the reform.

One aspect of the chapter will be particularly welcome to empirical public finance economists: the tabulation of the marginal-tax-rate changes that actually followed passage of the Tax Reform Act. Figures 12–1 and 12–3 summarize these results in an effective and compact way. A few years ago, Barry Bosworth and I attempted to survey the effects of tax reform for the *Journal of Economic Perspectives*.[1] Lyon's tabulations, had they been available, would have provided powerful evi-

---

1. Barry P. Bosworth, and Gary Burtless, "Effects of Tax Reform on Labor Supply, Investment, and Saving," *Journal of Economic Perspectives*, vol. 6 (Winter 1992), pp. 3–25.

dence about potential incentive effects of the 1986 reform. Instead, Bosworth and I calculated the changes in the marginal and average tax rates faced by a handful of "representative" households. If our selection of representative households was defective, we may have seriously misstated the theoretical effects of reform.

Lyon calculates the effects of the 1986 act on actual marginal rates using a straightforward and defensible procedure. He begins with the assumption that the same proportion of married taxpayers would have filed tax returns showing positive tax liabilities in both 1986 and 1990 if the reforms had *not* been enacted. He then compares the distribution of *actual* marginal rates on joint returns as reported in the *Statistics of Income* for the two years.

His comparison is limited to those families who would have faced positive tax liabilities in 1986. For 1990, this comparison includes some joint filers who were removed from the positive tax rolls as a result of the act. The analysis does not consider the fact that some joint filers who did not owe positive income taxes in 1990 (and in 1986) might still have faced a positive marginal income tax rate. Many people receive the earned-income tax credit who do not necessarily owe positive income taxes. For many recipients, the tax credit is reduced with each increment in wage earnings. Other recipients of the tax credit are in the credit *subsidy* range, implying that they face negative marginal rates on their earnings. It would be interesting to see the full distribution of marginal rates, including those faced by people receiving net subsidies under the earned-income tax credit.

Lyon's adjustments for the changing size of the tax-filing population are more successful for joint filers than for single filers. There was a decline in the number of joint filers between 1986 and 1990 because of an increase in the zero-bracket threshold. But for single filers, there was an unexpected 20 percent jump in the number of positive filers, compared with only a 6 percent rise in the number of unmarried adults. Lyon reasons that tax reform pushed 8 percent of 1990 filers into the system who would have been nonfilers under the law in effect in 1986. These unfortunate filers saw their marginal rates jump 15 percent in comparison with the rates they would have faced in 1986. Unfortunately, this estimate is just a plausible guess. Lyon might wish to perform a sensitivity analysis to see how his estimates would differ if he adopted different assumptions about the fraction of single filers brought into the positive tax system by the 1986 act.

Based on Lyon's current tabulations, joint filers apparently benefited from more generous marginal tax reductions than single filers. Nearly 70 percent of joint filers (versus only 40 percent of single filers) enjoyed reductions in tax rates. One-fifth of joint filers (versus nearly

249

one-half of single filers) experienced tax-rate increases. Weighing each return by taxable income, however, Lyon finds that both groups on balance experienced reductions in marginal tax rates. Joint filers saw rates fall six percentage points—or 20 percent—while single filers saw marginal rates fall two percentage points—or 9 percent.

How can the author's methods be used practically in distributional analysis? Strictly speaking, these exact methods cannot be applied to analyze a proposed piece of legislation. Since they depend on observing the *actual* distribution of marginal tax rates before and after implementation of the reform, the analyst (or policy maker) would have to wait several years before the actual distribution of postreform marginal rates is known. Nonetheless, analysts could use Lyon's methods to obtain a useful impression of the potential incentive effects of a proposed reform. After calculating the distribution of actual marginal tax rates faced by representative taxpayers under the assumption that the tax schedule and pretax incomes remain unchanged, the analyst could calculate the marginal rates these taxpayers would face under the proposed reform. The analyst could then display results using the same graphs prepared for this chapter.

What are we to make of the marginal-tax-rate reductions calculated by Lyon? Along with most public finance economists, Lyon believes the reductions improved economic efficiency. He cites predictions by Jerry A. Hausman and James M. Poterba[2] and estimates by Barry Bosworth and me[3] as well as by Martin Feldstein[4] to show that the effects of lower rates on work effort and taxable incomes had the predicted sign. I agree with Lyon's assessment. I am less certain about his evaluation of some of the other efficiency losses from the tax and transfer system.

It is not clear to me, for example, that "misperception" about marginal tax rates of the type that Lyon discusses is a serious problem. When deciding how much to work or save, even the best-informed filers usually have a rough idea of the full tax schedules they face. The amount of added uncertainty that occurs as a result of increasing differences in marginal tax rates between tax brackets from four per-

---

2. Jerry A. Hausman and James M. Poterba, "Household Behavior and the Tax Reform Act of 1986," *Journal of Economic Perspectives,* vol. 1 (Winter 1987), pp. 101–19.

3. Bosworth and Burtless, "Effects of Tax Reform on Labor Supply, Investment, and Saving."

4. Martin Feldstein, "The Effects of Marginal Tax Rates on Taxable Income: A Panel Study of the 1986 Tax Reform Act," Working paper no. 4496 (Cambridge, Mass.: National Bureau of Economic Research 1993).

centage points to thirteen points is probably small. This surmise, admittedly, is based on introspection. How many competent tax experts can state with confidence the cumulative marginal tax rate they faced *last year*? Now consider the range of responses we would obtain if we asked a random sample of filers to state the marginal tax rate they faced last year. If people cannot calculate their actual rate *last* year, it is hard to believe their error in forecasting *this* year's marginal rate would substantially reduce their welfare or affect their behavior. Fluctuations in income, which none of us control, substantially affect the exact rate taxpayers face on the margin. Rational economic agents probably determine their behavior on the basis of some "average" tax schedule they expect to face. Marginal tax rate changes of thirteen percentage points rather than four percentage points would not greatly affect their decision making.

Features of the Tax Code

In the third section of his chapter, Lyon discusses several arcane features of the tax code. He shows how some of these tax provisions can drive up actual marginal rates above the rates popularly advertised by the administration or in the press. Sometimes, the effect on actual marginal rates is startling. Contrary to a common assumption among economists, however, these exceptionally high rates seldom escape the attention of eagle-eyed lawyers and accountants who specialize in federal tax policy. The effects of even the most obscure provisions are explained in breathless (and sometimes misleading) detail on the Op-Ed or business pages of the nation's newspapers. In many cases, the significance of the provisions is misunderstood by the popular press—and even by sophisticated public finance economists.

This point can be illustrated by considering popular understanding of marginal tax rates under the largest public transfer program, social security old-age and survivor pensions. One of the most hated aspects of the pension formula is the so-called retirement earnings test. Under this provision, people who collect social security retirement benefits can have their monthly pensions reduced if their annual wage and self-employment earnings exceed a certain threshold (the annual exempt amount). This provision interacts with the income tax system in the case of some taxpayers whose social security benefits are subject to positive taxes. Under a narrow view of the law, the earnings test, along with income tax provisions that count part of social security benefits in taxable income, can yield extraordinarily high marginal tax rates on incremental earnings.

The interaction between the earnings test and the income tax law is extremely complicated. It can yield a relationship between adjusted gross income and marginal tax rates that is even more intricate than the tax functions illustrated in figures 12–6 and 12–7 in the chapter. Even though the relationship between the earnings test and the income tax system is complex, newspapers have offered explanations in Op-Ed columns and other parts of the paper that are read by people affected by the provisions. Usually, the explanations emphasize the extremely high cumulative tax rates pensioners face if their earnings are in the range where the retirement test is applied and if their adjusted gross incomes are above the threshold where part of social security benefits first become taxable.

Unfortunately, many popular explanations of the social security earnings test are incorrect, not just in detail but in substance. A major error was described by Alan Blinder, Roger Gordon, and Donald Wise in an academic article published more than a decade ago.[5] Workers who lose benefits in one year from application of the earnings test usually get back part or all of those lost benefits in subsequent years from an adjustment that is automatically made to their monthly pensions. For workers between sixty-two and sixty-four, the adjustment in subsequent benefits is intended to be actuarially fair. That is, it is supposed to be large enough to compensate workers fully for the temporary loss in benefits. Hence, there is *no* marginal tax rate on earned income above the earnings-exempt amount for these workers. For workers aged sixty-five and older, the marginal tax rate on earnings is often less than the 33 percent figure cited in most explanations of the earnings test.

Another point to understand about popular explanations of the earnings test is that, though incorrect, many older workers rely on them when deciding how much to work. Robert Moffitt and I as well as other economists, have demonstrated that an exceptionally high percentage of social security recipients—including recipients aged sixty-two–sixty-four—work almost exactly as much as required to earn the annual exempt amount; few workers earn more than the exempt amount.[6] If these workers understood the details of the earnings test, it is doubtful that so many would avoid having their pensions tempo-

---

5. Alan S. Blinder, Roger H. Gordon, and Donald E. Wise, "Reconsidering the Work Disincentive Effects of Social Security," *National Tax Journal*, vol. 33 (December 1980), pp. 431–42.

6. Gary Burtless, and Robert A. Moffitt, "The Effect of Social Security Benefits on the Labor Supply of the Aged," in Henry Aaron and Gary Burtless, eds., *Retirement and Economic Behavior* (Washington, D.C.: Brookings Institution, 1984), pp. 135–71; see especially pp. 155–57.

rarily reduced through application of the test. (In fact, Blinder, Gordon, and Wise show that under plausible assumptions, the social security formula actually *subsidizes* earnings received between ages sixty-two and sixty-four.)[7] In this case, workers' behavior is probably distorted by a misperception of the law, a misperception that is far more serious than the one mentioned by Lyon. People do not accurately understand how their pensions are affected by their current earnings. Sadly, this is a misperception created by inaccurate or incomplete descriptions of current law offered by "experts" who are critical of the earnings test and current tax law.

One feature of the tax code that draws intense criticism is the phase-in procedure used to include social security benefits in taxable income. The phase-in procedure is needed because social security benefits are excluded from taxable income in the case of taxpayers with low and moderate incomes, while 85 percent of benefits is included as taxable income for taxpayers with high incomes. For taxpayers in the phase-in range, a one-dollar increase in non–social-security taxable income can raise total taxable income by more than one dollar as an additional fifty cents of social security benefits are subject to ordinary income taxation. This phase-in procedure clearly raises marginal tax rates on *non–social-security* income above the nominal rates shown in official tax tables. If a taxpayer is in the phase-in range and happens to be subject to the social security earnings test, the apparent cumulative marginal tax rate might be very high indeed. Lyon's calculation of marginal tax rates under Aid to Families with Dependent Children, food stamps, and the earned-income tax credit shows a similar problem of high marginal rates in other income transfer programs.

While I usually agree that extremely high marginal tax rates should be avoided, I wonder whether the emphasis on high marginal rates in narrow income ranges is warranted. Only a small percentage of the population has incomes and earnings in exactly the ranges that generate the astronomical rates criticized in hostile press accounts. (Recall, too, that press accounts frequently offer poor guidance about who is actually affected by high tax rates.) Alternative procedures that yield a lower marginal rate on income often yield a wider range of income over which higher marginal tax rates would apply and would thus affect a larger number of people. Is it better to impose moderately high rates on a broad class of taxpayers or extremely high rates on a narrow class of filers? The apparent conclusion of many analysts is that extremely high rates should be avoided under all circumstances. It is not

---

7. Blinder, Gordon, and Wise, "Reconsidering the Work Disincentive Effects of Social Security."

clear to me that this conclusion is correct, either in theory or in practice. Perhaps the alternatives to current food stamp eligibility rules or the current phase-in procedure for taxing social security benefits would generate even greater efficiency losses.

Well-informed tax specialists are sometimes incorrect in their understanding of the laws that determine tax liabilities and transfer benefits. But there is often a bias in the way tax provisions are explained to the public. Conservative critics of the tax code as well as good public finance economists often highlight provisions of the law that yield extraordinary tax rates or perverse outcomes. This is fine if bad provisions of the law are thereby removed. But the critique is seldom evenhanded. Countless critics emphasize the work-discouraging effects of particular features of social security law and the income tax code. As noted, their explanations of the relevant law are not always reliable. Work-discouraging effects certainly occur. But social security also provides substantial incentives for extra work to a large fraction of the labor force, incentives that are rarely described by public finance economists or in the popular press.[8] Moreover, some of the tax provisions that discourage work among one group in the population actually preserve work incentives among other groups, for example, by keeping down marginal tax rates faced by low- or moderate-income families.

The general tenor of most discussion of federal tax policy might lead the public to conclude that the U.S. tax and transfer system is hopelessly biased against work and earned income (an inference that is hard to square with actual labor supply trends since the early 1970s). Many aspects of tax and transfer policy certainly discourage extra work and employment on the margin. It is not obvious that this effect of policy is as prominent as implied in the theoretical and popular literature.

---

8. For example, adults who have worked less than ten years in covered employment can ordinarily raise their expected lifetime incomes by working ten years and becoming fully insured under social security. Contrary to a popular complaint about social security, the system even provides positive expected benefits to secondary earners who are married to highly paid workers. These secondary earners can quality for generous social security disability pensions if they become and remain insured under the system.

Incentives, Disincentives, and Efficiency Issues

A Commentary by C. Eugene Steuerle

Andrew Lyon offers an interesting and comprehensive survey of recent changes in marginal tax rates and some of their effects on incentives. Let me begin by making a distinction between reporting on incentives and reporting on behavioral changes. The latter requires a great deal more information and relies upon many more assumptions than does the former. In general, the policy-making process does not even support the former adequately. As a practical matter, displaying the actual schedule of incentives is where I believe our efforts should mainly be directed in the near term.

Although the topic of the chapter is incentives, some of Mr. Lyon's most critical remarks seem aimed, at least implicitly, at violations of other standards and principles. There is nothing wrong with this; it merely indicates that reporting on incentives is but one among several items of information necessary to make policy conclusions.

Mr. Lyon appears, for instance, to be quite troubled by the back-door ways in which we have decided to raise tax rates in the current system. His objection is as much directed at the lack of transparency of the system as at the actual incentives. A transparent system is not necessarily less or more progressive, nor does it have greater or fewer disincentives to work and save.

Take the case of the personal exemption phaseout (PEP). This provision is the remnant of last-minute maneuvering in the 1986 tax reform, when there was a desire to claim that the top rate would be 28 percent—partly to respond to supply-side issues and partly to justify a common rate for ordinary income and capital gains (which are not adjusted for inflation). If the traditional style of progressive rates had been used, however, then a reform with a 28 percent top rate on all income would have lost revenues and shown up in the distributional tables as more regressive than the former law. (By traditional structure, I refer to one with consistently higher marginal rates at higher incomes.) To solve the dilemma, an intermediate top rate of 33 percent was enacted before the taxpayer would reach a last rate (at highest income levels) of 28 percent.[1]

Most tax policy experts felt that this approach was misleading and an unnecessary complication. The IRS came back to Treasury a year or two later to determine whether or not the 33 percent rate should be shown directly in a rate schedule or hidden in a separate calculation. They were afraid of the political repercussions from showing the rate directly, but several of us at Treasury pushed successfully to do so; we won that battle, but only temporarily. Today's PEP and Pease (personal exemption phaseout and itemized deduction limitation) both require somewhat complicated, separate calculations that cannot easily be put into the rate schedules.[2]

If one were concerned only with incentives, however, one would probably like these personal exemption phaseouts. Why? For very high-income taxpayers, phaseouts create inframarginal, not marginal, taxes. That is, they often do not create marginal disincentives because the phaseout is already complete before getting to the taxpayer's last dollar of income. In Mr. Lyon's figure 12–5, we see where the PEP ends, and although today the last bracket rises again for other reasons, maintenance of the tax rate in the PEP would have made the top (and last) rate even higher still.

Would Mr. Lyon give up the PEP in exchange for a straightforward, revenue-neutral increase in the top rate? My guess is that he might—despite the greater disincentive effect of a higher top rate.

Rate Structure, Incentives, and Disincentives

This brings us to a related set of issues. Because efficiency losses associated with raising rates are more likely to be marginal than inframar-

---

1. The extra five percentage points were obtained by phasing out the value of both the personal exemption and what was called the value of the bottom rate brackets—that is, the difference between the actual rate and the top rate of 28 percent that could have been applied to all income. This effectively allowed the system to move to a final marginal and average rate of 28 percent. The rationale, I realize, requires a bit of metaphysics.

2. In addition, I would argue on equity grounds that a personal exemption at all income levels is a legitimate way of adjusting for different family sizes. Ignoring these family-size issues is equivalent to ignoring the argument for progressivity in the first place—which itself rests on the notion that some have greater ability to pay or fewer needs than others. If one is trying to maximize welfare in some sense, moreover, then taking a dollar away from the family of four might easily reduce consumption more than taking it away from the family of one, especially if there are economies of scale in consumption.

ginal, many economists are led to believe that fewer distortions arise the more regressive our rate structure is. Mr. Lyon goes through a number of calculations, for instance, that indicate the difference in incentives between a proportional and a more progressive tax structure. For instance, he points out that those just above the beginning of a new tax bracket may be affected even more strongly than others. These individuals are the ones with the fewest dollars taxed inframarginally at the higher rate. Hence the disincentive for additional work is large, but the revenue gain is small.

Let me be a heretic here and argue that regressive taxes are not necessarily more efficient. To make this argument, I will refer to two separate issues: (1) the size of the rates that are adopted at different income levels; and (2) what is done with the money.

Concerning the first point, take the case of welfare recipients today. Most recipients of Aid to Families with Dependent Children (AFDC) report zero wages. If they work, they often face tax rates that approach 100 percent. If they marry, their income and that of their spouses can fall by as much as 30 percent. Economists often argue that the welfare loss from taxes grows with the square of the marginal tax rate. This implies that there may be tax rates in the system so high that a more progressive structure could actually improve welfare. Thus, if the rate structure is 15 percent, 100 percent, 35 percent, it is not at all clear a priori whether a structure of 15 percent, 45 percent, 45 percent would not be a better one. Lowering the middle rate in this example brings large gains in reducing the distortions for those facing the 100 percent marginal rate; those gains are offset by the rise in the top rate for others—a problem compounded by the inframarginal cost of lowering the middle rate for this same group.

My second point relates to David Bradford's observation that we must consider transfers and taxes at the same time. I would elaborate and say more generally that we must consider what is being done with the money and what we would likely do differently if our tax rate structure were different.

One of the greatest difficulties with using distributional tables to analyze tax and expenditure packages is that the deficit is treated as belonging to no one. In political accounting, not economic accounting, deficit reduction involves only the identification of losers—those who get fewer government benefits or pay fewer taxes. If my share of the national debt is reduced, I am not treated as gaining anything. Note, by the way, that generational accounting also forces this issue to be engaged.

In terms of Mr. Lyon's calculation on incentives and disincentives arising from recent bills, this inclusion of the deficit in the calculation would mean that the consequences of demonstrating the distribution of tax changes are misrepresented in a deficit-increasing or deficit-decreasing bill. It is misleading to use the same analysis to calculate incentive changes caused by the 1981 act (deficit increasing), 1986 act (deficit neutral), and 1993 act (deficit reducing). Deficits, after all, represent liabilities, just like taxes, except that the payers have not yet been identified.

Progressivity in Tax and Expenditure Programs

Next consider whether progressivity in the tax structure substitutes for other expenditures. Suppose, for instance, that as a society we reached consensus on what we were willing to accept as the top marginal rate of tax for the highest-income persons. Then the issue arises, how much should we lower rates for those in brackets below this top rate?

It turns out that the more we lower rates in brackets below the top bracket, the smaller is the tax collection available to the government. Most people associate progressive taxation (defined narrowly as higher rates at higher incomes) with growth in government, which, indeed, was correlated with growth of the income tax over the first few decades after adoption. Over the past few decades, however, most industrial societies have raised the level of government activity by lowering the top rate, raising rates in the middle and the bottom with bracket creep in the individual income tax, and increasing value-added and sales taxation. Strangely enough, progressive taxes in the traditional sense turn out to be a conservative instrument of policy in that they often support smaller, not larger, government.

In the same view, ask yourself: What is government going to do with the money from a proportional tax system? Suppose it returns the money to taxpayers in the form of cash, and phases out that cash benefit as income rises. What has it done? It has simply created a net tax-expenditure system that might have been approximated just as easily by a progressive tax that was abandoned for the sake of establishing a proportional tax. If we help the poor, for instance, we might rebate the amount of income tax they would pay under a proportional tax. But then we have simply created a zero-rate bracket or a personal exemption or credit—the very type of structure previously attacked because it involved an increase in tax rates as income increases.

Another efficiency issue also has to be engaged. Taxes are spent on something. We can provide cash to people, or we can provide in-kind services. If we conclude that it is cash that is required, then we may decide administratively to implement that rebate through a more progressive tax rate structure. The alternative provision of in-kind services on a progressive basis, though, will not be included in an examination of the incentive effect of taxes by themselves. Are in-kind goods more efficient than cash? A substantial literature often argues just the opposite.

Expenditures are almost inevitably progressive—even more progressive than what is implied in a typical tax-rate structure by itself. This is almost inevitable, as long as one of government's functions is to respond to social needs. Accordingly, assessing progressivity and incentives by looking at the tax system per se is simply inadequate.

Moving beyond High-Income Taxpayers

Once we engage the incentives in the tax and expenditures system together, the issue becomes quite challenging. Mr. Lyon mentions some of these problems in his chapter, but, interestingly enough, he is able to perform calculations mainly for taxes on high-income taxpayers. Quite frankly, this is because there is no existing estimate of combined tax and expenditure incentives faced by low-income taxpayers—only anecdotal examples. I am working on this problem, right now, with Linda Giannarelli and others at the Urban Institute. We are not far from producing a comprehensive estimate of the weighted marginal rates faced by AFDC recipients, for example—taking into account AFDC, food stamps, Medicaid, some forms of housing assistance, EITC, federal income tax, and state income tax.[3]

The problem, however, is quite complicated, and not only because there are many sources of implicit and explicit taxation. The calculation of "average marginal" rates themselves is controversial. Almost all AFDC recipients, for example, report zero income. Because of "disregards" in welfare programs, all these individuals technically face a zero tax rate on their first dollars of income. If they work full-time jobs, however, they will gain little. My belief is that the best way to show these incentive effects is to derive the entire schedule of marginal rates and to perform the calculation for discrete choices such as taking a minimum-wage job. This means that discrete choices, not just marginal

3. Linda Giannarelli and Eugene Steuerle, "The Twice-Poverty Rate: Tax Rates Faced by AFDC Recipients," paper presented at the Association for Public Policy Analysis and Management Annual Research Conference, October 27–29, 1994, Chicago.

choices from some starting point, must be examined to understand incentive effects fully.

Other Comments

These are some other random observations in response to Mr. Lyon's chapter.

• The assumption that taxes can be assessed in a lump-sum fashion is quite naive and can lead to all sorts of unwise policy. It supports, for example, both rent controls on the existing housing stock and tax rates of 100 percent backed up by investment credits on new capital. Initial presentations of incentive effects should not presume so easily that such taxes can be assessed in a lump-sum manner without behavioral reaction.

• One of the most important effects of high tax rates may be in "tax-sheltering" activity, not in reduction of hours of work or dollars saved. For low-income persons, this may mean work that is off the books and personal relations that avoid the legal commitments and tax penalties associated with marriage. The problems of tax-sheltering activity go far beyond standard efficiency measures; they strike at the heart of government's ability to act and the sense of fairness required for a society to function well.

• A personal exemption sometimes reduces marginal tax rates by pushing people into lower brackets. In terms of incentives, it cannot be compared strictly with a tax credit.

• The Treasury does reduce its estimate of revenues from that which might be derived from a pure static number. See Gerald Auten and Robert Carroll.[4]

• The assumption that incentive effects are proportional to income is just that: an assumption. For high-income persons, for instance, it may be more difficult to reduce hours of work in a job. Conversely, for these same persons, a spouse's option not to work or to retire early may be greater.

• Mr. Lyon's conclusion objects to widely divergent marginal tax rates in the same income class, but he lumps together sources of disparity such as marital status, personal exemptions, types of deductions, and sources of income. Many of these are quite justified on both efficiency and equity grounds and cannot all be treated the same.

---

4. Gerald Auten and Robert Carroll, "Tax Rates, Taxpayer Behavior and the 1993 Act," paper presented at the Eighty-Sixth Annual Conference on Taxation, St. Paul, November 7–10, 1993.

Conclusion

Although the issues are complicated, efforts such as Mr. Lyon's are vital. The simple presentation of incentives can be enormously important to the policy-making process. To perform the calculation more thoroughly, I have emphasized that one must also engage the issue of what is done with the money.

13

Distributional Effects on a Lifetime Basis

Don Fullerton and Diane Lim Rogers

Recent analyses of tax reforms have placed growing emphasis on determining the distributional effects of policies. Other chapters in this volume address various issues concerning the distributional tables that all government agencies charged with measuring the distributional effects of taxes use. As those studies show, agencies disagree about the unit of analysis, the measurement of income, the tax incidence assumptions, and the treatment of behavioral effects. In measuring both burdens and abilities to pay, however, all the agencies adopt a relatively short-run time horizon despite a recent emphasis in the academic literature on lifetime measures. The Congressional Budget Office has sometimes conducted analyses using consumption as a proxy for long-run income, and the Joint Committee on Taxation has recently adopted a five-year horizon for its calculations, but none of the agencies has embraced a full lifetime horizon. Categorizing households strictly according to annual income is still the norm. We attribute this apparent divergence between policy application and academic emphasis to concerns both philosophical and practical in nature. We discuss the various arguments against using the lifetime framework and respond to those criticisms later in this chapter.

We argue here that lifetime models of tax incidence can play a valuable role in the analyses of real-world tax reforms. The concept of the lifetime incidence of a tax simply suggests an additional examination, namely, of lifetime tax burdens relative to lifetime incomes. Our model generates distributional tables very similar to those that are already widely used in government circles. Because lifetime income may not reflect current ability to pay taxes, however, the lifetime framework can supplement rather than replace the traditional annual approach. In other words, policy makers might worry that current taxes reflect current ability to pay *and* that lifetime taxes reflect lifetime ability to pay.

The differences between annual and lifetime incidence have considerable bearing on certain policy issues. A good example is the continuing debate about the relative merits of consumption-based taxes versus income-based taxes. Proponents stress that a consumption tax would increase economic efficiency by removing the double taxation of interest income. Dynamic life-cycle models can calculate the welfare gains from removing those intertemporal distortions, so the lifetime perspective is likely to favor consumption taxes from an efficiency standpoint. Opponents stress that consumption taxes are regressive and place relatively greater effective tax rates on households with low income. They base their argument on an annual perspective. A consumption tax must be regressive with respect to annual income, since consumption makes up a high fraction of earnings for low-income groups. From a lifetime perspective, however, James M. Poterba[1] and others point out that if the present value of lifetime consumption equals the present value of lifetime income, then the lifetime incidence of a uniform-rate consumption tax is necessarily proportional. Thus, consumption-based taxes are likely to look much more desirable when using a lifetime model than when using an annual model, from both efficiency and equity standpoints.

A wage tax has steady-state effects much like a consumption tax, both in terms of efficiency and in terms of lifetime incidence. It differs in the transition, however, since older retired generations would prefer the switch to a wage tax rather than the switch to a consumption tax.

In this chapter we use a consumption tax and a wage tax as examples for measuring lifetime distributional effects, and we generate results that shed new light on the trade-off between intertemporal efficiency and distributional equity. We use a sophisticated general equilibrium model that we developed earlier[2] to calculate the economic incidence, that is, the distribution of real burdens from a consumption tax. Most important, we consider the regressivity of a consumption tax when individuals are classified not by their annual income but instead by lifetime income. Distinguishing among different lifetime-income categories, we are able to characterize the pattern of lifetime tax burdens relative to lifetime incomes by using utility-based "equivalent-variation" measures.

Within the model we have developed, the lifetime incidence of a uniform consumption tax is a bit more interesting than the purely

---

1. James Poterba, "Lifetime Incidence and the Distributional Burden of Excise Taxes" *American Economic Review*, vol. 79 (1989), pp. 325–30.

2. Fullerton and Rogers, *Who Bears the Lifetime Tax Burden?* (Washington, D.C.: Brookings Institution, 1993).

proportional outcome suggested by Poterba. In our model a consumption tax is typically not proportional on a lifetime basis for three reasons. First, some groups receive more bequests, which enable them to spend more than they earn. Second, individuals are classified by the present value of potential earnings, as a measure of well-being, so some groups may choose to work more and consume more taxed commodities instead of untaxed leisure. Third, the distributional effects of a consumption tax depend on which current tax it replaces.

To concentrate on issues regarding inherent regressivity, we consider a flat tax on all consumption at the same rate. We can interpret that uniform consumption tax as a proportional tax on individual consumption, as a national sales tax on all goods, or as a value-added tax at a single rate.[3] We thus ignore many differences in the administration of the tax, especially whether it is collected from individuals or from firms. And we ignore any progressivity that might be added into the system, either through graduated rates on an individual consumption tax base or through exemptions of necessities from a value-added tax base.

The next section describes current approaches that categorize households either by annual income or by age and how we combine those two approaches. We outline our efforts in five steps, and we summarize results. We then address a fundamental obstacle to the use of lifetime models in distributional analysis, namely, the lack of data on lifetime incomes. We explain how we tackle this problem by econometric estimation of lifetime incomes using panel data. Next we describe the general equilibrium nature of our model, which allows us to account for behavioral responses and price changes in calculating the distributional effects of tax policies.[4] We then simulate the replacement

---

3. An individual consumption tax could operate like the current individual tax, with the inclusion of all sources of income and the deduction of all forms of savings. Since all income must either be consumed or saved, income minus savings must equal consumption. That tax base can be applied to a progressive rate structure. In contrast, a value-added tax would apply to value added at each stage of production, measured by sales revenue minus the cost of all intermediate inputs. If full deductions are allowed for the cost of capital goods, then the value-added tax is a consumption-based tax. On each final product, the total revenue collected from a value-added tax is equal to the sum of amounts paid at each stage. Since the value of the final product is just the sum of value added at each stage, this consumption-based tax is equivalent to a retail sales tax. A specific proposal for a value-added tax may exempt certain goods and place different rates of tax on different industries. We do not consider these many variants.

4. Greater detail on our model can be found in Fullerton and Rogers, *Who Bears the Lifetime Tax Burdens?*

of each major U.S. tax with a uniform consumption tax and with a wage tax, and we determine the lifetime regressivity or progressivity of the various existing taxes relative to those two alternatives. Distributional tables show lifetime equivalent variations (tax burdens) relative to lifetime incomes (lifetime abilities to pay) under two parameterizations. After discussing some of the arguments against incorporating lifetime analysis into the policy arena, we present our conclusions.

How We Combine Existing Approaches

Existing studies of tax incidence fall into two general categories. The most common approach in policy analysis begins by dividing all households into groups based on some measure of their current annual economic income.[5] Such studies then collect data on the wages and salaries of households in each group, capital income such as interest and dividends, and expenditures on each commodity. We can then measure the effect of shifting tax burdens onto each group from estimated changes in wages, interest rates, and commodity prices.

A problem with that approach is that the group with the lowest annual income is a mixed bag. It includes some young workers just starting a career who are expected to earn more later, some retirees who had earned more earlier, some people with volatile income who just had a bad year, and, finally, the perennially poor. Yet the concern of policy must differ for those four types of individuals: some are really poor, some are comfortable, and some are actually very rich. Even if careful study shows that a particular tax change redistributes from a high-income group to a low-income group, little is known about what happens to the welfare of individuals who move among the annual income classes during their lives. Indeed, most of us move up the income scale during working years and then back to low income upon retirement.

The second approach proceeds by dividing all households into groups on the basis of their age. Such studies are typically based on the life-cycle model, that is, a specification of individuals' entire lifetime plans for saving and consuming during working years followed

---

5. This approach is exemplified by Joseph A. Pechman and Benjamin A. Okner, *Who Bears the Tax Burden?* (Washington, D.C.: Brookings Institution, 1974) and by Charles L. Ballard, Don Fullerton, John B. Shoven, and John Whalley, *A General Equilibrium Model for Tax Policy Evaluation* (Chicago: University of Chicago Press, 1985).

by dissaving and consuming during retirement years.[6] Analysts use such a model to calculate equilibrium prices over time and to report present value changes in lifetime tax incidence. Those studies focus on how taxes affect savings incentives, capital formation, and future productivity. They can also simulate a tax change, estimate effects on wage rates and interest rates, and measure redistributions between young and old.

A simpler, partial equilibrium version of the second approach is used in the generational accounting framework that Laurence Kotlikoff discusses in this volume. That framework focuses on what the government's intertemporal budget constraint implies about the intergenerational incidence of government policies. Effective tax rates can be computed for many different cohorts of households. For simplicity those measures assume constant prices and unchanged behavior, but the consequence is that generational accounts for alternative policies do not reflect predicted outcomes or changes in economic welfare. Generational accounting seems most valuable in addressing questions about current policies, such as the extent to which each generation pays for its own programs over its own lifetime—an assessment that annual deficit accounting clearly fails to provide.

A general problem with the second approach is that it considers only one kind of individual in each age group. Different generations are alive at one time, and the model can calculate effects on those different age groups, but individuals are not distinguished by level of well-being. Such a model misses the fundamental distinction between rich and poor, a distinction that plays prominently in any policy debate about the distributional effects of taxes.

To illustrate the distinction between the two approaches, suppose that the economy included only the two types of individuals depicted in figure 13–1. One type has relatively poor lifetime prospects and advances with age through points A, B, C, and D. The other type has relatively rich prospects and advances with age through points E, F, G, and H. The typical annual incidence study would take individuals at point G as the highest income group, lump together individuals at points F and C for the second group, lump together those at points E, B, and H for a third group, and add those at points A and D for the poorest group. The study might then find how taxes redistribute among those groups, but the results would convey nothing about what happens to either of the two types of individuals of concern.

---

6. Examples are Lawrence H. Summers, "Capital Taxation and Accumulation in a Life Cycle Growth Model," *American Economic Review*, vol. 71 (1981), pp. 533–44, and Alan J. Auerbach, Laurence J. Kotlikoff, and Jonathan Skinner, "The Efficiency Gains from Dynamic Tax Reform," *International Economic Review*, vol. 24 (1983), pp. 81–100.

FIGURE 13–1
Lifetime Income Profiles for the Poor and the Rich

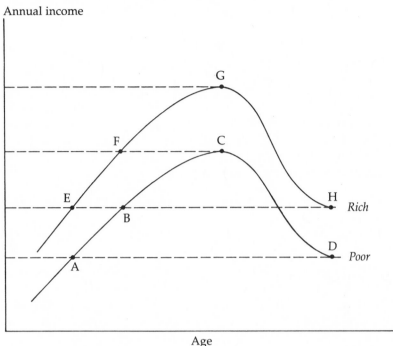

Annual income

Age

Source: Fullerton and Rogers, *Who Bears the Lifetime Tax Burden?* (Washington, D.C.: Brookings Institution, 1993), fig. 1–1, p. 3. Reprinted with permission of the Brookings Institution.

In contrast, the typical life-cycle or generational accounting study would lump together individuals at points *A* and *E* as one youngest group, those at *B* and *F* as another group, *C* and *G* as the next group, and *D* with *H* as the oldest group. The model could then calculate redistributions among the old, the young, and later generations, but not between rich and poor. Neither approach captures the fundamental distinction between the two types of individuals in this economy.[7]

---

7. Just a few studies have considered the incidence of taxes across different lifetime income categories. Using Canadian data, James B. Davies, France St-Hilaire, and John Whalley in "Some Calculations of Lifetime Tax Incidence," *American Economic Review*, vol. 74 (1984), pp. 633–49, construct lifetime histories of earnings, transfers, inheritances, savings, consumption and bequests. They then measure lifetime income, classify households, and add up the bur-

Our new model combines the two approaches. We distinguish between rich and poor, but we classify individuals on the basis of lifetime income. We use the model here to evaluate the lifetime incidence of a consumption tax and a wage tax. To avoid the debate about deficit reduction, however, we simulate the effects of using a consumption tax or wage tax to replace each existing U.S. tax, one at a time. This "differential incidence" depends on features of the tax being replaced, so we must specify details of personal income taxes, corporate taxes, and all other U.S. tax instruments.

We evaluate lifetime tax incidence in five major steps. First, we start with data from the University of Michigan's Panel Study of Income Dynamics,[8] including thousands of observations of individuals over an eighteen-year period. With all individuals together, we estimate the wage rate as a function of age and other demographic variables. We then construct a lifetime wage profile for each individual by using actual wage rates for available years and predicted wage rates in other years. With this wage profile we calculate the individual's present value of potential lifetime earnings. We rank individuals by lifetime income and classify them into twelve lifetime income groups.

Second, for each lifetime income group, we reestimate the wage profile as a function of age. We also estimate age-profiles for the personal income tax and for government transfers such as social security. The estimated wage profile rises and then falls over time for all groups, but the steepness and the timing of the peaks differ. Groups that earn relatively more of their income earlier in life must save more for retire-

---

dens under alternative incidence assumptions. Thus, they use the same basic approach as Pechman and Okner but extend it to a lifetime context. In "Lifetime Incidence and the Distributional Burden of Excise Taxes," Poterba focuses on sales and excise tax burdens in the United States. Appealing to the permanent income hypothesis of Milton Friedman in *A Theory of the Consumption Function* (Princeton: Princeton University Press, 1957), he uses current consumption as a proxy for lifetime income to classify households. He agrees with Davies, St-Hilaire, and Whalley that sales and excise taxes are less regressive in the lifetime context. Andrew B. Lyon and Robert M. Schwab use data from the University of Michigan's Panel Study of Income Dynamics in a model of life-cycle behavior to find that cigarette taxes are just as regressive, and alcohol taxes are slightly less regressive, when measured with respect to lifetime income rather than annual income. Andrew B. Lyon and Robert M. Schwab, "Consumption Taxes in a Life-Cycle Framework: Are Sin Taxes Regressive?" *Review of Economics and Statistics*, forthcoming.

8. University of Michigan, Institute for Social Research, *A Panel Study of Income Dynamics* (Ann Arbor: Institute for Social Research, 1987), data set, 1970–1987 survey years.

ment. Those groups are then likely to benefit more from a consumption tax used to replace any tax on capital income. Also, we add to each group an estimate of inheritances. They are highly concentrated at the top of the income distribution, and they also affect the incidence of replacing taxes on capital income.

Third, we use data from the Consumer Expenditure Survey[9] to estimate how people allocate their consumption among specific commodities. Those choices depend on age and income. If a uniform consumption tax replaces one that affects relative product prices, it may then burden some groups more than others.

Fourth, we build a general equilibrium simulation model that encompasses all major U.S. taxes, many industries, both corporate and noncorporate sectors within each industry, and consumers identified by both age and lifetime income. It is not a model of annual decision making, but a life-cycle model in which each individual faces a particular inheritance, a set of tax rules, a wage profile, and a transfer profile. Each then plans an entire lifetime of labor supply, savings, demand for each consumption commodity, and bequest. We also specify producer behavior, which determines each industry's use of labor, capital, and intermediate inputs. We can then simulate the effects of a tax change on each economic decision through time. We calculate new labor supplies, savings, capital stocks, outputs, and prices. With effects on all ages in all years, we can also calculate the change in economic welfare for groups ranging from those with low lifetime income to those with high lifetime income.

Fifth, we evaluate the effects of using a consumption tax or a wage tax to replace each U.S. tax. In our model those two replacement taxes are not equivalent. During the transition, retired individuals prefer the wage tax. Even in the steady state, because of inheritances, the present value of consumption for any individual exceeds the present value of wage income.[10] Thus, the consumption tax base is larger than the wage tax base, which allows a lower tax rate and a greater efficiency gain. Also, because those inheritances are concentrated in the higher lifetime income categories, the consumption tax is more burdensome than the wage tax on the lifetime rich.

---

9. U.S. Department of Labor, Bureau of Labor Statistics, *Consumer Expenditure Survey* (Washington, D.C.: Government Printing Office, 1985), data set, 1984–1985.

10. Individuals are born with an endowment of capital and must die with the same amount of capital, augmented by the rate of economic growth. Because the specified growth rate is lower than the specified interest rate, those bequests augment consumption possibilities.

Using either consumption or wage taxes, we find that replacement of the personal income tax is regressive, while the replacement of current sales and excise taxes would be progressive. The reason is that current sales and excise taxes place higher rates on goods like alcohol and tobacco that constitute a higher fraction of low-income groups' spending. Replacement of the payroll tax is also progressive, because the current tax is regressive.

Replacement of the property tax raises the net rate of return to capital in our model, so it helps high-income groups on the sources side. It also reduces the cost of housing, however, so it benefits low-income households on the uses side. Thus, the general pattern of gains is U-shaped across our lifetime income groups.

Our results for replacement of the corporate income tax are a bit surprising. In the standard analysis, replacement of the corporation income tax would raise the net rate of return to all owners of capital. Since those capital owners are in high annual income brackets, the change would be *regressive*. In our base year of 1984, however, the corporation income tax collects very little revenue.[11] Any tax that might have been collected on the return to equity is largely offset by interest deductions, investment tax credits, and accelerated depreciation allowances. The removal of the corporate tax system of credits and deductions hardly affects the total rate of return on the sources side. It does raise costs for industries that received more than the average amount of investment tax credits and accelerated depreciation allowances, however, and it therefore reduces the relative cost of other outputs such as tobacco and gasoline. Those goods constitute a high fraction of low-income budgets, on the uses side, so the change has a *progressive* effect in our model.

In general, our analysis emphasizes the estimation of lifetime incomes with panel data, the use of detailed consumption data to determine consumption patterns, and the general equilibrium determination of tax burdens. To apply the lifetime approach in routine policy analysis, we have developed ways to simplify the procedure. We shall discuss some of those possible simplifications below.

A Measure of Lifetime Income

To discuss how lifetime income can differ from annual income, we begin with a case in which the two measures are identical. If each per-

---

11. This revenue is calculated from observed capital stocks, an assumed 4 percent net rate of return, and effective tax rates that reflect the statutory tax rules for different assets under 1984 law. It thus reflects a long-run equilibrium, not short-run profit fluctuations.

son's income never changed over time, then annual income would accurately reflect permanent income. Each path in figure 13–1 would be flat, and individuals would not change annual income categories. In this case the poorest annual income category would include the same individuals as the poorest lifetime category.

The first difference between the two measures therefore arises from hump-shaped income profiles. Many studies confirm that incomes rise during early years, level off during later working years, and fall during retirement. That pattern puts young and old lifetime-rich individuals into groups with low annual incomes. The different groupings can affect incidence results.

A second difference can arise simply with income volatility. Self-employed individuals with a midrange permanent income might be placed into a category of high annual income or low annual income, depending on the year taken for study. Employed workers subject to temporary layoffs may experience similar fluctuations in annual incomes.

A third distinction is that, while the annual incidence of capital taxation depends on fixed capital endowments, the lifetime incidence of capital taxation depends on inheritances and on the shape of the *earnings* profiles. If that profile is steeply peaked, the individual must save more for retirement and bear more burden of capital taxation. In our results below, we find that incidence depends not only on the height of the peak but also on the timing of the peak. For example, we find that the earnings of middle-income groups tend to peak later in life, so those groups do not accumulate as much savings relative to richer and poorer groups. The burden of capital taxation falls on those whose earnings peak early and who therefore save more for later.

A fourth difference is that the composition of lifetime income varies less than the composition of annual income. Differences in the capital-share of annual incomes that arise from the average amount of life-cycle savings are not relevant in the lifetime perspective. The only relevant differences in the composition of lifetime income must derive from bequests and inheritances or from variations in the timing of earnings relative to consumption. Therefore, taxes that change relative factor prices have less effect on the sources side. Similarly, all individuals progress from one set of consumption goods when young to another set of consumption goods when old. The composition of spending may still depend on income, in the lifetime perspective, but it does not depend on age. Therefore, taxes that change the relative prices of goods have less effect on the uses side.

Those considerations suggest that *all* distributional effects of taxes are likely to be muted in the lifetime context. The progressivity of the personal income tax places low tax rates not just on the lifetime-poor, but also on the lifetime-rich who are young. In addition, high personal taxes may be paid by lifetime-poor individuals who happen to be at the top of their earnings hump. On the other hand, a progressive annual tax structure generates heavier burdens on individuals with more humped lifetime income profiles, all else equal.

To estimate lifetime incomes, we require longitudinal data for many individuals over many years. This analysis has only recently become possible because the University of Michigan's Panel Study of Income Dynamics has been asking the same questions of the same individuals now for over eighteen years. From that study we draw a sample of 500 households that includes 858 adult individuals and information on wages, taxes, transfers, and various demographic variables from 1970 through 1987. We include heads and wives in our sample, and for simplicity in defining the lifetime of a household, we exclude households whose marital status varied over the sample period. For heads and wives separately, we estimate the wage rate as a nonlinear function of age, so that for each individual in the sample we can predict the wage rate for years that come after as well as before the sample period, multiply the actual or estimated gross-of-tax wage rate by a total number of hours per year (for example, 4,000) to get the value of the endowment, and then calculate the present value of that endowment for each person. Thus, our level of well-being is defined by *potential* earnings, including the value of leisure. We use those levels to classify households into twelve groups according to lifetime ability to pay, where we define a household's lifetime income to be the average of the head's and wife's (if any) lifetime incomes. We start with ten deciles, but we separate the poorest 2 percent from the next poorest 8 percent, and we separate the richest 2 percent from the next richest 8 percent.

Also, we are interested in the timing of income, because the shape of an individual's lifetime income profile determines the composition of annual income. Therefore, we reestimate the nonlinear wage profile separately for each of the twelve groups. In addition, we require information on the time path of personal income taxes paid, and transfers received, to set up a consistent benchmark data set with a path of consumer spending out of total available net-of-tax income.

Thus, our lifetime income and classification differ from previous studies such as those by Joseph A. Pechman and Benjamin A. Okner[12] because of hump-shaped earnings profiles, volatility in annual income, the timing of the peak in earnings, the exclusion of capital income, the

12. Pechman and Okner, *Who Bears the Tax Burden?*

use of a life-cycle model, the use of heads and spouses (but not entire households) as the unit of account, and the decision to include leisure in the total value of endowment. The next logical question, therefore, is whether those issues really matter. How is lifetime classification different from the standard sort of classification?

We find that the annual income categories do not match up with the lifetime income categories for the same individuals. For each of our 858 individuals, we calculate annual income in 1984 for classification into annual income deciles. As it turns out, only 21.1 percent of those individuals are in the same annual and lifetime income deciles, and only 46.1 percent are within plus or minus one of the same decile. Most of the differences occur when someone who is lifetime-rich is very young or very old and earns low annual income. If we label the bottom 30 percent of the population the "poor" and the top 30 percent the "rich," we find that 13.8 percent of the annual poor are lifetime rich and 2.6 percent of the annual rich are lifetime poor. We conclude that annual and lifetime income classifications are too different to assume that annual and lifetime tax incidence will be similar.

We illustrate the final wage profiles for several of the lifetime income categories in figure 13–2. Each is the profile for a representative individual in the category. Groups 1 and 2 represent the lowest 2 percent and next lowest 8 percent of the lifetime income distribution, respectively. Group 4 represents individuals between the twentieth and thirtieth percentiles, and group 9 consists of those between the seventieth and eightieth percentiles. Group 12 is the top 2 percent of the population, and group 11 is the next highest 8 percent.

From figure 13–2 it is apparent that individuals in the higher lifetime income categories are characterized by wage profiles that are more peaked. The richest category (group 12) appears to be significantly more peaked than the second richest (group 11), which suggests that our split of the top decile is important. Because we use life-cycle consumption behavior in our model, the increasing peakedness implies that higher lifetime income categories will save more for retirement and will have higher ratios of capital to labor income. This ratio is key to determining the incidence of a consumption tax relative to capital taxes.

In figure 13–2 we can also see that those wage profiles peak at different points in the life cycle. For the first few income groups, the peak age has a slight upward trend, as group 2 peaks at age thirty-nine, group 4 peaks at age forty-seven, and group 9 peaks at age sixty-four. Then, at higher levels of income, the peak wage years come earlier, at age fifty for group 11 and at forty-seven for group 12. Thus, the middle-income groups, with the later earnings peaks, do not need

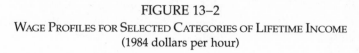

FIGURE 13–2

WAGE PROFILES FOR SELECTED CATEGORIES OF LIFETIME INCOME
(1984 dollars per hour)

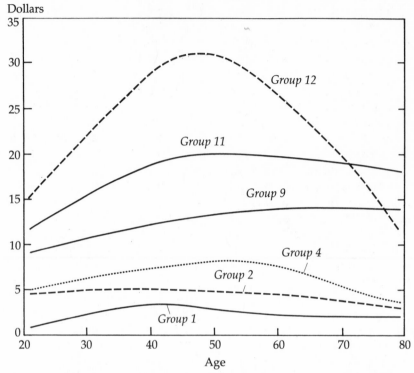

SOURCE: Fullerton and Rogers, *Who Bears the Lifetime Tax Burden?* (Washington, D.C.: Brookings Institution, 1993), fig. 1–3, p. 28. Reprinted with permission of the Brookings Institution.

to save as much for retirement. The lowest income groups and the highest income groups have earlier peaks, save more during life, and bear more burden of capital taxation.

The General Equilibrium Model

Our approach to analyzing lifetime tax incidence uses a rather sophisticated general equilibrium model to account for the behavioral effects and excess burdens taxes cause. We want to capture important influences of taxes on diverse household choices about labor supply, savings, and the consumption of different commodities. We therefore assume utility maximization to find demands for commodities and

274

supply of factors. We also want to capture effects of taxes on each producer's use of labor and capital, so we assume profit maximization to find demands for factors. We solve for general equilibrium prices to capture the net impact of taxes when those behaviors are considered simultaneously.

We assume that consumer decisions are made in stages. To begin, the individual calculates the present value of potential lifetime earnings. This endowment is supplemented by government transfers, reduced by taxes, discounted at the after-tax interest rate, and augmented by a fixed initial inheritance. For computational simplicity, we assume that the consumer expects the current interest rate to prevail in all future periods.

One part of this lifetime endowment must be saved for a bequest upon death. We avoid the many possible motivations for individual bequests or the many ways in which taxes might affect the size of those bequests.[13] Instead, we are concerned that life-cycle saving by itself can explain only about half the observed capital stock.[14] In our model part of the capital stock is attributable to the fact that individuals receive exogenous inheritances and are then simply required to leave comparable bequests at the end of life. Incidence results depend on the differences in those exogenous inheritances among groups. To achieve balanced growth, members of each group must add some additional savings to inheritance before they make their bequests.

The rest of the present value of income is available for spending. Decisions are made in stages. At the first stage, the consumer chooses how much to spend each period. That choice depends on our assumption for the individual's rate of time preference (.005 in the central case) and the elasticity of substitution among time periods (.5 in the central case). We later test the sensitivity of results to those parameters. The consumer's choice about how much to spend each period is also affected by changes in the net rate of return (which starts at .04 in the central case).

At the second stage the consumer allocates one period's "spending" between leisure and other consumption goods. That choice depends on our assumption regarding another elasticity of substitution (.5 in the central case). We allow individuals to "buy" more leisure at

13. B. Douglas Bernheim, "How Strong Are Bequest Motives? Evidence Based on Estimates of the Demand for Life Insurance and Annuities," *Journal of Political Economy*, vol. 99 (1991), pp. 899–927.

14. Laurence J. Kotlikoff and Lawrence H. Summers, "The Role of Intergenerational Transfers in Aggregate Capital Accumulation," *Journal of Political Economy*, vol. 89 (1981), pp. 706–32.

a price equal to the forgone net-of-tax wage, instead of buying other goods. That choice is affected by taxes, and it also depends on age. Individuals in this model never fully retire, but the weight on leisure increases with age after they reach sixty in a way that reflects actual choices.

In the third stage individuals decide how to allocate current consumption spending among seventeen particular goods (such as food, alcohol, tobacco, utilities, and housing). That decision function takes the form of a linear-expenditure system, which means that a consumer at a given age has to buy a set of seventeen "minimum required purchase" amounts and then allocates remaining spending according to a set of seventeen "marginal expenditure shares." We estimate those thirty-four parameters for each of twelve age categories by using data from the Consumer Expenditure Survey, as described thoroughly in Fullerton and Rogers.[15] The linear-expenditure framework has several important implications. By making a portion of spending nondiscretionary, it reduces the sensitivity of total consumption and saving to the net rate of return. In addition, because discretionary income may be spent in proportions different from minimum requirements, actual purchase proportions depend on total income. Required spending is relatively high for housing and gasoline, while discretionary spending is relatively high for clothing, services, and recreation. Thus, the rich and the poor buy different bundles and bear different burdens on the uses side.[16]

In the fourth stage of our consumer's allocation process, we divide the expenditure on each consumer good by fixed coefficients among components drawn from a list of producer industries. No real "decision" is made here, but this step allows us to match up consumption data using one definition of commodities with production data using

---

15. Fullerton and Rogers, *Who Bears the Lifetime Tax Burden?*

16. This framework also allows us to use the same utility function for everyone in the model. In previous efforts rich and poor individuals spend in different proportions because they have different preferences. But then the rich and the poor differ in fundamental characteristics and not just by the amount of income they receive. We feel that this assumption is very arbitrary: even if the poor were to receive additional income, they would still spend it as if they were poor, according to their unchanged proportions. It seems more natural, to us, that a poor person with more money would begin to behave like a rich person. That is, the primary distinction between rich and poor is the amount of income they receive. Therefore, in our model, everyone has the same preference parameters. The poor spend more on goods with high minimum required expenditures, because they are poor, and the rich spend more on goods with relatively high marginal expenditure shares.

a different definition. For example, expenditure on the consumer good "appliances" comprises portions from metals and machinery, from transportation, and from the trade industry.

Then, in the fifth and final stage of the decision tree, the consumer takes the spending on each industry output and allocates it between the corporate sector and the noncorporate sector. We assume that the corporate output is not identical to the noncorporate output in the same industry. Hand-carved furniture, for example, is not the same as manufactured furniture. We specify the consumer's choice of the amount of each by using a weighing parameter based on initial observed corporate and noncorporate shares of production within each industry and by using another elasticity of substitution (5.0 in the central case). That specification allows us to capture the observed coexistence of both sectors within an industry, despite different tax treatments. If the outputs were identical, then a higher tax rate would drive one sector out of production. The degree of similarity is reflected in the elasticity of substitution. The other purpose of that specification is to capture ways in which changes in corporate taxes affect relative product prices and quantities demanded of the outputs of each sector.

We employ a similar decision tree to model producer behavior in each sector of each industry. Many competitive firms produce each output in multistage production functions with constant returns to scale. Also, for computational simplicity, we assume no externalities, no adjustment costs, and no uncertainty.

In the first stage of production, output comprises a fixed coefficient combination of value added and intermediate inputs. Each of the nineteen industries uses the outputs of all other industries in fixed proportions. Thus, we capture the effect of one product price on another. In the second stage, value added is a function of labor and "composite" capital. We base the weighing parameters on observed labor and capital in each industry, and the elasticity of substitution varies by industry (between .68 and .96 in the central case). Thus, a tax on labor can induce the firm to use more capital instead and vice versa. The tax also raises the cost of production, and thus output price, in any industry that uses a high proportion of the taxed factor.

In the third and final stage of the production tree, composite capital is a function of five asset types—equipment, structures, land, inventories, and intangible assets. Those types are defined by important tax differences such as the investment tax credit for equipment and the expensing of new intangible assets created through advertising or research and development. We again base the weighing shares on the observed use of those assets in each industry, and we again specify the response to tax differentials by an elasticity of substitution (1.5 in the central case).

Government in this model conducts several functions. It pays transfers to individuals according to the estimated lifetime transfer profiles discussed in the previous section. It produces an output for sale through an industry called government enterprises, and it also produces a free public good through a composite combination of its use of labor, capital, and purchases of each private industry output. The weights in this combination are based on observed government purchases, and the elasticity of substitution is one. We hold the level of this public good fixed in all simulations, as any tax change is accompanied by an adjustment that ensures equal-revenue yield. A final government function, of course, is to collect taxes.

Each tax instrument enters the model as a wedge between the producer's price and the consumer's price. The payroll tax, for example, applies an ad valorem rate to each producer's use of labor, so the gross-of-tax wage the producer pays is higher than the net-of-tax wage the worker receives. Similarly, sales and excise taxes appear as ad valorem rates on each consumer good, so the gross-of-tax price the consumer pays exceeds the net-of-tax price the seller receives.

To capture the progressive effect of personal income taxes on tax burdens is more complicated. The actual U.S. personal tax system imposes higher effective tax rates on higher incomes through a graduated rate structure with a changing marginal tax rate. For some purposes, one must calculate the effects of individuals' choices at each different possible marginal tax rate to determine utility-maximizing behavior. Our primary goal, however, is to measure the distributional effects of the tax. For that purpose it is sufficient to use a set of linear tax functions that approximate the U.S. system with a negative intercept for each group and a single marginal tax rate (.3 in the central case). Although all individuals face the same marginal tax rate, average tax rates still increase with income owing to the negative intercepts. We do not model the myriad exemptions and deductions. The simpler, linear tax functions can replicate the observed data on personal taxes that each group actually paid.

The state and local property tax and the U.S. federal corporate income tax raise the producer's gross-of-tax cost of capital, for each asset type, relative to the investor's net-of-tax rate of return. A Hall-Jorgenson formula[17] shows how the cost of capital for each asset depends on the statutory corporate tax rate, depreciation allowances at

---

17. Robert E. Hall and Dale W. Jorgenson, "Tax Policy and Investment Behavior," *American Economic Review*, vol. 57 (1967), pp. 391–414.

historical cost, the rate at which inflation erodes those allowances, the rate of investment tax credit, and the required net rate of return for the firm. That required rate of return depends, in turn, on the going market rate and the personal taxation of interest, dividends, and capital gains. A similar cost of capital formula applies to the noncorporate sector. Such a treatment allows the producer's choice among assets to depend on relative tax rules, and the price of output in each industry to depend on the relative use of assets with different effective tax rates.

Other assumptions help to close the model in a way that accounts for all flows and that helps facilitate computation. We ignore international mobility of labor or capital, but allow for trade of industry outputs. Also, the value of imports must match the value of exports; the government's expenditures and transfer payments must match tax revenue; and the value of personal savings must match the value of investment expenditures. Producer investment is not the result of firms' intertemporal optimization, but instead follows personal savings from consumers' optimization. The amount of personal savings grows over time, because consumers' labor earnings increase through population growth and technical change. On the steady-state growth path, the capital stock grows at exactly the same rate as the effective labor stock.

Data for the model derive from many different sources, and we adjust them to represent 1984 as the base year. In addition to the survey data used to estimate wage profiles and preference parameters, we use the National Income and Product Accounts[18] for an input-output matrix, labor compensation by industry, government purchases, and international trade. We combine those data with other published and unpublished data, such as on capital allocations and inheritances.

For some parameters, such as the elasticities of substitution, we assume particular values. For other parameters, such as the linear-expenditure preferences, we have econometric estimates. Finally, for remaining parameters we calibrate from data on actual allocations. We use the demand functions and all initial prices and observed quantities to solve backwards for the value of the parameter that would make that quantity the desired one. Such a procedure establishes a benchmark equilibrium, with existing tax rules and prices, such that all consumers are buying the desired quantities and supplying the desired amounts of each factor, while producers are using their desired amounts of factors to produce the desired output.

Thus, using all those parameters together, we can solve for an

---

18. U.S. Department of Commerce, *Survey of Current Business* (Washington, D.C.: Government Printing Office, various years) and unpublished Commerce Department data.

equilibrium with unchanged tax rules that replicates the benchmark-consistent data. That provides an important check on the solution procedure. From the benchmark we can alter any particular tax rule and see how much more or less the consumers want to buy of each good. The solution algorithm then raises the price of any good in excess demand and lowers the price of any good in excess supply until it finds a set of prices at which the quantity supplied equals the quantity demanded for every good and factor. The algorithm simulates the effect of the tax change to calculate all new prices, quantities, and levels of consumer utility. Our measure of the change in tax burden is the equivalent variation—the dollar value of the change in utility measured in terms of benchmark prices. We compare the lifetime equivalent variations with each category's lifetime income to determine relative lifetime tax burdens and the lifetime incidence of the various taxes, relative to the consumption-tax or wage-tax replacement.

Results

As we discussed, the incidence of any additional tax within the general equilibrium model is defined relative to the tax it replaces. We focus on the lifetime incidence of a general consumption tax and of a wage tax. Although both types of replacement taxes are intertemporally efficient, the consumption tax base is larger than the wage tax base because of the presence of bequests. The timing of the two taxes also differs, because life-cycle behavior generates consumption paths that are smoother than the peaked wage paths. The two replacements therefore can produce very different transitional effects, but our results emphasize the long-run, steady-state incidence of taxes.

We measure the distributional effects between rich and poor by the gains to each lifetime income group in the steady state. The results for the consumption-tax replacement using our central parameterization appear in table 13–1. Total gains in the steady state appear at the bottom of each column in the table. That steady-state welfare gain is not a pure efficiency measure, because it includes redistribution to later generations from current generations, which may lose when the tax change is imposed. Indeed, we often find gains to future steady-state generations and losses to older transitional generations. For a general measure of "efficiency," at the bottom of the table we simply take the present value of all equivalent variations for all generations, discounted at the net rate of return.[19]

---

19. This procedure implicitly puts lower weight on later generations, but

Each table includes a column for each U.S. tax instrument being removed. We first discuss the consumption-tax replacement. In the first column of table 13–1, the effects of replacing the personal income tax range from a 5 percent loss of income for the poorest group to a 9 percent gain for the richest group. The pattern is clearly regressive. The bottom of the column indicates that this replacement would yield a total steady-state gain equal to 2.6 percent of income. That amount is also equal to 21 percent of the personal income tax revenue being replaced. The present-value gain is .7 percent of income (5 percent of revenue). The difference is caused by losses to transitional generations. Those who are near retirement at the time of the change would have paid low personal income taxes over the remainder of their lifetimes, but the consumption tax applies to all their remaining consumption.

We might consider the .7 percent efficiency gain substantial, especially since the personal income tax and the consumption tax *both* distort labor supply decisions. But progressivity makes the personal income tax more distorting. The personal marginal tax rate exceeds the total tax as a fraction of income, as is necessary for that average tax rate to rise with income. Distortions depend on the .30 marginal tax rate, while revenue depends on the average rate. Thus, the personal income tax is relatively distorting per dollar of revenue. In contrast, the uniform consumption tax needs a rate of only .12 to collect the same revenue.

In the second column we use a consumption tax to replace all existing U.S. sales and excise taxes. Contrary to initial intuition, the introduction of a consumption tax is clearly progressive. The explanation is that current sales and excise taxes are more regressive because they apply at nonuniform rates. Actual incidence depends on the pattern of tax rates and the pattern of goods consumed by the different lifetime income categories. Indeed, the point of our Stone-Geary specification is to allow for rich and poor households to purchase goods in different proportions. As it turns out, poorer households consume proportionately larger amounts of the highly taxed goods such as gasoline, alcohol, and tobacco. Poterba may be right that a uniform consumption tax would be proportional to lifetime income with no bequests, but the

---

the discounting is necessary to obtain a finite sum for a sequence that is growing over time because of technical progress and population growth. To avoid having a measure of efficiency that would increase with the number of individuals, we discount by population growth to calculate this present value equivalent variation, *EV,* for the size of the population alive at the time of the change.

TABLE 13–1
Welfare Effects of Using a Uniform Consumption Tax to Replace Each U.S. Tax, with Standard Parameters

Lifetime Income Category	Personal Taxes	Sales and Excise Taxes	Payroll Taxes	Property Taxes	Corporate Taxes	Entire Tax System
1	-5.09	1.70	0.73	0.60	1.14	-2.00
2	-0.34	1.27	0.48	0.55	0.89	3.19
3	-0.70	1.22	0.54	0.21	0.78	2.48
4	0.71	1.16	0.55	0.33	0.81	3.94
5	2.53	1.19	0.64	0.09	0.78	5.66
6	0.66	1.11	0.61	0.19	0.77	3.74
7	2.22	1.04	0.53	0.59	0.85	5.64
8	2.43	1.08	0.65	0.14	0.76	5.47
9	3.01	1.06	0.67	0.17	0.77	6.09
10	3.04	0.98	0.55	0.16	0.74	5.83
11	4.19	0.72	0.16	0.73	0.83	6.81
12	9.11	0.60	0.01	1.08	0.93	11.87
All twelve categories in steady state						
As % of lifetime income	2.57	1.02	0.50	0.36	0.80	5.58
As % of revenue	20.88	10.32	8.86	11.58	314.63	17.62
All generations						
As % of PV(lifetime income)	0.66	0.18	0.05	0.17	0.25	1.25
As % of PV(revenue)	5.10	1.76	0.80	5.04	84.14	3.75

PV = present value; EV = equivalent variation.
NOTE: EV as % of lifetime income for steady-state generations.
SOURCE: Authors' computations using Fullerton and Rogers (1993) model.

sales and excise taxes are not uniform.[20] The rate structure introduces regressivity.[21]

The difference between the 1 percent steady-state welfare gain and the total .18 percent efficiency gain indicates how much of the steady-state gain is attributable to effects in the transition.

The third column of table 13–1 considers the replacement of U.S. payroll taxes with a uniform consumption tax. Again, the consumption tax replacement is quite progressive on a lifetime basis. And again, that result conflicts with initial intuitions. In a simple life-cycle model with no bequests, each individual's present value of lifetime labor income exactly equals the present value of consumption. Therefore, a uniform consumption tax is equivalent to a flat wage tax. Here the equivalence is broken by bequests that rise as a fraction of total endowment for higher lifetime-income groups. Those high-income individuals are required to leave the same size bequest as they receive, but they get to consume out of the extra capital income during their lifetimes. Therefore, the consumption tax base exceeds the labor tax base for them. The simple consumption tax is more progressive than a labor income tax.

The switch from the payroll tax to a consumption tax hurts the elderly, raises revenue from them, and allows gains to subsequent generations. We show those intergenerational gains and losses in figure 13–3 for three of the tax change simulations. Lifetime effects of replacing the payroll tax on labor are represented by the bottom, solid line. Those born twenty to sixty years ago (with chronological age forty to eighty) incur small net losses. Net lifetime effects are positive and growing for those born later. The small bump for those born five years after the change is only an artifact of our five-year snapshots. Those born ten years after the change, and later, receive the steady-state gain equal to .50 percent of lifetime income. As in table 13–1, the present value of those net effects is a mere .05 percent of the present value of all lifetime incomes. Losses to transitional generations almost completely offset gains to steady-state generations, so the consumption tax is no more efficient than the labor income tax. Both distort primarily only labor supply decisions. The difference is purely distributional. The payroll tax is more regressive than the consumption tax.

In the fourth column of table 13–1, if the consumption tax replaces

20. Poterba, "Lifetime Incidence and the Distributional Burden of Excise Taxes."

21. Both the existing sales and excise taxes and the replacement consumption tax exempt untaxed leisure, but they both apply to spending out of inheritances. Fullerton and Rogers in *Who Bears the Lifetime Tax Burden?* show how those considerations affect the regressivity of all of the consumption taxes.

FIGURE 13–3

GAINS AND LOSSES TO EACH GENERATION WHEN A CONSUMPTION TAX
REPLACES EACH U.S. TAX (FOR ALL INCOME GROUPS,
WITH STANDARD PARAMETERS)

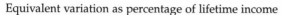

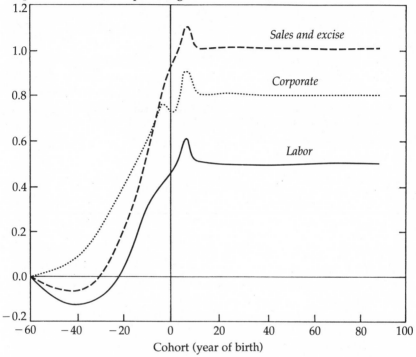

SOURCE: Fullerton and Rogers, *Who Bears the Lifetime Tax Burden?* (Washington, D.C.: Brookings Institution, 1993), fig. 7–1. Reprinted with permission of the Brookings Institution.

current property taxes, the distribution of gains is U-shaped. That replacement raises the net rate of return and affects owners of capital on the sources side. Because wage profiles peak later for middle-income groups in figure 13–2, they save less. Thus, the ratio of capital income to labor income is approximately U-shaped across the lifetime income groups. The property tax repeal also reduces the cost of housing and thus helps low-income groups on the uses side.

The efficiency gain is only .17 percent of income, for two reasons. First, the property tax applies primarily to use of capital in the housing sector and thus helps offset some of the misallocation due to high corporate taxes on other uses of capital. Thus, its repeal worsens intersectoral distortions. Second, the property tax is not a big tax. The last line shows that the efficiency gain is 5 percent of revenue, higher than for some other tax instruments.

Finally, in the fifth column we use the consumption tax to replace the corporate income tax. Gains are flat or just slightly U-shaped. All groups gain from that replacement, because the corporate tax is distortionary. The efficiency gain is a very high 84 percent of revenue, since the 1984 corporate tax in this model misallocates resources without raising much revenue.

An apparent implication is that the corporate tax should be repealed. It could be entirely replaced by a small consumption tax, with gains to every income group. While this simulation does indicate such a Pareto improvement, it does not indicate the best possible reform. The consumption tax replacement might be costly to introduce, it might be difficult to administer, and it might not be applied to all goods at a uniform rate as in this simulation. A different approach might "fix" the corporate tax to collect more revenue with less distortion. The Tax Reform Act of 1986 undertook such an attempt.

The last column of table 13–1 shows the distributional effects of replacing the entire U.S. tax system with a uniform consumption tax. The poorest lifetime income group would lose 2 percent of lifetime income, and the richest group would gain 12 percent of income. Thus, current U.S. taxes are progressive relative to the consumption tax. The first five columns indicate that most of the general progressivity is attributable to the personal income tax.

Under the standard parameters, replacing the entire U.S. tax system with a national value-added tax would generate an efficiency gain equal to 1.25 percent of lifetime incomes or 3.75 percent of tax revenues.

We now vary one of the key assumptions of the model, the intertemporal substitution elasticity. That parameter sets the degree to which consumers will switch between present consumption and future consumption, and it therefore helps determine the responsiveness of savings to relative prices such as the net rate of return to capital. Responsive savers can "avoid" a tax on capital by saving less, which ultimately decreases the marginal product of labor, decreases the wage, and "shifts" the burden to labor.

In the central case simulations, we used .5 for that elasticity. While we might consider that value on the high end of the estimates econometric studies produce,[22] it helps generate a capital stock in our model

---

22. See Robert E. Hall, "Intertemporal Substitution in Consumption," *Jour-*

that is close to the one actually observed in the benchmark data. If we simply reduced that elasticity from .5 to .25, the initial steady-state capital stock would fall to unreasonably low levels (about 32.5 percent of the measured capital stock). Therefore, we lower the elasticity and simultaneously lower the rate of time preference. In combination, those respecifications leave us with an initial capital stock close to that of the central case simulations.

Our "alternative" specification reduces the intertemporal substitution elasticity from .50 to .25, and it reduces the rate of time preference from .005 to −.005. As a theoretical matter, that rate of time preference may be either positive or negative. As an empirical matter, many readers may prefer a value that is even larger than the .005 we use in the standard case. The only way to achieve a higher rate of time preference with the same capital stock, however, is to raise the .5 value for the intertemporal substitution elasticity.

We report the results in table 13–2. Comparing the present values in that table with those in table 13–1, we see that the efficiency gains were larger under the standard parameters. In our alternative, replacement of the entire tax system with a value-added tax provides an efficiency gain of only .86 percent of lifetime incomes or 2.54 percent of tax revenues. That difference arises because the standard case uses a higher intertemporal elasticity. Thus, in the standard case, the savings distortions under current taxes are larger, and the efficiency gains from removing those distortions are higher. The contrast between efficiency effects in tables 1 and 2 is especially clear for replacing taxes on personal income or on property, since those taxes generate the biggest intertemporal distortions.

In tables 13–3 and 13–4 we report results for the wage tax replacement to emphasize the possible differences between consumption taxation and wage taxation. In general, the *intra*generational patterns of tax burdens under the wage-tax replacement are very similar to those under the consumption-tax replacement, with one exception. The uniform consumption tax looked progressive relative to current sales and excise taxes that place higher rates on goods purchased by low-income groups, but the wage tax in tables 13–3 and 13–4 appears to provide U-shaped welfare gains. Low-income groups still gain from removal

nal of Political Economy, vol. 96 (1988), pp. 339–57, and other studies cited in Alan J. Auerbach and Laurence J. Kotlikoff, *Dynamic Fiscal Policy* (New York: Cambridge University Press, 1987), pp. 50–51. Eric M. Engen's estimates in his Ph.D. dissertation, "Precautionary Saving, Consumption, and Taxation in a Life-Cycle Model with Stochastic Earnings and Mortality Risk," University of Virginia, 1992, fall between .30 and .38 for this parameter.

TABLE 13–2

Welfare Effects of Using a Uniform Consumption Tax to Replace Each U.S. Tax, with Alternative Parameters

Lifetime Income Category	Personal Taxes	Sales and Excise Taxes	Payroll Taxes	Property Taxes	Corporate Taxes	Entire Tax System
1	-5.58	2.01	1.05	0.64	1.34	-2.85
2	-0.79	1.29	0.50	0.37	0.83	2.56
3	-1.38	1.27	0.61	-0.11	0.69	1.49
4	0.09	1.21	0.61	0.03	0.73	3.03
5	1.76	1.26	0.72	-0.31	0.66	4.53
6	-0.06	1.17	0.69	-0.17	0.67	2.71
7	1.80	1.06	0.56	0.41	0.80	5.07
8	1.62	1.14	0.73	-0.24	0.65	4.31
9	2.24	1.13	0.75	-0.21	0.67	4.99
10	2.28	1.04	0.63	-0.20	0.64	4.71
11	3.19	0.72	0.17	0.65	0.79	6.36
12	9.11	0.57	-0.02	1.16	0.93	11.82
All twelve categories in steady state						
As % of lifetime income	1.96	1.06	0.55	0.09	0.72	4.71
As % of revenue	15.83	10.84	9.94	2.74	214.22	14.75
All generations						
As % of PV(lifetime incomes)	0.42	0.18	0.06	0.07	0.22	0.86
As % of PV(revenue)	3.22	1.78	1.02	1.97	54.84	2.54

PV = present value; EV = equivalent variation.

NOTE: EV as % of income for steady-state generations.

SOURCE: Authors' computations using Fullerton and Rogers (1993) model.

TABLE 13–3
WELFARE EFFECTS OF USING A UNIFORM WAGE TAX TO REPLACE EACH U.S. TAX, WITH STANDARD PARAMETERS

Lifetime Income Category	Personal Taxes	Sales and Excise Taxes	Payroll Taxes	Property Taxes	Corporate Taxes	Entire Tax System
1	-6.21	1.19	0.39	0.36	1.12	-5.86
2	-1.47	0.62	0.08	0.27	0.87	-0.80
3	-1.96	0.39	0.06	-0.11	0.76	-1.97
4	-0.55	0.33	0.07	-0.00	0.79	-0.55
5	1.15	0.19	0.07	-0.28	0.75	0.80
6	-0.69	0.15	0.07	-0.17	0.74	-1.03
7	1.01	0.22	0.07	0.27	0.83	1.32
8	0.97	0.02	0.06	-0.24	0.73	0.36
9	1.56	-0.02	0.07	-0.22	0.75	0.96
10	1.81	0.10	0.06	-0.16	0.72	1.43
11	3.77	0.59	0.06	0.62	0.82	5.00
12	9.03	0.75	0.08	1.06	0.94	11.12
All twelve categories in steady state						
As % of lifetime income	1.43	0.26	0.07	0.07	0.78	1.53
As % of revenue	6.54	1.29	0.65	1.14	162.55	2.26
All generations						
As % of PV (lifetime income)	0.60	0.14	0.02	0.14	0.25	0.93
As % of PV (revenue)	2.59	0.66	0.19	2.26	44.14	1.31

PV = present value; EV = equivalent variation.
NOTE: EV as % of lifetime income for steady-state generations.
SOURCE: Authors' computations using Fullerton and Rogers (1993) model.

TABLE 13–4
Welfare Effects of Using a Uniform Wage Tax to Replace Each U.S. Tax, with Alternative Parameters

Lifetime Income Category	Personal Taxes	Sales and Excise Taxes	Payroll Taxes	Property Taxes	Corporate Taxes	Entire Tax System
1	−6.80	1.42	0.66	0.38	1.31	−6.78
2	−1.96	0.59	0.08	0.07	0.81	−1.42
3	−2.75	0.33	0.05	−0.46	0.66	−3.12
4	−1.28	0.27	0.06	−0.33	0.69	−1.64
5	0.26	0.11	0.06	−0.72	0.62	−0.55
6	−1.53	0.08	0.06	−0.56	0.63	−2.28
7	0.55	0.19	0.07	0.06	0.77	0.73
8	0.03	−0.05	0.05	−0.66	0.60	−1.05
9	0.65	−0.09	0.06	−0.64	0.62	−0.37
10	0.94	0.03	0.05	−0.56	0.60	0.16
11	3.54	0.59	0.06	0.56	0.79	5.01
12	9.19	0.80	0.08	1.17	0.95	11.75
All twelve categories in steady state						
As % of lifetime income	0.77	0.22	0.06	−0.23	0.69	0.63
As % of revenue	3.46	1.05	0.60	−3.72	105.67	0.92
All generations						
As % of PV (lifetime incomes)	0.34	0.12	0.02	0.04	0.22	0.56
As % of PV (revenue)	1.47	0.55	0.18	0.55	27.85	0.78

PV = present value; EV = equivalent variation.
NOTE: EV as percent of lifetime income for steady-state generations.
SOURCE: Authors' computations using Fullerton and Rogers (1993) model.

TABLE 13–5

TAX RATES FOR EACH REPLACEMENT, WITH STANDARD PARAMETERS

Removal of	Consumption Tax Rate		Wage Tax Rate	
	First period	Steady state	First period	Steady state
Personal taxes	.1422	.1237	.1590	.1524
Sales and excise tax	.1104	.1073	.1469	.1457
Payroll taxes	.0642	.0627	.0741	.0738
Property taxes	.0384	.0328	.0460	.0414
Corporate taxes	.0058	.0026	.0075	.0034
Entire tax system	.4425	.3686	.4716	.4718

$(c_t = .5, \delta = .005)$.
SOURCE:.

of regressive sales and excise taxes, but high-income groups also gain because the wage tax does not apply to spending out of their larger inheritances. Also, note in tables 13–3 and 13–4 that the replacement of current payroll taxes with a uniform wage tax is not a neutral tax change because of the regressivity of the social security tax system and slightly different labor tax rates across industries.

The general levels of welfare gains to the steady-state generation are lower under the wage-tax replacement for two reasons. First, the smaller tax base of the wage tax necessitates a higher replacement tax rate. We report those tax rates in table 13–5. Second, the wage-tax replacement is relatively more burdensome to younger generations, because the consumption-tax replacement places a lump-sum levy on the elderly during the transition. As indicated in the bottom two rows of tables 13–3 and 13–4, total efficiency gains are lower under the wage-tax replacement.

Using the Lifetime Horizon in Policy Analysis

Our lifetime analysis has certain qualities that are desirable from an academic standpoint: the accounting for general equilibrium price effects, the use of utility-based measures of tax burdens that include excess burdens as well as taxes paid, the measurement of lifetime income to classify rich versus poor, and, finally, the measurement of lifetime tax burdens. Those four qualities need not always go together. One could use a general equilibrium model and utility-based welfare measures without lifetime income or tax burdens. Also, one could look at annual tax burdens on groups classified by lifetime income. Our model incorporates all four. Although those qualities are attractive from an academic standpoint, they might be viewed as obstacles from a policy standpoint. In particular, the lifetime perspective has often been criticized as impractical.[23]

The most fundamental criticism of the lifetime perspective is that it inappropriately presumes life-cycle behavior. Based on the life-cycle model of consumption, academic literature has often argued that lifetime income is a better indicator of a *current* ability to pay taxes. Moreover, the pure life-cycle model assumes perfect capital markets. It suggests that current consumption is proportional to lifetime income but independent of current income. Critics of lifetime measures point to a large literature with evidence that capital markets are far from perfect; liquidity constraints cause current consumption to track current income much more closely than the life-cycle model would predict. In the real world, then, high lifetime income does not necessarily allow high current consumption, and thus does not provide high *current* ability to pay taxes. We have argued, however, that lifetime income should *not* be taken as a measure of current ability to pay taxes.[24] It is simply a measure of lifetime ability to pay taxes. That interpretation applies even when the life-cycle model does not. It suggests that the lifetime perspective is a supplement to annual analyses—a way of assessing the long-run distributional effects of taxes. Policy makers might worry that current taxes reflect current ability to pay *and* that lifetime taxes reflect lifetime ability to pay.

That criticism of the life-cycle model does pertain to our particular general equilibrium model, however, because consumers maximize lifetime utility subject only to a lifetime budget constraint. Thus, the consumption paths generated in our model are almost certainly smoother than real-world data would suggest. We use the life-cycle model because no other model provides a simple theoretical foundation while tracking real-world observations accurately. We modify the standard life-cycle model by adding bequests and heterogeneous households, but we need the behavioral framework to simulate tax changes. Analyses of lifetime tax incidence do not, however, require the assumption of life-cycle behavior. One could use actual data on assets and consumption, perhaps merged with panel data on wage in-

---

23. Many of those criticisms are discussed in the methodology pamphlet produced by the U.S. Joint Committee on Taxation, "Methodology and Issues in Measuring Changes in the Distribution of Tax Burdens," Joint Committee Print, June 1993, pp. 32–33 and 83–86.

24. Fullerton and Rogers, *Who Bears the Lifetime Tax Burden?*

come to better reflect real-world data. Such a study could then make incidence assumptions such as those made by Pechman and Okner[25] or by James B. Davies, France St-Hilaire, and John Whalley,[26] but it could simulate behavioral changes in response to a tax change.

Another criticism of the lifetime perspective, as discussed by Thomas A. Barthold, is that tax policies never last a lifetime.[27] Indeed, the details of the tax code are modified very frequently. To analyze any particular reform, however, one cannot predict subsequent changes (or else those known future changes could be analyzed as part of the reform). We do not use the model to predict the future but to provide analytical insights and numerical magnitudes related to a particular policy. To address conceptional questions about that policy, we hold all other things equal. Besides, the reverse criticism could be levied against the *annual* perspective: major reforms last more than one year, so why look only at one-year effects?

Another frequent complaint about the lifetime perspective is that actual data on lifetime incomes are simply not available. Meanwhile, the procedure we describe above to infer lifetime incomes is thought to be too cumbersome. While measuring lifetime income is obviously much more complicated than measuring annual income, the use of proxies for long-run income might be considered a practical compromise. For example, as mentioned earlier, the Congressional Budget Office has used one year's total expenditure as a supplemental measure of the ability to pay taxes. With some kind of life-cycle smoothing behavior, total expenditures in one year would reflect long-run income. For this reason, however, the use of the total-expenditure proxy is subject to the same criticisms as the life-cycle model. If capital markets are imperfect, then consumption levels may track annual income more closely than lifetime income. The total-expenditure proxy may then better reflect *annual* income than lifetime income. An alternative, but still relatively simple proxy for lifetime income could be the level of education attained, or perhaps an estimated function of education, race, gender, and other age-invariant variables. Rogers and Erik Caspersen and Gilbert Metcalf investigate the latter approach.[28]

---

25. Pechman and Okner, *Who Bears the Tax Burden?*

26. Davies, St-Hilaire, and Whalley, "Some Calculations of Lifetime Tax Incidence."

27. Barthold, "How Should We Measure Distribution?" *National Tax Journal*, vol. 46 (September 1993), pp. 291–99.

28. Rogers, "The Distributional Effects of Corrective Taxation: Assessing Lifetime Incidence from Cross-Sectional Data," *Proceedings of the Eighty-sixth Annual Conference* (National Tax Association, 1994), pp. 192–202; Erik Caspersen and Gilbert Metcalf, "Is a Value-Added Tax Regressive? Annual versus

Finally, as the Joint Committee on Taxation suggested, computations generated by lifetime or infinite horizon models can be very sensitive to the choice of parameters.[29] In particular, numerical results strongly depend on parameters affecting intertemporal choice, such as the discount rate, rate of time preference, and interest elasticity of savings (or intertemporal elasticity of substitution). That criticism merely emphasizes the importance of conducting sensitivity analyses. Furthermore, annual horizon models still generate results that are sensitive to choices of other substitution elasticities. They only avoid sensitivity to intertemporal parameters by ignoring intertemporal effects. Thus, they are unable to shed light on the dynamic effects of policies.

In summary, lifetime tax incidence can play a valuable role in policy making, as long as it is viewed as a supplement to, and not a replacement for, calculations of annual tax incidence. We could easily simplify the particular analysis described in this chapter to avoid general equilibrium price calculations and utility-based welfare measures. Alternatively, we could make the analysis *more* complicated to account for imperfect capital markets, liquidity constraints, endogenous bequests, or other phenomena. Either way, our purpose here is just to emphasize the basic distinction the lifetime framework provides—the measurement of lifetime tax burdens with respect to lifetime abilities to pay taxes.

Conclusion

The model of lifetime tax incidence that this chapter describes provides new insights into the long-run effects of consumption or wage taxation. Our simulation results highlight the trade-offs between efficiency and equity in the debate about the choice between income-based and consumption-based taxes. For example, intertemporal efficiency is greatly improved by replacing the personal income tax with a consumption or wage tax, but such a switch is lifetime regressive in nature. A switch from either sales and excise taxes or payroll taxes to a uniform consumption tax is a progressive reform but generates a much smaller efficiency gain. Our results suggest that the removal of the 1984 version of the corporate income tax provided the largest gain in relation to the small bit of revenue lost. For such a tax switch, our distribu-

Lifetime Incidence Measures," *National Tax Journal*, vol. 47 (December 1994), pp. 731–46.

29. U.S. Joint Committee on Taxation, "Methodology and Issues in Measuring Changes in the Distribution of Tax Burdens," Joint Committee Print, June 1993.

tional results are somewhat surprising. The corporate tax replacement would be slightly progressive in nature, because the corporate tax applies higher effective rates to goods that low-income families consume.

While the academic community widely accepts the concept of lifetime tax incidence, government agencies that analyze tax policy have yet to implement the concept fully. We have attempted in this chapter to respond to some of the criticisms of the lifetime approach, as voiced by government economists, but further efforts are needed to bridge the current gap between the rather stylized, academic analysis we have presented and the data-intensive types of studies policy economists undertake. Only then will the lifetime framework be routinely incorporated, along with the annual perspective, into real-world analyses of tax policies.

The Lifetime Incidence of a Consumption Tax

A Commentary by Gilbert E. Metcalf

Probably very few public finance economists are unaware of the path-breaking work by Don Fullerton and Diane Lim Rogers in their recent book, *Who Bears the Lifetime Tax Burden?*[1] This chapter uses the model developed in that book to analyze a switch from one of a number of existing taxes to a uniform consumption tax. Such a tax could be a value-added tax (VAT) or a flat-rate consumed income tax. In the steady state, it would also be equivalent to a wage tax, though not in the transition. I will return to this point later.

Strengths of the Fullerton and Rogers Approach

One of the major strengths of the approach taken by Fullerton and Rogers is their explicit measure of lifetime income in a general equilibrium context. Their approach is quite flexible: they construct wage profiles by age for different lifetime income groups, an obvious advantage over other methods of measuring lifetime income. Moreover, this approach illustrates the importance of the lifetime saving profile. The steeper wage profile (and earlier peak) for higher-income groups has important implications for distributing the burden of capital income taxes. Specifically, income groups that save early in life will be more burdened by capital income taxes than income groups for whom the wage profile is relatively flat over their lifetime.

Note the importance of measuring wage rather than earned-income profiles. Measuring earned-income profiles allows the authors to

---

These comments were prepared for presentation at the American Enterprise Institute conference, "Distributional Analysis for Making Tax Policy," held in Washington, D.C., December 16–17, 1993.

1. Don Fullerton and Diane Lim Rogers, *Who Bears the Lifetime Tax Burden?* (Washington, D.C.: Brookings Institution, 1993).

value leisure and consider substitutions between taxable consumption and untaxed leisure in their model. This advantage is often ignored in discussions of consumption versus income taxation.

The general equilibrium nature of the study allows the researchers to work from primitives to determine incidence rather than make assumptions about forward or backward shifting of the tax. Working from primitives has advantages and disadvantages; for one thing, it is more difficult to isolate the important parameters that drive results. The authors vary some of the important parameters to illustrate their effect on the results.

Disadvantages of the Fullerton and Rogers Approach

One variation I would have liked to have seen would be to reduce the elasticity of substitution between consumption and leisure. Recent research by Thomas MaCurdy and others suggests that the labor supply elasticities estimated by Hausman are too high[2]; Fullerton and Roger's labor supply elasticity is about .1. Would a VAT distribution look different if the labor supply elasticity were closer to zero?

The sensitivity analysis here presents a puzzle that illustrates a general difficulty with computable general equilibrium (CGE) models. Their base-case intertemporal substitution elasticity is set to 0.5, somewhat high considering the results from econometric studies. Yet, if they reduce this elasticity, the initial steady-state capital stock falls precipitously. CGE models in general are so complex that it is difficult for an outsider to understand or evaluate anomalies such as this. Does this puzzle indicate some conceptual flaw in the model or a minor glitch? One cannot say without a thorough dissection of the model.

Consumption versus Other Forms of Taxation

Having said that, the results that are presented make so much sense that one is inclined to believe the model and write off such concerns as minor quibbles. Moreover, they illustrate very dramatically two important points that are often neglected in the discussion over the appropriate choice of tax base. First, by providing a differential incidence

---

2. See T. MaCurdy, "Work Disincentive Effects of Taxes: A Reexamination of Some Evidence," *American Economic Review*, vol. 82 (May 1992), pp. 243–49; and J. Hausman, "Labor Supply," in *How Taxes Affect Economic Behavior*, Henry Aaron and Joseph Pechman, eds. (Washington, D.C.: Brookings Institution, 1981).

analysis, the authors remind us that consumption taxes are progressive or regressive *relative* to other taxes.

Switching from a personal income tax to a uniform consumption tax is highly regressive in Fullerton and Roger's model, a probable result of the progressive nature of the existing income tax rather than any inherent regressivity in the consumption tax. A switch from sales and excise or payroll taxes would be unambiguously progressive. The authors argue that the progressivity of the switch from payroll taxes follows from the nontaxation of bequests. Let me note in passing that incorporating the capping of the social security and Medicare tax base in their model would substantially increase the progressivity of a switch from payroll to consumption taxes. Finally, property and corporate taxes burden the poor and the rich relative to a uniform consumption tax. Poor people gain on the uses side (housing costs fall if the property tax falls), while rich people gain on the sources side.

Second, Fullerton and Rogers illustrate that transitional effects are very large. While the steady-state gain from a switch from income to consumption taxation is over 2.5 percent of lifetime income, the gain to all generations is only .7 percent of lifetime income. The difference measures the losses to the owners of old capital (primarily the current elderly) in the transition. The transitional loss is even more stark if payroll taxes are eliminated. The steady-state gains are ten times the gains to all generations, indicating that almost all the gain to future generations comes at the expense of the current owners of capital. The political economy implications of such a policy proposal are obvious.

Shifting from an income-based tax system to a consumption-based system causes two conflicting problems. First, as illustrated in the chapter by Fullerton and Rogers, the uniform consumption tax includes a one-time lump sum levy on existing capital. In one sense, this is a virtue of this form of a consumption tax: the welfare losses of the tax are reduced through the lump-sum component.[3] Current owners of capital, however, will surely argue that the levy is unfair.

Second, many are likely to see unfairness in the fact that consumption taxes omit capital income from the tax base. The experience of the Tax Reform Act of 1986 is relevant here. One of the driving factors for tax reform was the report by the public interest group, Citizens for Tax Justice, which documented the fact that 128 out of 250 large and profitable firms paid no federal income taxes between 1981 and 1983—no matter that these corporations often engaged in costly activ-

---

3. For more on this point, see Alan Auerbach, Laurence Kotlikoff, and Jonathan Skinner, "The Efficiency Gains from Dynamic Tax Reform," *International Economic Review*, vol. 24 (1983), pp. 81–100.

ity to reduce their tax liability.[4] Put differently, the implicit tax paid by corporations was far from zero. Whether this is appropriate tax policy or not, the public has little understanding of the difference between statutory and economic tax burdens.

Would the public support a change in the tax system that gave large tax breaks to capital-intensive firms? Maybe. Whether they would or not, they would probably not favor a wage tax that exempted current owners of capital from further taxation—this, despite the capital-levy component of a uniform consumption tax.

A related issue in the transition affects what kind of consumption tax is feasible. If we wish to replace an existing tax with a consumption tax, a VAT or an X-tax or a BTT would be a possibility. If we wish to implement a new consumption tax to increase revenues, however, either to decrease the federal deficit or to finance health care reform, only the VAT is viable. It is hard to imagine merging a BTT with the existing corporate income tax.

This last point suggests a way to deal with the political problem presented by the transitional burden on current owners of capital. A shift to a consumption tax may be politically feasible if the revenues are linked to an existing program serving the current elderly (for example, Medicare) that is expected to experience financing problems without some infusion of new funds (or cutback in benefits).

The recent analysis of distribution methodology that the Joint Committee on Taxation put out raises an issue that Fullerton and Rogers do not appear to consider.[5] The implementation of a VAT could lead to a rise in the price of goods (forward shifting) or to a fall in factors (backward shifting). Which one occurs will depend in part on the response of the Federal Reserve. Moreover, this will affect the incidence of the tax, given the prevalence of untaxed transfer payments at the bottom of the income distribution (primarily Aid to Families with Dependent Children). If the Federal Reserve does in fact tighten money to prevent prices from rising, the effect will be a redistribution toward transfer recipients (excluding social security, since these benefits are indexed) as well as creditors. It would be interesting to see how the results Fullerton and Rogers report change if output prices are held constant through monetary policy.

---

4. For a highly entertaining description of the tax reform process, see Birmbaum and Murray, *Showdown at Gucci Gulch* (New York: Random House, 1987).

5. Joint Committee on Taxation, *Methodology and Issues in Measuring Changes in the Distribution of Tax Burdens*, June 14, 1993.

Bequests

Finally, to return to the issue of bequests in the Fullerton and Rogers model, the authors note that a uniform consumption tax departs from proportionality because leisure and bequests are untaxed. (It also departs from proportionality because one must consider what tax the consumption tax is replacing. Let's ignore this point for the moment and consider a consumption tax that finances additional spending.) While bequests are central to the results, the model has an ad hoc motive for bequests: that individuals must leave to their heirs as large a bequest as they received (adjusted for productivity and population growth). This should not be construed as a criticism of the model. Indeed, there are substantial debate and confusion in the profession over why bequests occur. Whether bequests should be in the tax base or not (and whether they are implicitly subject to a consumption tax when omitted from the base) depends on the bequest motive.

Whether bequests are implicitly included in the tax base of a consumption tax is perhaps easiest to see in the case of a VAT. To begin, we can characterize bequests as either accidental or intentional. Accidental bequests follow from a precautionary bequest motive in which there is uncertainty as to the age of death. Consumption is diminished to avoid running out of assets before death.[6] This model takes the view that bequests have no value per se. One could argue that this form of bequest is a form of an annuity. The elderly receive piece of mind (albeit less consumption) in return for a lump-sum payment at death—the bequest. Consider implementing a VAT. To maintain the same level of consumption is now more expensive. Moreover, saving against unanticipated longevity must increase as each year of additional life will be more costly. The expected bequest should thus increase. Since the bequest has no value to the decedent and is simply a payment for peace of mind during the elderly years, one can view the change in bequest amount as a tax burden levied on the individual.

The notion that an accidental bequest has no value to the decedent is extreme. Even with a precautionary element to the bequest, it is likely that there is an intentional element also.[7] Thus we should con-

---

6. James B. Davies was an early proponent of this point of view; see "Uncertain Lifetime, Consumption, and Dissaving in Retirement," *Journal of Political Economy*, vol. 89 (1981), pp. 561–77.

7. Furthermore, Bernheim presents strong evidence against the accidental bequest motive; see Douglas Bernheim, "How Strong Are Bequest Motives? Evidence Based on Estimates of the Demand for Life Insurance and Annuities," *Journal of Political Economy*, vol. 99 (1991), pp. 899–27.

sider intentional bequest motives. Broadly speaking, there are three views why bequests occur: bequests serve as terminal consumption, bequests are driven by altruism, and bequests are strategically motivated. Let me begin by considering the first two view in one model.

The view that bequests are terminal consumption has been posited by Blinder among others.[8] Alan Blinder incorporates a utility-of-bequest function into his lifetime utility equation with after-inheritance tax wealth as the argument. Later, he provides a motivation for this formulation by having the utility derive from "the knowledge that the bequest buys consumption for future generations of the family." This suggests that what is important is the purchasing power of the bequest rather than the amount per se. Viewed this way, the fact that future generations will be subject to the tax lowers utility for the decedent: the bequest has been implicitly taxed by the VAT.[9]

The altruistic motivation for bequests follows from work by Gary Becker[10] and Robert Barro[11] among others. Here, the utility of children enter the utility function of a parent. In this case, bequests can be an optimal strategy when parents wish to increase the utility of children. Like the previous case, utility for the parent is diminished by the reduced purchasing power available to children (and hence lower utility for these beneficiaries).

A simple illustration shows the results for these two models. Consider a parent who has a utility function with arguments consumption (c_p) and the utility of a child (U^k). Labor supply (and hence income) is fixed. Parents are concerned about their children (the children's utility is in the parent's utility function, but children are not concerned about their parents). Parents are deciding how much to consume (one period) and how much to leave to their children. The model is

$$U^p(c_p, U_k(c_k)) \equiv V(c_p, c_k)$$
$$\text{subject to}$$
$$y_p = c_p + B \text{ and } y_k + B = c_k$$

We can draw the budget constraint for the parent in the space of (c_p, c_k) (figure 14–1). Absent the tax, the budget constraint is linear with slope equal to 1 (line AA'). For simplicity, let's assume that $y_k = 0$. If the

8. A. Blinder, *Toward an Economic Theory of Income Distribution* (Cambridge: MIT Press, 1974).

9. Ibid., p. 28.

10. G. Becker, "A Theory of Social Interactions," *Journal of Political Economy*, vol. 82 (1974), pp. 1063–93.

11. R. Barro, "Are Government Bonds Net Wealth?" *Journal of Political Economy*, vol. 82 (1974), pp. 1095–17.

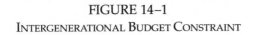

FIGURE 14–1

INTERGENERATIONAL BUDGET CONSTRAINT

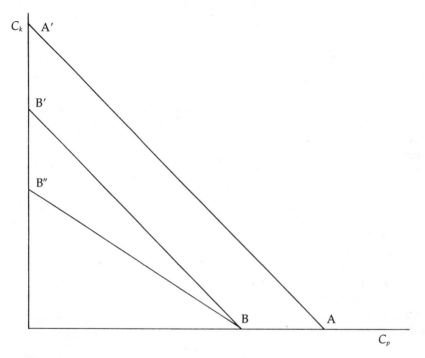

SOURCE: Author.

parent leaves no bequest, the outcome is $(y_p, 0)$. Alternatively, the outcome $(0, y_p)$ is possible. Now consider a VAT implemented at rate t. The budget constraints become

$$y_p = (1+t)c_p + B$$
$$y_k + B \equiv B = (1+t)c_k$$

The new budget constraint in (c_p, c_k) space is shifted inward in a parallel fashion (line BB'): no bequest leads to outcome $(qy_p, 0)$, and complete bequest leads to $(0, qy_p)$ where $q = (1+t)^{-1}$. Two important points emerge from this diagram. First, even if the parent pays no consumption tax explicitly (that is, $c_p = 0$), his utility has been reduced. This follows from the reduction in purchasing power available to his children. Thus, models that ignore the utility derived from the purchasing power resulting from bequests will understate the progressive shift when moving to a consumption tax.

301

Moreover, explicitly taxing bequests induces a distortion between parents' consumption and children's consumption. To see this, consider the budget constraint if bequests are treated as taxable consumption:

$$y_p = (1+t)(c_p + B)$$
$$y_k + B \equiv B = (1+t)c_k$$

Now the budget constraint rotates in on the point $(qy_p, 0)$ (line BB''). The new intercept is $(q^2y_p, 0)$. The inclusion of bequests in the tax base now creates an efficiency loss as parents substitute current consumption for consumption by their children. The intuition is simple. If bequest motives of either altruistic type posited by Becker or Blinder hold, including bequests in the tax base subjects them to double taxation for the parent: directly through the explicit tax on the bequest and then indirectly through the reduction in the value of the bequest to the children.

Different results emerge from the strategic bequest theory of Douglas Bernheim, Andrei Shleifer, and Lawrence Summers.[12] The basic point in this model is the possibility that bequests are used to elicit some action on the part of the child. Typically, the actions are a substitute for leisure on the part of the children (visits, personal services, and the like). It is more difficult to sketch out a simple model to illustrate the effects of consumption taxation on bequests. Let me make the following points. First, from the parent's point of view, the services received from children are excluded from the tax base. Hence, this encourages a shift from consumption to services. This is likely realized through an increased bequest. From the children's point of view, the tax induces a shift toward more leisure and less consumption. Since leisure must be forgone to provide services to receive a bequest, there is likely to be a fall in the supply of services to the parent; the value of the bequest has fallen in the presence of the VAT. It is not clear a priori whether equilibrium bequests will rise or fall. Moreover, it is not clear whether bequests belong in the tax base or not. To the extent that behavior is driven by the parent's utility function and budget constraint, bequests should be included in the tax base as they are an expenditure for a consumption good.

There is a complication, however, in that the strategic bequest model has untaxed services not only in the parent's utility function but also in the children's utility. The inclusion of the children's utility brings us back to the altruistic model and the view that bequests

---

12. Douglas Bernheim, Andrei Shleifer, and Lawrence Summers, "The Strategic Bequest Motive," *Journal of Political Economy*, vol. 93 (1985), pp. 1045–76.

should not be included in the tax base. The end result, I believe, is that neither inclusion nor exclusion of bequests from the base is precisely correct. One has to weigh the relative importance of the services aspect of the bequest and the altruistic component to determine how to construct the base.

It is striking, however, that almost all studies of bequests indicate that parents divide their estate equally among their children. While the strategic bequest theory does not suggest this should occur, it is a possible outcome. Perhaps more likely, however, parents are concerned for the utility of their children, and unequal bequests will lead to dissension in the next generation, which reduces utility uniformly. To the extent that altruism dominates strategic considerations, the optimal consumption tax excludes bequests from taxation, and incidence studies should recognize and measure the implicit tax associated with bequests when consumption taxes like a VAT are analyzed.

Index

A NOTE ON THE BOOK

This book was edited by the
publications staff of the American Enterprise Institute.
The index was prepared by Shirley Kessel.
The text was set in Palatino, a typeface designed by
the twentieth-century Swiss designer Hermann Zapf.
Coghill Composition Company, of Richmond, Virginia,
set the type, and Data Reproductions Corporation,
of Rochester Hills, Michigan, printed and bound the book,
using permanent acid-free paper.

The AEI PRESS is the publisher for the American Enterprise Institute for Public Policy Research, 1150 17th Street, N.W., Washington, D.C. 20036; *Christopher DeMuth*, publisher; *Dana Lane*, director; *Ann Petty*, editor; *Leigh Tripoli*, editor; *Cheryl Weissman*, editor; *Lisa Roman*, editorial assistant (rights and permissions).